Exorcism and Deliverance Ministry in the Twentieth Century

An Analysis of the Practice and Theology of Exorcism in Modern Western Christianity

STUDIES IN EVANGELICAL HISTORY AND THOUGHT

Exorcism and Deliverance Ministry in the Twentieth Century

An Analysis of the Practice and Theology of Exorcism in Modern Western Christianity

James M. Collins

Foreword by Ian Stackhouse

WIPF & STOCK · Eugene, Oregon

Wipf and Stock Publishers
199 W 8th Ave, Suite 3
Eugene, OR 97401

Exorcism and Deliverance Ministry in the Twentieth Century
An Analysis of the Practice and Theology of Exorcism
in Modern Western Christianity
By Collins, James M.
Copyright©2009 Paternoster
ISBN 13: 9781498255424
Publication date 10/29/2009
Previously published by Paternoster, 2009

"This Edition published by Wipf and Stock Publishers
by arrangement with Paternoster"

Series Preface

The Evangelical movement has been marked by its union of four emphases: on the Bible, on the cross of Christ, on conversion as the entry to the Christian life and on the responsibility of the believer to be active. The present series is designed to publish scholarly studies of any aspect of this movement in Britain or overseas. Its volumes include social analysis as well as exploration of Evangelical ideas. The books in the series consider aspects of the movement shaped by the Evangelical Revival of the eighteenth century, when the impetus to mission began to turn the popular Protestantism of the British Isles and North America into a global phenomenon. The series aims to reap some of the rich harvest of academic research about those who, over the centuries, have believed that they had a gospel to tell to the nations.

Series Editors

This book is dedicated to Naomi, Katie and Michael and my many friends at Morden Park Baptist Church

CONTENTS

FOREWORD

Those of us committed to charismatic renewal are caught in something of a dilemma. On the one hand we want to affirm the place of the supernatural (after all, what kind of faith would we talking about that is not supernatural?); on the other hand, we don't want to affirm it too much that we end up living in a 'parallel universe'. Sadly, however, this is often what transpires when a church 'goes supernatural', so to speak. In fact, as Andrew Walker points out, with reference to the specific ministry of deliverance, the Christians often end up in these supernatural settings not simply inhabiting a 'parallel universe' but a 'paranoid' one: a world in which everything is either of God or of the devil.

It is an unhealthy position, to be sure, and one that is unbiblical, because, as one wise teacher put it: in the world of the Bible there is weather that is from God, weather that is of the devil, and weather that is just weather. To put it simply: some days we just feel depressed. It is not a dark night of the soul, nor an attack of the devil. We just feel fed up. But if we insist on rejecting this natural theology of 'just weather' as a viable middle position, then paranoia is really all that is left to us. It is either God or the devil. Indeed, one of my very first pastoral visits was to a couple who were convinced their son was demonised, when anybody could have told you that he was simply crying out for love.

Which brings me to James Collins' book: because it is precisely this problem of religious paranoia that James exposes in his treatment of contemporary models of deliverance ministry. What Collins chronicles, with an enviable methodological thoroughness, is the rise of deliverance ministry over the twentieth century, rooting both charismatic and fundamentalist expressions of deliverance - and even to some degree the sacramental form of deliverance ministry - in Ronald Knox's classical definition of enthusiasm. Deliverance ministry, he argues, particularly its more recent expressions, conforms to the tidal waves of charismatic faddism, precisely because it is rooted in a non-rational enthusiasm, rather than in any coherent, biblical theology.

What I like about James is the fairness of his treatment. He is anxious to affirm where possible. Indeed, on reading this book, strangely enough I feel more keen, not less, to develop in our church a ministry of healing and deliverance. But then again, this is one of the questions he raises: where are the churches that will develop this, as opposed to the plethora of books, tapes and conferences by itinerant ministries? After all, he argues, itinerant deliverance ministry thrives on its own internal logic: that is, the very nature of itinerancy, and the need to hold one's own on the charismatic circuit, requires ever more sensational results in order for it to continue (reminding me of Pete Ward's comments about the logic of the contemporary worship industry: that given the need to sell worship, Christian music is bound to be driven more by commercial interests than overtly theological ones). And it is precisely this need for results that spills the theology of these itinerants over the edge into paranoid Christianity. Thus, if a credible deliverance ministry is to develop, one that avoids the kind of paranoia that attends a 'Pigs in the Parlour' type of supernaturalism, my sense, from reading this timely book is that it will need to be far more rooted in a congregational setting, and driven by the pastoral and theological sensitivities of local practitioners.

I hope James's book is read widely. Furthermore, I hope it will be received as the work of a passionate charismatic. James, like many other Christian leaders of our generation, is simply seeking to promulgate a vigorous form of charismatic Christianity 'without the hype'.

Ian Stackhouse
Guildford
April 2009

PREFACE

My interest in all things 'charismatic' goes back to my upbringing in the Pentecostal churches where I witnessed and participated in a liberal mixture of sincere, zealous and occasionally foolish Christian spirituality. I would not change my formative Christian experience for the world, but since I passionately believe that zeal is improved by knowledge I offer this study in the hope that it will make a helpful contribution to improving the depth of Christian reflection upon the practice of exorcism and deliverance ministry and associated subjects such as sanctification and pastoral care.

This study, originally my PhD thesis, is unashamedly focused on 'grass roots' Christianity. I believe that the gap between popular and academic theology has grown far too wide and pray that the coming years will see a reversal of this trend.

I am very grateful for the assistance of many scholars and institutions. I would like to thank Rev Dr Derek Tidball and Dr Meic Pearse for their encouragement and the many helpful suggestions they made during the course of my study. I would also like to place on record my gratitude to Professor Andrew Walker, Dr David Garrard of the Donald Gee Centre, Alastair McKitterick, Prof Michael Collins, Dr Ian Randall, and Rev Dr Nigel Wright for their time and advice. I owe a very good deal to the members of Morden Park Baptist Church who generously allowed me to complete this study whilst I had the privilege of serving as their minister. Finally, I sincerely thank God for the gift of my family who have been an ever-present source of support to me.

James Collins
Redhill
April 2009

CHAPTER 1

Introduction

In 1973, during the heyday of the Charismatic Movement, Frank and Ida Hammond published *Pigs in the Parlour*, subtitled *A Practical Guide to Deliverance*.[1] In many respects it was typical of much of the popular theological material produced by Charismatic writers around this time, predominantly anecdotal, exegetically naïve and simplistic in outlook. It sold like hot cakes and proved profoundly influential. It, and others like it, fuelled the already burgeoning interest in the exorcism of evil spirits.

Exorcism, or as non-sacramentalist practitioners usually prefer, deliverance ministry, is a widely accepted though controversial practice. Many Christians continue to advocate this ministry to a greater or lesser extent. Others, usually from a more rationalistic perspective (perhaps dubious about the existence of a personal devil or demons, and/or appalled at the sensational nature of this ministry and its potential for grievous results) are less confident or even opposed. Actually this represents only the crudest analysis of the debate – there is in fact a spectrum of alternative views on and methods of deliverance and exorcism. These include the traditional, Sacramental, liturgical rite, Charismatic and Fundamentalist strains of deliverance ministry, and hybrids of these emerging towards the end of the twentieth century.

Christian Enthusiasm

It is the key contention of this study that whenever the practice of exorcism / deliverance grows in popularity, it invariably does so within those forms of Christianity that might accurately be labelled 'Enthusiastic'. In other words enthusiasm is a necessary (but not sufficient) cause of exorcism / deliverance. The term 'enthusiasm' and those associated with it ('enthusiasm', 'enthusiast') have an interesting history. Their etymology is in a Greek term meaning 'in God', however, they have often been used as a term of little more than abuse aimed at excitable, emotional expressions of faith. In 1949 R. A. Knox published a classic study of Christian enthusiasm in the seventeenth and eighteenth centuries, providing a clear description of the bundle of repeating characteristics that make up the enthusiastic tendency. The characteristics he

---

[1] F. and I. Hammond, *Pigs in the Parlour: A Practical Guide to Deliverance* (Kirkwood: Impact Books, 1973).

observed include immanent spirituality, anti-rationalism, imminent eschatology, ecstatic manifestations, extremes of antinomianism and ethical rigorism / perfectionism and absolutism, female emancipation, faddism and schism.[2] It is important to recognise that Knox describes enthusiasm as a tendency rather than as a discrete quality. Therefore, no one might be said to be a pure enthusiast. Where such a claim is made in this study it should be understood to indicate that this tendency is a significant presence.

Some of the characteristics of enthusiasm identified by Knox seem to be of greater significance than others; in particular (and certainly for this study) immanent spirituality and imminent eschatology play explanatory rather than merely descriptive roles in understanding Christian enthusiasm. Rather than focus on Knox's descriptors, it is perhaps preferable, in building a definition of enthusiasm, to highlight these driving assumptions of spiritual immanency and eschatological imminency. These assumptions lead to the tendency towards simplistic spiritualised explanations of experience and events and a further tendency to invest such experience and events with great spiritual significance. These lie in contrast to rational attempts to categorise experience and events in terms of natural cause and effect which would be included in a more balanced faith perspective. In short, in the present study enthusiasm should be understood as a tendency towards immanent spirituality, imminent eschatology and a parallel trend away from human reason.

David Middlemiss contends convincingly that the Charismatic Movement matches exactly the features of enthusiasm as outlined by Knox, highlighting in particular the experiential, anti-rational aspect of enthusiasm.[3] Since exorcism / deliverance is usually practised within a broadly Charismatic environment, Middlemiss's study raises the possibility that exorcism / deliverance may be an innately enthusiastic practice. Although Knox does not specifically draw out exorcism / deliverance as a characteristic of enthusiasm, he does mention several specific cases in his historical analysis,[4] and tellingly comments that the 'traditional enthusiast over-emphasises the distinction between "the spirit" and "the flesh."'[5] This is immediately pertinent to the study undertaken here, at the very least indicating that enthusiasm is an environment conducive to the practice of exorcism / deliverance. Actually the case can and will be presented in much stronger terms as the evidence is examined.

It is important to realise that enthusiasm is certainly not confined to discrete

---

[2] R. A. Knox, *Enthusiasm: A Chapter in the History of Religion* (Oxford: Oxford University Press, 1949) 2-4, 14-16, 20, 48, 403, 565 and 570.

[3] D. Middlemiss, *Interpreting Charismatic Experience* (London: SCM, 1996).

[4] Knox, *Enthusiasm*, 150, 314, 325, 519, 521-523. Since the focus of Knox's study was by no means upon exorcism / deliverance these references are of great significance. There can be little doubt that he would have found many more examples to report among the groups he studied had he been looking for them.

[5] Knox, *Enthusiasm*, 93.

movements but is fundamentally a paradigm that manifests itself wherever faith is defined in contra-distinction to reason.

Context

This study aims to examine exorcism / deliverance within Western Christianity during the twentieth century. This is admittedly a difficult boundary to maintain since the Western Church clearly does not exist in a vacuum and the influence of Christians and churches operating within other, usually animistic, cultural settings should and will not be ignored entirely. Nevertheless, this is a story about Western Christian enthusiasm and one of its persistent characteristics. The story of the forms of Christian exorcism that are *primarily* influenced by factors alien to mainstream, post-Enlightenment Western culture (such as animism) will have to be told elsewhere. Specifically, it is for this reason that attention is not paid to exorcism / deliverance within black majority churches, despite the fact that this is of great public interest at the current time.[6]

Furthermore, this is not a study of the various Christian approaches to spiritual warfare which is in many respects the wider category of Christian theology of which exorcism / deliverance is a sub-category. Some years after the heyday of exorcism / deliverance in the 1970s and 1980s, a new emphasis upon 'Strategic Level Spiritual Warfare' emerged. Proponents usually incorporated exorcism / deliverance within their highly influential schemas and therefore some attention is devoted to them, but this study will not broaden its focus to include all of their interest.

Christian doctrine and praxis are not developed in a vacuum. It is important to identify and consider influences working upon Christians in the area of study. In order to do so some examination of simultaneous religious trends such as the Occult Revival, the New Age Movement and the emergence of New Religious Movements is included. The growth in popularity of Christian enthusiasm (and the often concomitant practice of exorcism / deliverance) is to some extent fruit of the same sociological tree as these movements; a deeper perspective on the former is gained by an understanding of these and the fiery reaction they often provoked from Christian enthusiasts.

Another temptation is to widen the focus of study to examine the broader theological and ecclesial trends which affect development of thought regarding deliverance ministry and exorcism. It should be recognised that to a certain extent this is desirable and so there will be some examination of (for example) the development of the Pentecostal / Charismatic Tradition.[7] This is not,

---

[6] This is not because the current author does not consider this to be important. On the contrary, it is of such importance and complexity that separate study is required.

[7] This development is by far the most significant ecclesiological development for this study fuelling not only a distinctive form of Charismatic deliverance ministry but

however, the main focus of the study. Where necessary some familiarity with scholarly analysis will be assumed.[8]

Definition of Terms

It is necessary to use several terms in a specified manner in order to maximise clarity. Of primary importance is the distinction between two terms at the heart of this study, namely, exorcism and deliverance ministry.[9] In a Christian context, 'exorcism' is a term more suitable for the *sacramental* rite by which an evil influence, more specifically, an evil personality which has in some sense taken possession of a human subject, is removed. 'Deliverance' ministry is a 'charisma' ministry; it relies less upon received forms and more upon the charismatic enduement of the practitioner. It is usually a less formal (though sometimes lengthy) procedure aiming to alleviate some form of 'demonisation'.[10] When it is desired to group these alternatives together in a single term, reference will be made to exorcism / deliverance.

Affliction by evil spirits has traditionally been termed 'possession', namely, that condition in which individuals suffer episodes during which a demon completely takes over their personality; possession also carries the connotation of some kind of legal ownership.[11] The alternative term, 'demonised' came to the fore during the twentieth century due to a revision of the translation of *daimonizo*, the Greek term translated by the KJV 'possessed'. To be demonised is to be oppressed, influenced or, even, controlled by demons in some way. 'Demonised' is a much broader term than 'possessed' and enables an understanding of demonic activity even amongst Christian people without implying demonic ownership (a belief which most Christians could not

---

another parallel but antagonistic form amongst those Christian enthusiasts that rejected the early Pentecostal movement.

[8] Suitable sources for studying these wider concerns will be indicated where appropriate.

[9] Cf S. Hunt, 'Deliverance: The Evolution of a Doctrine' *Themelios* 21.1 (October, 1995) 12. Cuneo light-heartedly refers to deliverance ministry as the 'charismatic renewal movement's... sort of bargain-basement alternative to full-fledged exorcism.' M. W. Cuneo, *American Exorcism* (London: Bantam, 2001) 81. Powlison proposes a new term, 'Ekballistic Mode or Ministry' or EMM. This nomenclature owes more to Powlison's cessationist theology than to a genuine attempt at clarity. D. Powlison, *Power Encounters* (Grand Rapids: Baker Books, 1995) 27-29.

[10] The words charisma and charismatic are used here in their accepted sociological (rather than ecclesiological) sense. This is a technical but important point because, as will become clear there are groups practising deliverance ministry who would certainly not define themselves as part of the Charismatic Movement.

[11] Hence the concept of the 'Faustian pact' in which one's soul is 'sold' to the Devil in exchange for some temporal advantage.

countenance).[12]

Categorising the Progress of Twentieth Century Enthusiastic Exorcism / Deliverance

At first glance, exorcism appears to be a minority interest among Christians at the beginning of the twentieth century and this proves to be largely the case, with some important exceptions. It is evident that interest grew throughout the twentieth century as institutional Christianity faltered and declined and Christian enthusiasm developed and, in time, came to dominate the horizon.

Schema for understanding the various strands of praxis of exorcism / deliverance have been proposed by Cuneo (based upon a purely Americo-centric study), Powlison and Hunt. Cuneo divides his study of the practice of exorcism in late twentieth century America as involving four streams: 'Charismatic Deliverance Ministry', 'The Rough-and-Ready School' which appears to be a particularly extreme version of the former stream,[13] 'Evangelical Deliverance' and 'Roman Catholic Exorcism'.[14] Powlison identifies four (different) 'varieties' namely: Charismatic, Dispensational, 'Third wave' and 'broadly evangelical'.[15] Sacramental exorcism is notable by its absence from this schema; this is because Powlison is not so much writing history or sociology as he is presenting a cessationist polemic for the evangelical constituency. In a short article, Hunt examines the 'evolution' of Christian deliverance ministry in the UK identifying its place within 'Classical Pentecostalism', 'the mid century itinerant healing ministries', 'The Fort Lauderdale Five', 'The Renewal Movement' and 'Restoration, postmillenarianism'.[16] All of these are in fact sub-categories of Charismatic deliverance ministry. To his credit, Hunt's brief study remains a decent (though brief) scholarly and disinterested attempt to chart some history of Charismatic deliverance. With the exception of cursory examinations by Nigel Wright and Andrew Walker[17] which make some relevant analysis, this present survey has

---

[12] Cf J. White, *When the Spirit Comes with Power* (London: Hodder and Stoughton, 1992) 208-211.

[13] This 'stream' appears to be perpetuated by adherents of 'Word-Faith' doctrine. I regard these to be better understood a subset of Charismatic Deliverance Ministry.

[14] Cuneo, *American*, 99-323.

[15] Powlison, *Power*, 32-33.

[16] Hunt, 'Deliverance', 10-13. Although Hunt asserts that his study is of deliverance in the UK much of his study is of American development since this is where most developments regarding deliverance have emerged.

[17] N. G. Wright, *A Theology of the Dark Side* (Carlisle: Paternoster, 2003) 103-109; cf N. G. Wright, 'Charismatic Interpretations of the Demonic' in A. N. S. Lane (ed.), *The Unseen World* (Carlisle: Paternoster, 1996) 149-155; A. Walker, 'The Devil You Think You Know: Demonology and the Charismatic Movement' in T. Smail *et al* (eds.), *Charismatic Renewal* (London: SPCK, 1995) 86-105.

reached the outer limits of scholarly engagement with an issue that has been of fair significance within the century in question.[18]

The present study will, subsequent to briefly drawing attention to significant events antecedent to the period under examination, study the development of Christian exorcism under three broad headings which form the titles for three chapters: 'Charismatic deliverance' (to include all deliverance practiced within the categories identified by Hunt and not simply that associated with the Charismatic Movement), 'Evangelical Fundamentalist deliverance', and 'Enthusiastic Sacramental exorcism'. In each case it is to be understood that exorcism manifests itself within the broader emergence of the enthusiastic impulse and one should not therefore imagine that exorcism is ever a ubiquitous characteristic of any of these streams of ecclesiology. Neither should it be thought that these categories are intended to be watertight, however, they will hold enough water to be useful channels into which to divide attention. A final chapter will aim to demonstrate that the last couple of decades see the waters muddied considerably as ecumenism (partially motivated by cross-denominational Charismatic movements) and late Modern pragmatism increasingly undermine Modernity's impulse towards theological and ecclesiological consistency and sectarianism.

The story of twentieth century Christianity is to a large extent the story of twentieth century Christian enthusiasm. At the beginning of the century that enthusiasm is restricted to particular movements and usually excluded from powerful and rationalist Christian institutions. By the end of the century these institutions were failed or failing and enthusiasm had infiltrated and in many cases overturned the power centres of Christianity. Enthusiasm is a favourable climate for various theological impulses, not least demonology and exorcism. As these enthusiastic impulses have taken root within different streams of Christianity and as these streams have intermingled, old categories have become irrelevant and diverse; colourful fusions of belief and praxis have emerged.

Methodology

Before proceeding to the study itself two important issues of methodology must be identified and understood. Firstly, the primary sources used for this study are almost exclusively published books and booklets. I have steered away from using recordings of sermons for three reasons:

- Firstly, the sheer quantity of recorded material militates against a fair and comprehensive analysis.

---

[18] Which begs the question, why? The answer must lie in academic theology's disengagement from popular Christianity particularly where the latter strays into areas that do not sit comfortably within a rationalistic framework.

- More importantly, the value of spoken sources is questionable since it is hard to establish the extent to which they represent the considered opinion of the speaker.
- Quotations from and references to written sources are easier to verify and less prone to be taken out of context.

Secondly, whilst a fairly comprehensive history is attempted, the primary thrust is to establish enough history to confidently ascertain the relationship between exorcism / deliverance and Christian enthusiasm. This is primarily a story of the main loci of Western Christian enthusiasm in the twentieth century, namely, the Pentecostal / Charismatic Movements and the groups of Evangelical Fundamentalists who found their identity in opposition to these. Nevertheless a somewhat less comprehensive analysis of exorcism among enthusiastic Sacramentalists is included, not so much in order to square off the history (although it certainly goes some way towards doing so) as to establish that different forms of Christian enthusiasm still prove conducive to exorcism / deliverance.

CHAPTER 2

Exorcism and Enthusiasm in Late Nineteenth Century Christianity

The nineteenth century was in many respects the high tide of Modern scepticism. Whilst general culture remained highly religious, belief in evil spirits was no longer taken seriously within academic circles. One is hard pressed to find any leading Christian theologian or church leader making any reference whatsoever to demonology or exorcism.[1] However, this is not to say that exorcism was not taking place among the enthusiastic streams of Christianity, merely that these streams are less open to historical enquiry.[2] Nevertheless, as with any rule there are important exceptions. This chapter is in no way designed to be a thorough study of nineteenth century exorcism, merely an indication that the rite was not completely redundant. The two individuals identified and examined are also of particular significance in twentieth century practice of exorcism / deliverance.

Johann Cristoph Blumhardt (1805-1880)

Blumhardt was a Lutheran pastor of good reputation who came to exert a wide influence. He is best known for his encounter with a demon possessed girl named Gottlieben Dittus while he served as pastor in the village of Möttlingen in the Black Forest.[3] After a two-year battle of gothic proportions against the evil spirits inhabiting Dittus, and latterly her family, they were finally restored to their right minds in December 1843.[4] The successful eviction of these evil spirits proved to be the catalyst for an enthusiastic revival in his parish.[5]

---

[1] The obvious reason for this is that the nineteenth-century church was dominated (at least from the perspective of a century or two later) by rationalistic institutional faith.

[2] Enthusiastic Christians are far less visible to the Church historian since they rarely keep records and their praxis is intuitive and therefore much harder to trace.

[3] See F. Zuendel, *The Awakening* (Robertsbridge: Plough, 1999) for a full account.

[4] Zuendel, *Awakening*, 23-63.

[5] Zuendel, *Awakening*, 67-90.

John Livingstone Nevius (1829-1893)

As has been frequently pointed out, the rationalism of Modernity is not particularly effective in presenting Christ to peoples with animistic world views.[6] This problem and its resolution appear to have been first committed to print by John Livingstone Nevius, just prior to his death in 1892.

Nevius, a graduate of Princeton Seminary, was a Presbyterian minister and missionary to China for approximately 40 years. He wrote several books including a history of China. He also developed a missionary strategy called the 'three-self plan' that was widely used in China and most effectively in Korea.[7]

Whilst serving as a missionary in China, Nevius became aware of the frequent cases of exorcism performed by the native Chinese converts.[8] After researching the issue he published his findings in *Demon Possession and Allied Themes*.[9] Despite the fact that he went to China disbelieving in evil spirits, Nevius became convinced of their reality as a result of his experience and his research. He later discovered that the same was true for many of the missionaries to inland China.[10] In short he became convinced that the possessions and Christian exorcisms he had discovered were identical to those recorded in the New Testament.

Typically, he discovered that Chinese Christians were often confronted with people troubled by symptoms that they readily attributed to evil spirits. In many cases the symptoms were successfully alleviated through Christian prayer.[11] He further discovered that similar incidents had occurred in India, Japan and Africa.[12] Finally, turning his attention to the so called 'Christian lands', he marshalled evidence (including the Dittus case) and records of mental illness particularly 'demonomania'.[13] He also observed the phenomenal growth of Spiritualism and concludes that its adherents are in contact with evil spirits.[14]

---

[6] E. F. Murphy, *The Handbook for Spiritual Warfare* (Nashville: Thomas Nelson, 2003) 3-13.

[7] The 'three self-plan' was to organise 'self-supporting, self-governing and self-extending indigenous' churches. B. Stanley, *The Bible and The Flag* (Leicester: Apollos, 1990).

[8] Cf. H. Taylor, *Pastor Hsi: Confucian Scholar and Christian* (London: Lutterworth, 1900). His was an early Chinese convert who, convinced of the reality of the Christian's battle with demonic forces took the nickname 'Demon Overcomer'. He regularly carried out exorcisms and his method and experience seem to align very closely with that of Nevius.

[9] J. Nevius, *Demon Possession and Allied Themes* (London: Revell, c.1894).

[10] Nevius, *Demon*, 134-136, cf. 110. It is at least arguable that this transition amounts to the conversion of Western missionaries to a Christianised version of the religious enthusiasm of the peoples to whom they were ministering.

[11] Nevius, *Demon*, 12f., 17-94, 395-426.

[12] Nevius, *Demon*, 95-110.

[13] Nevius, *Demon*, 111-133.

[14] Nevius, *Demon*, 321f.

Nevius did not address the question of whether a Christian can be possessed by an evil spirit. It seems likely that he would have thought not.[15] However, he laid the foundation for others to conclude differently by observing that the term and concept of *demonisation* is to be preferred to *possession*.[16] He outlined a four-stage model of demonisation: obsession ('the introductory or tentative efforts of the demon'), struggle (where 'the unwilling subject resists'), subjection (where the demon periodically assumes control) and cooperation (where the subject is willing to be used by the demon).[17]

Another issue that Nevius did not examine closely is how an exorcism should be performed and whether it was a crisis or a process. His case studies present numerous alternative methods for exorcism though usually involving prayer.[18] Whilst instantaneous deliverance does occur, many of his studies indicate a possibly unsuccessful process, particularly if the freed does not assume Christian faith. Nevertheless, Nevius frequently presented a very positive view of the success of Christian exorcism.[19]

The remainder of his book is largely an argument for the existence and operation of evil spirits in the light of widespread Modern scepticism. Nevertheless, two other points are noteworthy. With regard to the origin of evil spirits, Nevius acknowledges some doubt,[20] although he approvingly quotes Gall's theory that:

> Satan and the demons who are his subjects, are the disembodied spirits of a pre-Adamic race, who once lived on this earth... This race sinned, and fell... He [Satan] was naturally envious of the race which succeeded him, and plotted and compassed its fall. After Adam's fall... Satan reasserted his claim to it by right of precedence. He still contests the claim; the final issue of the contest being suspended on the success or failure of the redemption and restoration of men.[21]

The implications of such a view cannot be analysed here. However, it should be noted that it is a good foundation for Nevius' understanding of evil spirits and their *modus operandi*. Finally, Nevius frequently highlights the value of

---

[15] His evidence is somewhat equivocal. For example, 'as the Holy Spirit entered my mother's heart the demon went out.' Nevius, *Demon*, 90. Cf. 36, 51f. and 391.

[16] Nevius, *Demon*, 264. Nevius appears to be the first to make this point. It will be made repeatedly throughout the twentieth-century usually in order to establish a Biblical case for the possible demonisation of Christians.

[17] Nevius, *Demon*, 285-287. This appears to be similar enough to the model adopted later by Kurt Koch and other evangelical fundamentalist practitioners of deliverance ministry that we are entitled to assume some influence here.

[18] For various examples see Nevius, *Demon*, 30-40, 73-94 and 395-426.

[19] Nevius, *Demon*, 71 and 258.

[20] Nevius, *Demon*, 342.

[21] Nevius, *Demon*, 270f.

exorcism for Christian mission. In a pre-Modern, animistic setting, successful Christian exorcism represents a demonstration of Christ's power over the spirits that frequently leads to acceptance of Christianity. [22] Demons speaking through their human host often acknowledge Christ's lordship.[23]

Nevius' book represents a significant new direction in Christian demonology. Emerging from the experience of an intelligent and thoroughly Modern interaction with an animist setting it carried weight with Evangelicals in the Modern West that was itself experiencing the first stirrings of an anti-Modern, occult revival. Nevius adopted a Modern methodology to establish an anti-Modern conclusion regarding the existence and activity of evil spirits. His work was (and still is) powerfully attractive to many Evangelical Fundamentalists who held to a Modern epistemology but maintained an anti-Modern, conservative biblical spirituality.[24] Nevius's influence over later advocates of deliverance ministry, particularly of the evangelical fundamentalist variety should not be underestimated.

Exorcism and the Holiness Movement

Towards the end of the nineteenth century Christian enthusiasm was to be found in greatest concentration among adherents of Holiness teaching. Earlier in the century the camp meeting had provided American evangelicals with opportunity for distilled enthusiasm[25] and this tradition continued in the campaigns of holiness revivalists although it is fair to say that the emotional conservativism of the late nineteenth century, particularly in Britain, often restrained the enthusiastic impulse towards unfettered emotionalism.

In the latter decades of the nineteenth century many enthusiastic holiness groups emerged with varying perspectives on such issues as the charismata, the baptism in the Holy Spirit, perfectionism and eschatology. As will become clear, several of these holiness streams were to coalesce in the Pentecostal movement whilst others found common identity in their settled opposition to the latter.

There is no evidence to suggest that exorcism or deliverance ministry was at any stage a primary characteristic of any nineteenth century holiness group (the main issue at stake among these groups during the latter decades of the nineteenth century was divine healing). Nevertheless, it is unarguable that these

---

[22] Nevius, *Demon*, 51, 57, 76-94, 87 and 413.

[23] For example, Nevius, *Demon*, 27.

[24] See, for example, M. Unger, *Biblical Demonology* (Grand Rapids: Kregel, 1994) 28, 57, 87.

[25] K. S. Latourette, *A History of Christianity Volume 2: Reformation to the Present* (London: Harper and Row, 1975) 1037, 1266. For a brief treatment of the history of camp meetings and an intriguing report from a contemporary example see R. Balmer, *Mine Eyes Have Seen the Glory* (New York: OUP, 2000) 226-245.

groups were dualistic in their theology and, as the subsequent arguments over Pentecostalism were to demonstrate, had a tendency to demonise that which they opposed. This was the soil out of which sprang both Charismatics and their *bête noir* the Evangelical Fundamentalists each of which would provide deliverance with its hour in the sun.

CHAPTER 3

Charismatic Deliverance Ministry

The twentieth century witnessed an explosive global expansion of enthusiastic Christianity, initially centred on the emergence of Pentecostalism. In this section attention is given to the place of exorcism within those branches of Christian enthusiasm that find their roots in the Pentecostal awakening. Taken in turns these may be grouped in four broad stages of development: the early Pentecostals, mid century itinerant healing evangelistic ministries, the Charismatic Renewal and post-Pentecostals of various types. It is reasonable to apply the term 'Charismatic' as a catch-all to all these groups.

It is inappropriate to think of any of these groups practising 'exorcism' since their approach was usually in no way sacramental; on the contrary their praxis was marked by the complete absence of traditional liturgical form. Charismatics usually glorify spontaneity and despise routine and tend to favour straightforward expressions of faith rather than the aesthetic appeal of liturgical forms.[1] Therefore, in the context of Charismatic praxis, it is more appropriate to speak of 'deliverance ministry'. For the sake of consistency this term will be used throughout this chapter even though strictly it may not have been in regular parlance until the 1970s.

Charismatic Deliverance Ministry among the Early Pentecostals

The Origins of the Pentecostal Movement

Charting the origins of the various Pentecostal groups that emerged in the opening decade of the twentieth century is both straightforward and of great complexity. Straightforward, in that early Pentecostals were simply radical evangelicals holding to a fusion of existing Holiness beliefs that quickly evidenced mass appeal.[2] Complex, in that emerging Pentecostalism was a

---

[1] This tendency is of course rather easy to expose as fallacious since it is naively ignorant of the unavoidable problem of routinisation. Nevertheless, one cannot get under the skin of Charismatic identity without an awareness of this instinct towards novelty.

[2] See G. Wacker, *Heaven Below: Early Pentecostals and American Culture* (Cambridge: Harvard, 2003) 2 for a helpful description of the various streams of Holiness teaching antecedent to Pentecostalism.

dynamic and entrepreneurial grass roots movement; the religious pioneers who
drove the movement forward were not given to carefully recording their
activities and any influence other than that that came from above.[3]

Pentecostalism, particularly in its earlier stages, is usually identified with the
belief that glossolalia is the initial evidence of the 'second blessing'
(subsequent to conversion) of the Baptism of the Holy Spirit.[4] Hence its origin
is usually traced to the first modern record of speaking in tongues attended by
this belief in 'subsequence', namely that of Miss Agnes Ozman.

Miss Ozman was a student at Charles Parham's Bethel Bible College.
Although Parham is usually identified as the original formulator of Pentecostal
doctrine, it was not until another student of his, William Seymour, took
Parham's teaching to Azusa Street, Los Angeles that Pentecostalism developed
mass appeal.[5] Since the early days of Seymour's ministry, Pentecostalism's
popularity has burgeoned; in only a century it has become a significant, global
force.

Pentecostalism has been so closely identified with glossolalia that its other
distinctives sometimes go unnoticed. Dayton identifies a 'four-fold pattern' that
is 'well-nigh universal within the movement, appearing in all branches and
varieties of Pentecostalism'.[6] Put simply and generally, the early Pentecostals
recognised varying combinations and permutations of four vital characteristics
of Jesus; Saviour, Baptiser with the Holy Spirit, Healer and coming King. All
of these emphases were of course present within the pre-existing Holiness
Movement, it was this unique combination of them tied to the characteristic

---

[3] The standard reconstruction of the emergence of Pentecostalism is certainly still that of
Robert Anderson, R. M. Anderson, *Vision of the Disinherited: The Making of American
Pentecostalism* (New York: Oxford University Press, 1979) although Grant Wacker has
recently presented a very well argued alternative taking a somewhat more elevated view
of the social standing of the early Pentecostals. Wacker, *Heaven*, (and particularly, 197-
216).

[4] M. R. Hathaway, 'The Elim Pentecostal Church: Origins, Development and
Distinctives' in K. Warrington (ed.), *Pentecostal Perspectives* (Carlisle: Paternoster,
1998) 4.

[5] Hathaway, 'Elim', 4f. For this reason Hollenweger asserts that 'this Azusa Street
Mission is regarded... as the place of origin of the world-wide Pentecostal movement.'
W. J. Hollenweger, *The Pentecostals* (Massachusetts: Hendrickson, 1988) 22. 'Parham's
pioneering role in the movement was eclipsed in the explosive growth that followed.'
Hathaway 'Elim', 5. For a brief account of the Azusa Street revival and Seymour's
ministry see R. Owens, 'The Azusa Street Revival: The Pentecostal Movement begins in
America' in V Synan (ed.), *The Century of the Holy Spirit* (Nashville: Thomas Nelson,
2001) 39-68. For a powerful and persuasive assertion that Seymour is the father of
Pentecostalism see R. G. W. Sanders, *William Joseph Seymour* (Sandusky: Alexandria,
2003).

[6] D. W. Dayton, *Theological Roots of Pentecostalism* (Metuchen: Hendrickson, 1987)
21f.

emphasis upon speaking in tongues that lies at the heart of Pentecostalism.

A Significant Proto-Pentecostal: The Story of Alexander Dowie and Zion City

John Alexander Dowie is of great significance to the emergence of Pentecostalism. He was one of the great pioneers of healing evangelism – a ministry that was to come to the fore in the middle of the twentieth century.[7] He was also the inspiration behind Zion City which runs like a golden thread in the background of many an early Pentecostal leader. Furthermore, there is concrete evidence that Dowie understood divine healing in terms of liberation from the power of Satan and therefore a form of deliverance ministry.

Born in 1847 in Scotland, Dowie grew up in Australia. The early years of his career were unspectacular; he was ordained as a Congregational minister in 1872 before leaving to pioneer his own church in Melbourne in 1878. In 1882 Dowie made divine healing the centrepiece of his ministry, 'this teaching was his theme in attracting followers'. [8] Dowie's ministry was popular but also generated a great deal of controversy and opposition.[9]

In 1885 Dowie announced his intention to take his message to the whole world inside three years.[10] In 1888 he departed Australia for the United States.[11] By 1893 he was preaching to thousands in the 'Zion Tabernacle' which he had erected in Chicago. Dowie's popularity grew and grew partially due to the publicity generated by the controversy surrounding his ministry.[12]

At the turn of the century (at midnight on New Year's Eve) Dowie announced plans to build a city to be called Zion.[13] Zion City was built approximately 50 miles north of Chicago. Dowie planned to establish a city

---

[7] D. E. Harrell, *All Things are Possible* (Bloomington: Indiana University Press, 1975) 13. The best biographical information on Dowie is to be found in G. Lindsay, *John Alexander Dowie* (Texas: Christ for the Nations, 1986) and P. L. Cook, *Zion City, Illinois: Twentieth Century Utopia* (New York: Syracuse University Press 1996) though the former is somewhat hagiographical. See also *Voice of Healing* (August, 1951) 'How God gave John Alexander Dowie the Ministry of Healing' 4-5.

[8] Harrell, *All*, 13.

[9] G. Wacker, 'Marching to Zion: Religion in a Modern Utopian Community', *Church History* 54 (December 1985) 498.

[10] Hollenweger, *Pentecostals*, 116.

[11] Hollenweger notes that in 1888 Dowie described his teaching as the 'full gospel', a term which was later in common use among Pentecostals. Hollenweger, *Pentecostals*, 116, cf. 123.

[12] Wacker, 'Marching', 500. The parallels between Dowie's Zion and the Anabaptist debacle at Munster are striking, particularly once allowance is made for the massively divergent cultural contexts from which they emerged. See G. H. Williams, *Radical Reformation* (Kirkville: Sixteenth Century Journal, 1992) 553-588.

[13] Hollenweger, *Pentecostals*, 17. Within a month Dowie publicly claimed to be 'Elijah the Restorer' Cook, *Zion*, 57.

where 'all aspects of personal and social existence [are brought under] theocratic direction'.[14] The city's slogan was 'Where God rules, Man prospers'.[15] By 1905 the town had a population of around 7,500.[16]

Dowie was expelled from Zion City in 1906. From 1903 the town had suffered economically[17] whilst Dowie's standard of living had become progressively extravagant.[18] Furthermore, his integrity and personal morality was persistently brought under suspicion and his health suffered a setback in 1905 when he was the victim of a stroke.[19] He died a lonely death in March 1907.[20]

Dowie was a genuine maverick and an inspirational leader. Whilst many of his beliefs and practices were highly idiosyncratic others such as his stand against racism and his evident concern for social justice were magnificent. His view of his own ministry grew more eccentric and egocentric towards the end of his life.[21] In common with the early Pentecostals, he was restorationist and premillenialist.[22] In Zion 'sale of drugs, medicinals, liquors, tobacco, swine's flesh, or the keeping of swine within the corporate limits of the city' were prohibited on pain of losing the title to one's property.[23] Unlike many enthusiasts Dowie was not opposed to academia *per se*. He appears to have had a reasonable grasp on academic theology,[24] moreover, education in Zion

---

[14] Wacker, 'Marching', 501. Of course Dowie was to be the sole administrator of the theocracy! Cook, *Zion*, 103-115.

[15] Wacker, 'Marching', 501.

[16] Wacker, 'Marching', 502.

[17] Orr attributes Dowie's demise to the ill-fated evangelistic meetings in Madison Square Gardens. 'Something snapped in his brain one night and out of his mouth there flowed "a seething torrent of defiling invective"'. Cf. Hollenweger, *Pentecostals*, 117. Orr also notes that the campaigns were a financial disaster 'leaving Zion $300,000 in debt'. J. E. Orr, *The Light of the Nations* (Exeter: Paternoster, 1965) 195.

[18] Wacker, 'Marching', 507.

[19] Wacker, 'Marching', 496, 507.

[20] Wacker, 'Marching', 508.

[21] This increasing egocentricity is a marked feature in the lives of some high profile religious figures. It seems likely that it is a response to the marginalisation of their ministry combined with a deepening sense of insecurity about its significance. Weaver points out that William Branham went through a parallel process to Dowie in the latter stages of his ministry. C. D. Weaver, *The Healer-Prophet* (Macon: Mercer University Press, 1987) 173.

[22] That Dowie had an imminent eschatology is clear, not least from the 1,100 year leases issued on property in Zion. These allowed for Christ's millennial rule after he returned according to Dowie before the year 2000. This allowed 100 years to 'build other Zion cities, reclaim Jerusalem, and literally establish the kingdom of God here on earth preparatory to his second coming.' Cook, *Zion*, 55.

[23] Cook, *Zion*, 51, cf. 55. Dowie had an extremely negative view of medicine.

[24] Hollenweger notes that Dowie put academic theology 'to his own use'. Hollenweger, *Pentecostals*, 117.

included all the mainstream academic disciplines. Whilst Dowie was an undoubted enthusiast one should not infer that he was an unintelligent or uninformed man.

Dowie's emphasis upon divine healing was clearly his main focus, but this in itself led to the beginnings of a demonology that would become pronounced in the ministries of later healing evangelists. In short, Dowie asserted that sickness was *always* to be considered of diabolic origin.[25] In time, and in combination with other factors, this teaching served to bring demonology to the foreground of his thought. Whereas mainstream Christian faith portrays the Devil leading humanity to destruction via temptation and sin, Dowie presented a Satan that lay behind *every* physical affliction.[26] This widened the Devil's sphere of activity and laid the foundation for a revival of a superstitious, dualistic Christianity that perceived the Devil behind every misfortune. Moreover, in common with many of his enthusiastic contemporaries Dowie had a very prominent concept of spiritual warfare; Satan and the demonic feature heavily in his thought.[27]

Dowie believed in 'demonic possession' lying behind problems such as addiction and deception.[28] It appears that Dowie did not consider the Christian to be immune from demonic assault: when his daughter's alcohol lamp exploded with fatal consequences, Dowie interpreted it as a satanic attack made possible due to her disobedience of his instruction regarding the prohibition of the use of alcohol.[29]

Dowie did not groom a successor and had no immediate link with any of the great healing evangelists of the 1940s and 50s. Nevertheless, Harrell observes that 'the indirect ties were many and important.'[30] Several important healing evangelists emerged from Zion including John Lake, the Bosworth brothers and Raymond T Richey. Gordon Lindsay also 'carried the mark of Zion'.[31] Charles Parham visited Dowie in 1900 and then again *en route* to Azusa Street in 1906;[32] Vreeland notes that 'many of those involved in the Azusa Street revival came from Zion, Illinois after the death of Dowie.'[33] Hollenweger observes that 'many of his followers in Switzerland, Holland, South Africa, and the USA

---

[25] Cook, *Zion*, 8, 14.

[26] An inevitable consequence of this belief is that healing ministry begins to merge into a form of deliverance ministry

[27] For example, Dowie embarked upon 'Three Months Holy War Against the Hosts of Hell in Chicago'. Cook, *Zion*, 20.

[28] Lindsay, *Dowie*, 101, 144.

[29] Cook, *Zion*, 120f.

[30] Harrell, *All*, 14.

[31] Harrell, *All*, 14.

[32] Sanders, *Seymour*, 63, 108.

[33] D. Vreeland, 'John Alexander Dowie', http://www.derekvreeland.com/history2.htm 3 (May 2003).

were leading Pentecostal preachers.'[34] John Alexander Dowie is a highly significant figure in the emergence of the Pentecostal movement[35] and his influence lies behind the healing revival of the 1940s and 50s. His enthusiastic credentials are exemplary. Given the above, the stress upon imminent eschatology and immanent spirituality could hardly be clearer.

Early Pentecostal Deliverance Ministry

Deliverance Ministry was a persistent secondary feature of early Pentecostalism inherited from the pre-existing radical evangelical groups from which the former emerged.[36] An article describing the Azusa Street Revival written in 1906 (perhaps authored by Frank Bartleman) makes the following statement:

> In the center of the big room is a box on end, covered with cotton, which a junk man would value at about 15 cents. This is the pulpit from which is sounded forth what the leader, Brother Seymour, calls old-time repentance, old-time pardon, old-time sanctification, *old-time power over devils and diseases*, and the old-time "Baptism with the Holy Ghost and fire."[37]

Two important implications may be drawn from this quote. Firstly, deliverance from devils was a part of the 'old-time' Gospel; hence deliverance was not an innovation at Azusa but a pre-existing component of the received

---

[34] Hollenweger, *Pentecostals*, 119.

[35] E. L. Blumhofer, 'Dowie, John Alexander' in S. M. Burgess and E. M. Van Der Maas (eds.), *The New International Dictionary of Pentecostal and Charismatic Movements* (Grand Rapids: Zondervan, 2002) 587.

[36] References to the eviction of evil spirits is extremely common in early Pentecostal journals. I have identified 30 references to such activity in *The Apostolic Faith Magazine* (which was the official publication of the Azusa Street Revival) and 27 in *Confidence* (which was published by A. A. Boddy as the voice of natal British Pentecostalism). For precise references see Appendix 1. Wacker makes five specific references to deliverance ministry in his study despite the fact that this subject is tangential to his area of study. Wacker, *Heaven*, 38f., 64, 65 (referring to hundreds of deliverances), 88 and 91-93. Cf. F. Bartleman, Azusa Street (New Kensington: Whittaker House, 1982) 66 and J. G. Lake, *John G Lake: His Life, His Sermons, His Boldness of Faith* (Fort Worth: Kenneth Copeland, 1994) 149f. Early Pentecostals were eager to stress their ability to evict demons, not only in order to demonstrate their spiritual competence, but also to overcome the objections of their opponents who accused them of giving reign to satanic activity through their lack of discernment regarding pneumatic manifestations and glossolalia in particular (See below chapter 4). Hence the following outraged sentiment 'This Pentecostal work *is* discovering and exposing the devils' *Confidence* (June 1910) 15.

[37] F Bartleman (?) *Way of Faith* (October 1906) quoted by Owens, 'Azusa', 51. Italics added for emphasis.

radical evangelical tradition. Secondly, deliverance was closely allied and ran parallel to physical healing due to a belief that at least some diseases were demonic in origin.[38] Nevertheless, it is important to bear in mind that emphasis upon divine healing does not inevitably lead to a similar emphasis upon deliverance; nevertheless, it usually does because there is often a concomitant belief that at least some disease is demonic in origin.

The early Pentecostals held to a conservative demonology and frequently indulged in theological dualism envisaging the Christian life as a battle against Satan and his demonic powers.[39] In addition to physical disease, a range of other problems might be attributed to their pernicious activity. Nevertheless, early, mainstream Pentecostals did not usually become preoccupied with the demonic.[40] Walker identifies three factors within early Pentecostalism that prevented the movement from adopting the sort of obsessive demonology apparent among Charismatics later in the century:

> First... it [early Pentecostalism] was essentially evangelistic in nature: its revivalistic impulse was heaven-bent on saving souls. Its evangelism therefore kept it outward-looking and Christ-centered, leaving its demonism in the wake of its excitement and enthusiasm. It was there alright, but it was peripheral and virtually out of sight. Second, Pentecostalists were too entranced with their own Pentecost – with its tongues, healings, and singalong songs – to be bewitched by beguiling theories of demonism. And third, Pentecostalists may have been educationally disadvantaged, but they were not stupid. What they lacked in cultural finesse they made up with working-class common sense.[41]

Much may be said to expand Walker's argument. Firstly, it is important to note that Walker rightly acknowledges that 'demonism' was present; this should not be underestimated – 'demonism' and deliverance was certainly a secondary characteristic of the movement. The key point that Walker is making is that it did not at this stage become a primary characteristic for the reasons he outlines.

Walker's analysis misses one major motive for Pentecostal optimism regarding the threat of the demonic. Their opponents accused them of opening

---

[38] Wacker, *Heaven*, 92. See Lake, *Lake*, 341-384 for some examples of healing defined as deliverance from demons.

[39] Wacker, *Heaven*, 24, 33, 35, 38, 59, 61, 63, 66 and particularly 91-92.

[40] There were exceptions most notably among Pentecostals ministering overseas. One example of this tendency is Lars Jeevaratnam whose mission work in India was marked by an emphasis upon deliverance from demons. See his publication L. Jeevaratnam, *Concerning Demons (Questions and Answers)* Allahabad: Mission Press, no date available, and his regular contributions to Redemption Tidings during the 1920s.

[41] Walker, 'Devil', 90.

the doorway to Satanic activity due to their acceptance of various pneumatic manifestations and so the Pentecostals were understandably at great pains to dismiss the threat of demonic activity. Hence they were keen to prove that they could evict demons from non-believers (usually as a component of conversion) and equally determined to indicate that demons could not possess a Spirit-filled Christian which for this reason went on to become a tenet of most Pentecostal denominations.[42]

Of the reasons given by Walker for this, the most compelling is that the early Pentecostals had a very optimistic view of the effects of both conversion and, particularly, the baptism of the Spirit. It was therefore unthinkable to most early Pentecostals that a 'Spirit-filled' Christian could be seriously afflicted, let alone, demonised – their sense and understanding of God's presence in their lives was too immediate.[43] Consequently, deliverance ministry to Spirit-filled believers did not easily gain a foothold among the Pentecostal communities. That it did so from time to time is evident from the manner in which the young Pentecostal denominations frequently ruled out the belief that a 'Spirit filled Christian' could be demonised.[44] If no one had been teaching otherwise there would have been no need to make this assertion.[45] Early Pentecostals however uniformly believed in the possibility of demon possession for non-Christians and would have been unperturbed, delighted even, by deliverance ministry being practised in this context. This point militates against Walker's view that

---

[42] Early Pentecostal references to the security of the spirit filled believer are frequent. Some have already been observed, for a host of others see Appendix 1. A somewhat technical issue that emerged from this contention about the Pentecostal manifestations is that of 'pleading the blood'. The Pentecostals placed great emphasis upon this procedure since it appears to have been a common place device for gaining protection from evil spirits in the Holiness milieu out of which sprung the Pentecostals and their opponents. Numerous examples of this particular emphasis in the journals of early Pentecostalism can be found in Appendix 1. Penn-Lewis recognises this Pentecostal move and counters it by asserting that 'pleading the blood' will not 'prevent Satan from working on the ground that he has a right to'; such ground may be gained by Satan through ignorance of how he seeks to counterfeit true Christianity with demonic [a.k.a. Pentecostal] manifestations and consequent demonic deception. Penn-Lewis, *War*, 78f., 64f. and 27-29.

[43] 'I believe before God there is not a devil that comes within a hundred feet of a real God-anointed Christian.' Lake, *Lake*, 146.

[44] These denominational assertions were at least partially a refutation of the suggestion that allowing spiritual manifestations to run wild was dangerous due to the possibility of being invaded by an evil spirit. This was the consistent accusation made by radical evangelicals outside of Pentecostalism (see the next chapter). See Lake, *Lake*, 145, 150 for a typically upbeat Pentecostal response.

[45] And of course many enthusiastic non-Pentecostal Holiness people were making this allegation precisely (see chapter 4). The Pentecostal contention that Christians cannot be demonised was largely motivated by the way they defended themselves from this critique.

the evangelistic nature of the early Pentecostals protected them from paranoid preoccupation with the demonic – it is precisely in the evangelistic context that Pentecostals were most likely to, and often did, practise deliverance.

This Pentecostal spiritual confidence and optimism also meant that they were less inclined to feel threatened spiritually by the demonic. Consequently deliverance ministry when practiced was usually conducted in a simple and straightforward manner with a degree of confidence.[46]

Finally, Walker may speak better than he knows when he asserts that the early Pentecostals' common sense safeguarded them from preoccupation with the demonic. He appears to suggest that this common sense acted as a substitute for a good education. However, in the light of the widespread adoption of deliverance ministry by middle-class, highly educated Charismatics later in the century, it seems likely that 'working-class common sense' is the best defence in any case.[47]

In addition to all of this it is undoubtedly the case that a degree of routinisation of charisma took place among the early Pentecostals.[48] In the very early days of Azusa Street revivalism the atmosphere was much the same as that of the camp meeting – unrestrained enthusiasm.[49] It was simply not possible to define the community of the Spirit-filled, consequently everyone was a potential subject for deliverance. As Pentecostal communities bedded down into more stable and static groups this revivalistic fervour died down and (particularly among second generation Pentecostals (frequently economically upwardly mobile)) became altogether less attractive. Hence, the prohibition of deliverance ministry on members of the 'Pentecostal community' was to some degree a result of the institutionalisation of the maturing Pentecostal movement.[50] Conversely, whilst the Pentecostal congregations experienced

---

[46] See Lake, *Lake*, 149f.

[47] The working class people who were drawn to early Pentecostalism were too busy trying to survive to be much interested in the kind of highly introspective deliverance ministry favoured by many Charismatics later in the century. To be sure, they might view their problems in terms of theological dualism but their problems were not usually in same categories as those of middle-class Charismatics. Of course the common characteristic was the need for physical healing but even here a difference is evident – if an early Pentecostal got sick she would ask for prayer and go to the doctor only if her theological conviction and financial status allowed it; when a late century Charismatic got sick he would certainly go the doctor and then ask for prayer if the condition was serious. One can immediately see why early Pentecostals were inclined to view physical ailments as a demonic attack.

[48] Bartleman, *Azusa*, 56f. Cf. Lake, *Lake*, xxxiiif.

[49] For an interesting transcript of sermons taken from a nineteenth-century camp meeting see A. Wallace, *A Modern Pentecost* (Salem: Convention, 1970).

[50] On routinisation and institutionalisation see Weber's classic study, M. Weber, *The Theory of Social and Economic Organisation* (New York: Free Press, 1947) and

routinisation there were still many 'old-time' itinerant healing evangelists keeping the flames of enthusiasm burning, generating new Pentecostal converts. Hence the story of early pre-war Pentecostalism is best understood as one of 'creative tension' between the increasingly routinised denominational congregations and the enthusiastic evangelists. It seems certain that deliverance ministry was more commonly practised by the itinerants rather than by the denominational leaders though this is extremely difficult to prove.[51]

Early Pentecostalism contained a number of characteristics that are powerfully conducive to the emergence of deliverance ministry. However, for the reasons outlined above most early Pentecostals could not conceive that Christians, particularly 'Spirit-filled' Christians, could be possessed by demons. Consequently, whilst the deliverance of non-Christians was very common, [52] it was not practised on existing members of the Pentecostal communities. The majority of the denominational hierarchies asserted clearly that a spirit-filled Christian was invulnerable to demonic possession. Deliverance ministry was significant without being central to early Pentecostal doctrine or practice and was largely practised within an evangelistic context.

Charismatic Deliverance Ministry and the Post War American Healing Revival

Itinerant Healing Evangelism Comes of Age

The late 1940s and the 1950s witnessed a remarkable surge in the popularity of the itinerant healing evangelists. Whilst this was primarily an American phenomenon, several figures rose to international fame including (pre-eminently) Oral Roberts, William Branham and Tommy Lee Osborn.

This sudden rise to prominence of the itinerant healing evangelists represented a rebellion against the perceived institutionalisation of Pentecostalism. The evangelists cast themselves as the preachers of the 'old-time Gospel'. Consequently, relations with the mainline Pentecostal denominations were often strained.

(applied to a specific Pentecostal context) M. Poloma, *The Assemblies of God at the Crossroads* (Knoxville: University of Tennessee, 1989).

[51] One noted exception to this generalisation is the case of Lewi Pethrus the well known Swedish Pentecostal pastor who believed that Christians were vulnerable to demonic possession where they were not baptised / filled with the Holy Spirit. L. Pethrus, *The Wind Bloweth Where it Listeth* (Chicago: Philapdelphia, 1945) 25-30.

[52] Hunt argues that it was the dualism inherent to the emergent Pentecostal movement that 'fostered an acceptance of the active nature of demonic forces' which in turn prompted the widespread exorcism of non-Christians. Hunt, *Themelios*, 11.

It was within the earthy, enthusiastic and fervent atmosphere of the healing revival that popular attention was drawn to the need for widespread deliverance ministry. A seed was planted in the Charismatic consciousness which took root and would eventually flower some decades later. This emphasis in the ministry of the healing evangelists was a bone of contention between them and the Pentecostal denominations who continued to vigorously reject the need for Spirit-filled Christians to be delivered from demons. However, the influence of the evangelists was such that the scene was set for obsession with the demonic and deliverance ministry found wide acceptance. Three prominent healing evangelists are examined below: William Branham who was the pioneer of the healing revival, Oral Roberts who was the most prominent of the healing evangelists and A A Allen who was, arguably, the most extreme.

Three Leading Healing Evangelists of the Post-War Revival

WILLIAM BRANHAM (1909-1965)[53]

William Branham was the first great healer evangelist of the post-War period achieving legendary status in the process. He emerged from a humble background to successfully serve as an independent Baptist minister. Ruined financially by the great depression of the 1930s, Branham's wife and child were killed in a flood in 1937. His great success as a healing evangelist was apparently initiated by an encounter with an angel on May 7 1946. The angel told him that 'God has sent you to take a divine gift of healing to the people of the world. IF YOU WILL BE SINCERE, AND CAN GET THE PEOPLE TO BELIEVE YOU, NOTHING SHALL STAND BEFORE YOUR PRAYER, NOT EVEN CANCER.'[54]

It appears that even prior to this crisis experience Branham's spirituality was characteristically esoteric.[55] This 'estranged him from the more sedate independent Baptists of his community' during his early ministry.[56] At this time Branham established some links with Pentecostals, primarily the controversial 'Jesus only' or 'Oneness' faction. He finally decided not to get involved with the latter due to their 'dubious social reputation.'[57] This was a decision he came to regret, believing that the death of his wife and son were God's judgement on his snobbery.[58]

Within a month or two of the angelic visitation Branham was preaching to

---

[53] There is a fair amount of literature on Branham, most of it hagiographical. Worthy of serious consideration is Weaver, *Healer*, Harrell, *All* and Hollenweger, *Pentecostals*.

[54] Lindsay, *Branham*, 77 cited by Harrell, *All*, 28.

[55] Weaver, *Healer*, 22-35.

[56] Harrell, *All*, 29.

[57] Harrell, *All*, 29.

[58] Weaver, *Healer*, 33.

thousands of people. His message was one of 'old-time' miracle power.[59] Gordon Lindsay, the administrative brain behind the healing revival attended a Branham meeting in 1947. He decided to work with Branham and was able to broaden Branham's appeal beyond the Oneness Pentecostals to a wider Pentecostal constituency.[60] Under Lindsay's guidance Branham's reputation grew rapidly; a fortnight of meetings in Vancouver attracted 70,000 people.[61] His itinerary was punishing and he began to suffer the effects of exhaustion; according to Weaver he lost forty pounds in the space of a year.[62]

In May 1948, with his popularity reaching fever pitch, Branham suddenly withdrew from public ministry on the grounds of ill-health (caused by exhaustion).[63] Lindsay, who had just launched a magazine to promote Branham's ministry, felt 'deserted'.[64]

Branham resumed his healing evangelism after a period of about five months, armed with a fresh revelation from the 'angel of the Lord' encouraging him to take his message around America and then to the wider world.[65] His popularity was not damaged by his brief sojourn. He commenced a series of campaigns including a visit to Zion city where he preached in Dowie's Shiloh Temple.[66] F. F. Bosworth, a former resident of Zion City, was a 'loyal supporter' of Branham from January 1948 until he [Bosworth] died ten years later.[67] Harrell notes this line of influence stretching from Dowie to Branham: 'without question Branham received inspiration and instruction in Pentecostal doctrine and campaigning techniques from Bosworth.'[68] In 1950 Branham travelled to Europe holding campaigns in Finland, Norway and Sweden.[69] Two

---

[59] Harrell, *All*, 30.

[60] Harrell, *All*, 32. He worked closely with both Oneness and Trinitarian Pentecostals for the rest of life. Harrell, *All*, 31.

[61] Harrell, *All*, 32. According to Weaver, Branham claimed 'that 35,000 persons received during the first year of his ministry.' Weaver, *Healer*, 47.

[62] Weaver, *Healer*, 48.

[63] The parallel with the early ministry of Evan Roberts (see chapter 5, above) is intriguing. The fact that Branham made a swift recovery and returned to the revival scene with renewed vigour suggests that he was not as emotionally vulnerable as Evan Roberts. I am grateful to my friend Meic Pearse for this observation.

[64] Harrell, *All*, 33.

[65] Harrell, *All*, 33.

[66] Harrell, *All*, 33. It was around this time that the famous photo of 'Branham with halo' was taken. Branham took this remarkable development in his stride. Harrell *All* 34f.

[67] Harrell, *All*, 34. Branham and Bosworth ministered together in late 1948 See *Voice of Healing* (December, 1948) 1-2.

[68] Harrell, *All*, 34. Gordon Lindsay also provided a line of influence from Dowie to Branham. Lindsay not only lived in Zion as a boy but had worked with John Lake, one of Zion's most prominent exports. D. D. Bundy, 'Lindsay, Gordon' in S. M. Burgess and E. M. Van Der Maas (eds.), *The New International Dictionary of Pentecostal and Charismatic Movements* (Grand Rapids: Zondervan, 2002) 842.

[69] Harrell, *All*, 35.

years later he was in Africa, he visited India in the following year and in 1955 he made another trip to Europe.[70]

During these years (1948-55) of his popularity 'Branham filled the largest stadiums and meeting halls in the world.'[71] However, as the healing revival tailed off in the late 1950s Branham went through a few lean years. He experienced financial difficulties[72] but nevertheless remained a significant and successful campaigner. He worked closely with the emerging Full Gospel Business Men's Fellowship International (FGBMFI) and its president, tycoon Demos Shakarian. The latter held Branham in great esteem.[73] This is a good illustration of the oft-neglected influence of the healing evangelists on the Charismatic Movement and its key leaders.

As Branham's popularity diminished in the late 1950s he began, like Dowie before him, to develop increasingly sensational, unpredictable and egotistical doctrines. His communication style became that of a prophet frequently using the Biblical phrase 'Thus saith the Lord' to lend his message more gravitas.[74] During this period of ministry, Branham condemned trinitarianism and denominationalism as diabolic, castigated women (allied to his infamous doctrine of the 'serpent's seed'), attacked the emergent prosperity of Pentecostals and his fellow revivalists, developed a heretical Christology, an imminent and extremely unconventional eschatology, and finally, in an intriguing and alarming parallel with Dowie, staked an implicit claim to be the prophet Elijah whose appearance was prophesied in Malachi 4:5-6.[75] Branham's followers though fewer in number were not short on commitment. A radical fringe asserted Branham's divinity, baptising converts in his name.[76]

Branham died in 1965, the victim of a head-wound sustained when he was hit by a car driven by a drunk driver. Hollenweger notes that he had predicted the manner of his death.[77] It was an enigmatic and tragic end to an enigmatic and often tragic life. Kenneth Hagin, no stranger to controversial doctrines himself, also claimed to have prophesied the death of Branham and declared that God removed the evangelist due to his heretical teaching.[78]

Branham's Influences
Three major streams of influence lie behind the ministry of William Branham. Firstly one can see a great deal of John Alexander Dowie's teaching on well-

---

[70] Pement, 'Family'. Cf Harrell, *All*, 35.

[71] Hollenweger, *Pentecostals*, 354.

[72] Difficulties began in 1955 when Branham was unable to meet his expenses. Pement, 'Family'.

[73] Harrell, *All*, 161.

[74] This attracted criticism from Pentecostals. Weaver, *Healer*, 140.

[75] Weaver, *Healer*, 119-121, 114-118, 109-113, 123-126, 109, 125f., 126-139.

[76] Weaver, *Healer*, 103.

[77] Hollenweger, *Pentecostals*, 354.

[78] Weaver, *Healer*, 105.

being and his stress upon the supernatural and prophetic. Dowie's influence was mediated by both Bosworth and Lindsay who were both products of Zion City. Furthermore, the teaching of E. W. Kenyon regarding 'faith, confession and healing' which lies at the root of the word-faith movement seems to have been incorporated into Branham's theology and practice.[79] Another influence upon Branham was the oddball evangelist Franklin Hall whose teaching was 'the initial impetus of the Latter-Rain movement.'[80] Hall taught that fasting was the key to extraordinary, supernatural Christianity.[81] Branham along with the other healing evangelists accepted, practised and propagated this teaching.[82]

Branham's Angel
Branham's angelic advisor apparently granted him two signs with which to convince people of his message. Firstly, taking someone's left hand Branham was able (via 'vibrations') to diagnose spiritual and physical oppression. Where Branham encountered an afflicting spirit his reaction was sufficiently strong to be visible and to 'stop his wrist-watch instantly'.[83] When the spirit was evicted one could 'see Brother Branham's red and swollen hand return to its normal condition.'[84] The second sign was Branham's use of the so-called 'word of knowledge'. Inexplicably, he appeared able to identify facts about people that he could have no natural way of knowing. In particularly Branham would identify the sins that held people back from receiving their healing. The evangelist would identify these sins quietly in order to protect privacy.[85] Remarkably, as well regarded an authority as Hollenweger, who 'knew Branham personally and interpreted for him in Zurich, is not aware of any case

---

[79] R. M. Bowman, *The Word-Faith Controversy: Understanding the Health and Wealth Gospel* (Grand Rapids: Baker, 2001) 87f. F. F. Bosworth was the link between Kenyon and Branham.

[80] Bowman, *Word*, 87, 89. Cf. Hollenweger, *Pentecostals*, 140-148. Instructively, Hollenweger notes the prevalence of demonology within the movement and the similarity between 'Dowie's Christian Catholic Church and a Pentecostal Church in the early stages of its development.' Hollenweger, *Pentecostals*, 144f., 145. For details of the Latter-Rain movement see R. M. Riss, 'Latter Rain Movement', in S. M. Burgess and E. M. Van Der Maas (eds.), *The New International Dictionary of Pentecostal and Charismatic Movements* (Grand Rapids: Zondervan, 2002) 830ff. Branham's teaching was also a catalyst in the emergence of the Latter Rain movement. Bowman, *Word*, 87f.

[81] Harrell, *All*, 80-82.

[82] Bowman also observes that, like Hall, Branham was involved in 'Christian astrology.' Bowman, *Word*, 87.

[83] F. F. Bosworth, *The Voice of Healing* (March, 1950) 10 cited by Harrell, *All*, 37.

[84] Bosworth cited by Harrell, *All*, 37.

[85] Hollenweger, *Pentecostals*, 354. Cf. Harrell, *All*, 38 and D. E. Harrell, 'Healers and Televangelists after World War II' in V. Synan (ed.), *The Century of the Holy Spirit* (Nashville: Thomas Nelson, 2001) 326.

in which he was mistaken in the often detailed statements he made'.[86]

Branham's Demonology and Practice of Exorcism[87]

None of the major historians/analysts (Hollenweger, Harrell etc) identify deliverance ministry as a chief characteristic of Branham's ministry. This is primarily due to the fact that their interest lies elsewhere. In fact, a close inspection reveals that Branham was a regular practitioner of deliverance and placed great emphasis upon it even from the start of his ministry. Three factors should be considered here:

a) Explicit exorcism was definitely a feature of his ministry[88] and this was seen by his colleagues and followers as highly significant. Lindsay records an occasion where Branham exorcised a man who approached him during a campaign meeting with murderous intent. In order to display the power of Christ, Branham commanded the man to bow at his feet. Lindsay also recalls a separate exorcism affected by Branham. There is no doubt that Lindsay sees these events as indicative of God's special anointing on the evangelist.[89] Weaver describes this story as one of Branham's 'favourite miraculous events' which he often recounted when preaching. This emergence of the use of exorcism as vindication is of key significance and offers a motive for the increasing obsession with the demonic and the inspired minister's authority among the healing evangelists. In the highly competitive world of healing evangelism a graphic and dramatic spiritual power encounter testimony would sensationally and convincingly convey the authority of the evangelist.[90]

b) Demonology was a prominent part of Branham's thinking. He believed in a personal devil and personal demons claiming to have conversed 'face to face' with the latter.[91] Moreover, in a typical enthusiastic dualism Branham tended to collapse human experience into two spheres of supernatural agency; events were either of God or of the Devil. Hence, confronting the demonic became a key aspect of his ministry whether through deliverance or, more commonly, through exposing 'demonic' doctrines,[92] philosophies[93] or behaviour. He also wrote pamphlets and preached on the subject of demonology.[94] According to

---

[86] Hollenweger, *Pentecostals*, 354.

[87] In 1976 Branham published a book entitled *Demonology* (which was largely transcripts of sermons delivered on the subject in the early/mid 1950s). His justification for belief in Satan is typically enthusiastic, that is to say based upon a claim to first hand experience that is so explicit that it is not open to any other interpretation. W. Branham, *Demonology* (Jefferson: Spoken Word, 1976) 9.

[88] Weaver, *Healer*, 61-63.

[89] G. Lindsay, *The Gordon Lindsay Story* (Dallas: CFN, 1992) 149f.

[90] On this point see also A. Finlay, *Demons!* (London: Blandford, 1999) 37.

[91] Weaver, *Healer*, 61.

[92] Such as trinitarianism! Weaver, *Healer*, 120.

[93] Weaver, *Healer*, 113f.

[94] For example, Branham, *Demonology*.

Weaver Branham believed that uncontrollable sin, insanity and even 'temper tantrums' were attributable to demon-possession[95] the clear implication being that a (Pentecostal, spirit-filled) Christian could be demon possessed.[96]

c) Like Dowie and the pre-war healing revivalists, before him Branham believed that all sickness was demonic.[97] The fact that Branham's ministry (and that of his contemporaries) was often called 'deliverance' suggests that, broadly, they viewed their healings as a form of exorcism.

Two facets of Branham's demonology that recur frequently in later charismatic teaching are transgenerational demon possession (demon possession is due to sin committed by the victim's forebears) and the danger of transference (that demons be ousted from one body only to occupy that of someone nearby).[98] Moreover he held that evicted demons tried to gain access to human beings via the eyes. This teaching is a prototype of the more developed idea of 'entry points' held by later practitioners of deliverance ministry. Moreover Branham identified 'insanity and temper tantrums as demons.'[99] Hence, all the basic strands of deliverance ministry may be found in the teaching and practice of Branham.

One should not conclude that Branham was the innovator behind deliverance ministry. Deliverance ministry played a prominent part in the ministry of many of the itinerant Pentecostal healing evangelists and had done for decades.[100] However, it was Branham's sheer influence and the dramatic nature of his deliverance ministry itself that initiated its wider adoption.

It has already been noted that the early Pentecostals would have rejected the concept of deliverance ministry since they were too enamoured with the benefits of Spirit-baptism to contemplate the possibility that a 'Spirit-filled believer' could simultaneously be demonised. Whilst Branham might well have concurred, his obsession with the demonic effectively overtook this. Effectively his demonology grew to the point where it overtook his optimism regarding the benefits of Spirit baptism. Again, he was not the first to make this journey but he was undoubtedly the most influential.

William Branham remains an elusive and enigmatic character. As the initiator of the post-war healing revival he remains a mysterious, almost

---

[95] Weaver, *Healer*, 62. Actually, Branham believed that the mass of sinful humanity as well as nominal Christianity was all subject to the influence of 'enticing spirits' Branham, *Demonology*, 79f.

[96] Branham makes this point clearly in a 1953 sermon. Branham, *Demonology*, 23.

[97] Weaver, *Healer*, 62. Of course this view was and is not uncommon among Pentecostals and indeed contemporaries of Dowie in the Higher Life tradition. In a 1953 sermon Branham outlined this doctrine in a hopelessly naïve manner, Branham, *Demonology*, 21-39.

[98] Weaver, *Healer*, 62f.

[99] Weaver, *Healer*, 62.

[100] Examples include John Lake. G. Lindsay (ed.), *The New John G Lake Sermons* (Dallas: CFN, 1979) 29f. and 57f.

mythical figure:

> Branham's sermons were indeed simple; hundreds of extant recordings demonstrate that. And yet, the power of a Branham service – and of Branham's stage presence – remains a legend unparalleled in the history of the charismatic movement.[101]

Branham was not by any means innovative in his practice of deliverance, however, his popularity and influence ensured that the other healing evangelists that followed him would also practice deliverance from demons. As a result deliverance came to play a much more prominent role within Pentecostalism and indeed the emergent Charismatic Movement.

ORAL ROBERTS (1918-)

If Branham's ministry gave the initial impetus to the post-War healing revival then it was Oral Roberts who became its leading light. Rising to prominence just after Branham, the ministries he initiated continue to expand and grow, even to the present day. His significance for this study lies in the progression of the emphasis he placed upon deliverance ministry compared to the ministry of Branham and his more prominent role in the emergence of the Charismatic Movement.

Biography[102]

Born in 1918, Roberts was raised in a poverty-stricken family. His father owned a small-holding, but in 1916 sold it and embarked upon a career as a minister / evangelist of the Pentecostal Holiness Church.[103] In 1935 Roberts contracted tuberculosis which cut short his teenage rebellion and threatened to cut short his life. The turning point came when he was taken to a healing revival conducted locally by Geo W Moncey.[104] Roberts believed that he was

---

[101] Harrell, *All*, 162.

[102] Roberts has written autobiographical accounts including O Roberts *My Story* (Tulsa: Summit, 1961); O. Roberts, *My Twenty Years of a Miracle Ministry* (Tulsa: Oral Roberts, 1967); O. Roberts, *The Call: An Autobiography* (New York: Doubleday, 1972). The only serious academic treatment of his life and significance is that of David Harrell. His analysis is to be found in D. E. Harrell, *Oral Roberts: An American Life* (Bloomington: Indiana University Press, 1985) and to a lesser extent in his previous study of the post-War healing revival, Harrell, *All*.

[103] Harrell, *Oral*, 15.

[104] Harrell describes Moncey as 'one of that generation of roving revivalists who continued to fight the devil in the depths of the Depression after such stalwarts of the 1920s as Aimee Semple McPherson, Charles Price, B. B. Bosworth and Raymond T. Richey had retired to the shelter of local churches.' Harrell, *Oral*, 5. It is important to remember that Pentecostalism spread through the ministries of the itinerant evangelists. This study focuses on the most prominent of these, but for every Dowie, Bosworth or

healed as Moncey 'delivered' him from the 'tormenting disease',[105] although his recovery was gradual.[106]

During his illness Roberts underwent a Christian conversion, and his healing experience was enough to prompt him to join his father in itinerant evangelism.[107] His reputation grew rapidly and he swiftly rose to prominence within his native denomination.[108] By 1947 Roberts was the pastor of the congregation at Enid, Oklahoma.[109] Growing dissatisfied with the apathy of this congregation, Roberts became preoccupied with divine healing. At the climax of a month of concentrated prayer and study of the Gospels and Acts he heard God say to him, 'from this hour your ministry of healing will begin. You will have my power to pray for the sick and to *cast our devils.*'[110] Consequently, Roberts began to hold healing services, firstly in his own church and thereafter in a larger building in 'downtown Enid.'[111] The popularity of these meetings was such that Oral decided to resign his pastorate and embark upon an itinerant ministry of healing and evangelism.[112] Shortly afterwards, in July 1947, the Roberts family moved to Tulsa which has been the headquarters of their operation ever since.[113]

For the next decade or so Roberts enjoyed almost uninterrupted success as the 'leader of the [post-war] salvation- healing revival.'[114] However, as the 1960s approached and the revival began to run out of steam, even 'America's premier healing evangelist'[115] found his appeal waning. Although the campaigns continued in the 1960s, they tended to be shorter and latterly the attendances began to fall away.[116] The last crusades were held in 1968/69[117]; thereafter Roberts focused his attention on his two other major ministries, Oral

---

Branham there were thousands of humble itinerant ministers of the 'Full Gospel'. The advent of mass media curtailed this characteristic of Pentecostalism but did not eradicate it.

[105] Harrell, *Oral*, 7. Note the manner in which healing and deliverance are fused. This was typical of the thinking of the healing revivalists. To be healed is to be delivered from a demonic affliction. Cf (for example) Roberts, *Story*, 19.

[106] Harrell, Oral, 35-37.

[107] Harrell, *Oral*, 36.

[151] Harrell, *Oral*, 37f., 41-44.

[152] Harrell, *Oral*, 62.

[153] Harrell, *Oral*, 67, italics added for emphasis.

[154] Harrell, *Oral*, 68

[112] Harrell, *Oral*, 69

[113] Harrell, *Oral*, 80f.

[114] Harrell, *All*, 41f

[115] P. G. Chappell, 'Roberts, Oral Granville' in S. M. Burgess and E. M. Van Der Maas (eds.), *The New International Dictionary of Pentecostal and Charismatic Movements* (Grand Rapids: Zondervan, 2002) 1024.

[116] Harrell, *Oral*, 253-261.

[117] Harrell, *Oral*, 261.

Roberts University and televangelism.

Roberts first made television programmes in 1954 but decided to stop in the mid 1960s. In March 1969 he returned to this medium in a bold new format with 'an entertainment quality... and an informal atmosphere.'[118] Although the racy style attracted some criticism from traditional Pentecostals the shows were an outstanding success.

Roberts' greatest achievement is undoubtedly the establishment of ORU (Oral Roberts University) and the $250m City of Faith (a medical and research centre). These have been established on an overtly Charismatic Christian and ethically rigorous base. By the mid-80s ORU housed several major faculties, offering numerous graduate and post-graduate programmes. It had an established track record in both academic and sporting arenas.

Roberts' startling success lies in his uncompromising commitment to excellence and his ability to make decisive and radical shifts when required to by changing circumstances. From humble origins he progressed from small-time Pentecostal pastorates to become one of the world's leading revivalists, the pioneer of modern televangelism (achieving media-celebrity status in the process) and the driving force behind a leading academic institution. Small wonder that Harrell asserts that Roberts 'has been one of the most influential religious leaders in the world in the twentieth century'.[119] His significance is probably only superseded by his friend Billy Graham.

Roberts' Role in the Progress of Charismatic Deliverance Ministry
Roberts' significance for this study revolves around two key factors; firstly, his overt emphasis upon exorcism/deliverance ministry[120] and secondly, his pre-eminent role in healing revivalism and his ability to take his emphases beyond the strictures of the Pentecostal subculture into the emergent Charismatic Movement.

Reflecting on his early ministry, Roberts writes:

I had only one fear as we prayed for the sick, and that was praying with those who were 'demon possessed'. Papa always warned me to be careful when dealing with these unfortunate people, for the demon, when cast out, may strive to enter someone else. He told me never to pray for any of them until I felt a special anointing of God's power. His warnings frightened me so that I prayed for only a few in my early ministry. But I had the desire and urge to pray for them. It was difficult to restrain

---

[118] Harrell, *Oral*, 268.
[119] Harrell, *Oral*, vii.
[120] See his article on the subject, O. Roberts, 'Demon Possession' in *Voice of Healing* (November, 1951) 8, 23, and, much later, O. Roberts, *How to Resist the Devil and His Demons* (Tulsa: Oral Roberts, 1989) which nevertheless includes stories from much earlier in his career.

myself, for I loved them and 'felt' for them. I can see now the wisdom in Papa's warning and his care for me. I was not yet twenty years old, and he knew I must wait until I became more mature.[121]

Harrell notes that for Roberts:

Demons loomed large in his early healing ministry. The sensitivity in his right hand gave him the 'power to detect the presence, names and numbers of demons' in afflicted people. Concerning demons, he wrote: 'A demon is a strange, abnormal personality of evil. He lost his celestial body, spiritual illumination, godly knowledge and balance. He is now a miserable, disenfranchised, homeless, psychopathic creature.' Roberts believed that demons were responsible for insanity, one of man's most formidable enemies.[122]

In the earliest years of his healing ministry, Oral, and his audiences, seemed spellbound by demons and their relation to human sickness. He thought his sermon on demon possession usually turned 'the tide of the meeting'; his audiences marvelled at Oral's command over the evil spirits.[123]

All this is of singular importance since it highlights the existing emphasis on deliverance within pre-War Pentecostalism and the fact that some of the features so common in later Charismatic deliverance ministry are already explicit here. One can note the danger of demonic transference, the discernment of the number and names of demons to facilitate their eviction. Furthermore, the naïve association of insanity with demonisation is reflected in the approaches of the early Charismatic practitioners. There can be little doubt that this emphasis upon deliverance from evil spirits made a significant impact upon the emergent Charismatic leaders. Inevitably, Roberts found himself involved in the deliverance of existing Christians which proved to be such a decisive

---

[121] Roberts, *Story*, 39f. Note that deliverance was clearly a feature of his father's ministry.

[122] Harrell, *All*, 50. Cf. Roberts, *Resist*, 26-30. Note how the overlap in technique between Roberts and Branham. Branham used his left hand whilst Roberts used his right. Roberts also discerned the presence of demons by observing 'the leering and gleaming in the eye of the individual' and 'the breath or odour of the body... [even] if a person is five or six people away.' Harrell, *Oral*, 453.

[123] Harrell, *Oral*, 453. Note also the comments of O. E. Sproull in Roberts' early and popular *If You Want Healing Do These Things* (Tulsa: Healing Waters, 1954 (but first published in 1947)) viff. Whilst there is some evidence to suggest that Roberts moderated his interest in the demonic it was still an important issue when the City of Faith was developed. Harrell, *Oral*, 454.

move in the subsequent ministries of Charismatic practitioners.[124] This conclusion is further supported when one is aware of Roberts' strategic role in the emergence of the Charismatic Movement itself.[125]

It has already been observed that Roberts was able to make decisive shifts in his ministry when he felt they were required. Towards the end of the 1950s Roberts' began to disassociate himself from the more extreme healing evangelists and increasingly attempted to portray his ministry as within the orthodox, Evangelical Protestant tradition.[126] There can be no doubt that his image improved and his appeal broadened to include many Christians from outside the Pentecostal churches. His status as the undisputed leader of the healing revival left him well placed to make an impact on the emergent Charismatic Movement, but this impact was enhanced by Roberts' chameleon-like ability to adapt to new surroundings. Whilst Branham had gradually faded from sight, unable to effectively relate to the new breed of middle-class Charismatics, Roberts underwent a major metamorphosis which culminated, in 1968, in leaving the Pentecostal Holiness church and transferring his ministerial credentials to the Methodist church.[127] From 1963, Roberts played host to a significant series of conferences in the 1960s that were 'important stimuli to the budding Charismatic Movement.'[128] ORU went into operation in 1965 amidst hot opposition from the largest Pentecostal denomination, the Assemblies of God, whose own plans to build a similar university were undermined. This opposition provided further reason for the University to make its primary appeal towards charismatics in the established denominations. ORU was another important factor in Roberts' growing credibility and influence as a mainstream Christian leader.

By the end of the 1960s Roberts had left Pentecostalism trailing in his wake whilst maintaining largely orthodox Pentecostal doctrines. He was positioned as an influential and respectable Christian leader within the established denominations. His ministry won admirers and supporters from right across the Christian spectrum. There can be no doubt Oral Roberts played a significant role in cultivating and establishing the Charismatic Movement helping to

---

[124] Roberts, *Resist*, 26-30.

[125] Chappell notes that Roberts 'was ... influential in the formation of the Full Gospel Business Men's Fellowship International in 1951 as well as a leading figure in laying the foundation for the modern charismatic movement.' Chappell, 'Roberts', 1024.

[126] Harrell, *Oral*, 178.

[127] Harrell, *Oral*, 293-298. One is left with the impression that Oral Roberts simply outgrew Pentecostalism. His vision was too extensive and his influence too pervasive to remain restricted by his undeniable sense of loyalty towards Pentecostalism in general and the Pentecostal Holiness church in particular. When the opportunity arose to penetrate mainstream evangelicalism Roberts grasped it with both hands taking his message of healing and deliverance ministry with him.

[128] Harrell, *Oral*, 216. Roberts, like Branham but to more significant extent, was a major influence on the emergence of the FGBMFI.

embed an emphasis upon deliverance ministry in the process.

A. A. ALLEN

Biography[129]
Asa Alfonso Allen was born in 1911 in deprived circumstances. He inherited a
drink problem from his father that appears to have stayed with him throughout
his career as a healing evangelist. Allen was converted in 1934 and became a
Pentecostal pastor two years later.[130] His ministry developed slowly, however,
he came to prominence as a healing revivalist during the post-War revival.

In the mid-1950s Allen's relations with his own denomination, the
Assemblies of God, grew tense, as they felt embarrassed by the increasingly
sensational nature of his ministry. This came to a head in late 1955 when he
was arrested on suspicion of drink driving which prompted his departure from
both his denomination and the loose affiliation of healing revivalists, *Voice of
Healing*. Despite his best attempts, Allen never really managed to shake off the
suspicion that he persistently drank to excess.[131]

Allen remained faithful to traditional campaigns of healing revivalism even
when the revival began to decline towards the end of the 1950s. He excoriated
other healing evangelists for changing their methods when things got tough[132]
and asserted that the 'old-time religion is still the newest thing around'.[133]
Despite this he was not afraid to add new styles to his campaigns such as
'gospel rock music' while continuing to lay on 'an endless array of spectacular
miracles.'[134] Increasingly his ministry drew support from the poor and
marginalised; Allen enjoyed a particularly good rapport with the black racial
minorities.[135]

By the mid-1960s Allen's drink problem was becoming more obvious,
causing him to miss revivals. In 1967 he divorced his wife. Three years later he
died alone of sclerosis of the liver in a San Francisco Hotel 'while his team was
conducting a revival in Wheeling, West Virginia.'[136]

---

[129] There is no comprehensive scholarly biography of Allen available. Apart from one
brief article (S. Shemeth, 'Allen, Asa Alonso' in S. M. Burgess and E. M. Van Der Maas
(eds.), *The New International Dictionary of Pentecostal and Charismatic Movements*
(Grand Rapids: Zondervan, 2002) 311f., the only trustworthy material available is to be
found in Harrell, *All*, 66-75 and 194-206.
[130] Shemeth 'Allen' 311.
[131] Harrell, *All*, 70-72.
[132] Harrell, *All*, 194.
[133] Harrell, *All*, 195.
[134] Harrell, *All*, 198f.
[135] Harrell, *All*, 201f.
[136] Harrell, *All*, 202. Cf. Walker, 'Devil', 91.

Allen's Obsession - Extreme Deliverance Ministry
If Branham was the pioneer of the revival and Roberts was its popular face, then Allen exemplifies its extreme sensationalism. Harrell concludes that once '[the daring healing evangelist] Jack Coe died, he had no rival as the boldest of the bold'.[137] Accordingly, Allen's ministry demonstrated a preoccupation with demons and ministry to those they afflicted.[138] He published numerous books and pamphlets on the subject of demon possession, deliverance and other related topics.[139] Allen attributed a great deal of spiritual and physical problems (including mental illness) to demonic possession[140] and encouraged sufferers to attend one of his revival meetings or failing that to write to him for a specially anointed cloth.[141] He also suggested that sufferers should 'name the kind of demon from which you desire to be set free, (if known).'[142] His preoccupation with the demonic led Allen to publish eighteen pictures of demons as seen and drawn by a demon possessed woman'[143] and recordings of what Allen claimed to be a demon speaking and indeed revealing important information.

A. A. Allen represents the extreme end of the healing revival. His example demonstrates how great a significance deliverance ministry may take on in excessive versions of Charismatic ministry. Its sensational and dramatic nature lends credibility to the practitioner where appeal is based upon charismatic endowment and spiritual authority. Due to his extremism, Allen is a very clear illustration of this trend.

Enthusiastic Christian Ministry and the Logic of Competitive Itineracy

Enthusiastic Christian professionals/activists (in both the technical and non-technical senses) are always predisposed towards itinerant ministry. It promises the opportunity to focus on those areas of ministry that capture the attention of the practitioner. Itinerancy also offers liberation from the stifling routinised institutionalism and often risk averse nature of the settled congregation with its

---

[137] Harrell, *All*, 68.

[138] Harrell, *All*, 88. Cf *Voice of Healing* (October, 1954) 22f.

[139] Including, principally, A. A. Allen, *Demon Possession Today and How to be Free* (Miracle Valley: A. A. Allen, 1953). Reading this book, one is struck by its close similarity to the publications of Charismatic practitioners writing twenty years later. See also A. A. Allen, *Invasion from Hell* (Miracle Valley: A. A. Allen, 1953), A. A. Allen, *The Tormenting Demon of Fear* (no publication details available), A. A. Allen, *It Pays to Serve the Devil* (no publication details available), A. A. Allen, *Witchcraft, Wizards and Witches* (Miracle Valley: A. A. Allen, 1968). The latter appears to narrowly predate the SRA obssession which was to emerge among Charismatics and EFs in the 1970s and 80s.

[140] Allen, *Demon*, 36-41.

[141] Allen, *Demon*, 143-152.

[142] Harrell, *All*, 88.

[143] Harrell, *All*, 88.

denominational structures. However, these freedoms come at a price.

The post-War healing revival was an extremely competitive environment and the evangelists themselves were not beyond behaving in a sub-Christian (sometimes petty and bizarre) fashion in seeking to establish themselves. They often advertised their ministry in a manner designed to make clear their pre-eminence in the revival, not least by frequent assertions that they were in possession of the biggest campaign tent.

Certainly the emphasis upon the demonic was part of a general tendency towards the sensational which was part of the appeal of the evangelists. Moreover, the frequent relation of successful and spectacular power encounters certainly helped to establish the spiritual authority of the evangelists when they were often under attack from each other (and the mainline denominations). Below is a fairly typical example of a narrative functioning in this way:

> One night I was praying for people in the healing line. Several were present to be delivered from demons. I always ask people to be reverent, to remain seated with heads bowed. A man over on my right would not bow his head; he was making fun and sitting there saying, 'There's nothing to all this.' I warned him, as I warn everybody when I come to cast out demons. I know that you might make fun of some things but don't ever make fun of the real power of God. You are digging your own grave when you do that; besides you are getting mighty close to blaspheming the Holy Spirit when you make fun of the works of the Holy Ghost. I warned him, I warned the crowd, urging everyone to be reverent. But the man sat there and looked at me. I said, 'All right, you'll take your responsibility, I won't. If you'll do as I say, I'll take responsibility for you and nothing will happen to you.' He took his own responsibility. Through the power of God, I cast the demons out of the man I was praying for. The dispossessed demons went through the audience seeking someone to enter. They struck this irreverent man a blow and knocked him completely out of his chair onto the ground. The ushers found him writhing and twisting and biting his own tongue and trying to scream out his misery. I told the ushers to bring him to me. They picked him up and carried him to me on the platform. It took me five minutes to get him delivered by the power of God. When he walked off that platform he was a different man. He will never make fun again. That has happened several times in our meetings.[144]

---

[144] O. Roberts, in *Voice of Healing* (November, 1951) 8f. For more examples of deliverance narratives functioning to establish the spiritual credentials of the revivalist see *Voice of Healing* (October, 1952) 6; A. A. Allen 'Demon Possession Today' in *Voice of Healing* (May, 1953) 23; Allen, *Demon*, 19-21. See also a case of deliverance ministry in the Philippines: L. Sumrall, *The True Story of Clarita Villaneuva* (Manilla:

It seems likely therefore that the emphasis upon deliverance ministry was driven in part by the competitive nature of the ministry during the revival which demanded continual evidence of the evangelists' elevated spiritual status and increasingly spectacular evidence of God's presence and power.

Assessment: The Healing Evangelists' Contribution to the Progress of Deliverance Ministry

The key advocates of healing revivalism in the American post-War healing revival often referred to their message and ministry as one of 'deliverance'. Whilst this term was undoubtedly widely used prior to their use of it their popularity was the key factor in bringing it to common parlance and (perhaps unwittingly) placing their ministries in the context of spiritual warfare. Moreover, some figures on the fringes of the revival placed great emphasis upon deliverance from demons in a manner that greatly resembles that of the later Charismatic practitioners, occasionally including the possibility that Spirit filled believers require such ministry.[145]

Lester Sumrall, 1955). Sumrall claims to have delivered this young girl from two demons one of which was attacking her physically, leaving behind visible bite marks. As Sumrall presents the case, the supernatural elements involved were of such an obvious nature that the deliverance 'WAS THE MIRACLE THAT OPENED THE HEARTS OF THE PEOPLE OF MANILA TO THE FULL GOSPEL, AND PREPARED THE WAY FOR THE GREAT REVIVALS WHICH FOLLOWED.' Sumrall, *Clarita*, 103. Cf. *Voice of Healing* (October, 1953) 10. Regarding Sumrall's approach to and experience of deliverance ministry see also L. Sumrall, 'An Evil Spirit was Starving a Girl to Death' in *Voice of Healing* (September, 1955) 6 and L. Sumrall, *The Gates of Hell* (South Bend: World Harvest Press, no date available). Lester Sumrall was very influential in the establishment of another advocate and practitioner of deliverance ministry, that of Norvel Hayes. N. Hayes, *How to Cast out Devils* (Tulsa: Harrison, 1982) 7f. Sumrall first encountered Hayes via the Full Gospel Business Men's Fellowship International.

[145] H. A. Maxwell Whyte is the clearest example. His understanding was featured in *Voice of Healing* (July, 1953) 14, 25. Cf. 'Delivering a Haunted House' in *Voice of Healing* (November, 1958) 8. Among Whyte's many publications in the field of deliverance see H. Whyte, *The Kiss of Satan* (Monroeville: Whitaker, 1973); *Return to the Pattern* (no publication details but with a foreword by Derek Prince on whom see below); *The Body is for the Lord* (first published in 1969, no other publication details); *Pulling Down Strongholds* (no publication details); *Dominion Over Demons* (Monroeville: Banner, 1973 – with a foreword by Don Basham). See also, T. N. Foster, 'Divine Deliverance in the Local Churches' in *Voice of Healing* (September, 1953) 2; L. C. Harris, 'Deliverance from Evil Spirits' in *Voice of Healing* (July, 1954) 11 and 19; H. Hampel, 'I Met the Devil Face to Face' in *Voice of Healing* (June, 1956) 9f. By the late 1950s almost all of the healing evangelists had published something in the area of demonology; competence in this area had become an expected component of healing revivalism. Gordon Lindsay published various pamphlets including an extended one that

The healing evangelists were keen to establish their spiritual credentials by demonstrating and then advertising their expertise in dealing with evil spirits. This desire, so evident in the examinations of Branham, Roberts and Allen above, to establish their spiritual competency not only lay behind their emphasis upon deliverance ministry, but also indicates their enthusiastic tendency towards spiritual immanency. This, combined with their clear and typical impulse towards feverish, imminent eschatology squarely locates them within the category of enthusiasm. Therefore the emphasis upon deliverance ministry served to validate the enthusiastic ministry of the healing evangelists and was consequently of increasing importance to the healing revival as a whole.

In his discussion of Charismatic demonology Walker states that:

> we could trace the influence of Allen... and Roberts on modern Charismatics, but I [Walker] think a more profitable line to follow would be to show the personal and theological link between Branham... and the group known as 'The Fort Lauderdale 5.'[146]

Actually both streams of influence are of great significance for this study. Firstly, (as will become very clear) the healing revival of the late 1940s and 1950s 'stood at the cradle' of the birth of the Charismatic Movement.[147] Hence the Charismatic Movement bears the stamp of the healing revivalists such as Branham, Allen and Roberts, including their key emphasis upon deliverance ministry. Secondly, Branham (via his close associate Ern Baxter) exerted influence on the Fort Lauderdale Five.[148] The latter were the driving force behind the Restorationist movement of the 1970s and 1980s and were an important factor in the great popularity of deliverance ministry among Charismatics during the same period.

It should be clear that the term 'deliverance' pre-dates the healing revival; it

---

bears many similarities to those of the Charismatic practitioners G. Lindsay, *Satan, Fallen Angels and Demons (and how to have power over them)* (Dallas: The *Voice of Healing*, no date available).

[146] Walker, 'Devil', 91.

[147] Paul Cain's name may be added to the list of those who featured in the healing revival and went on to play significant parts in the Charismatic Movement See P. Cain, 'I was not disobedient to the Heavenly Vision' in *Voice of Healing* (August, 1951) 16. Cf. *Voice of Healing* (January, 1952) 3. Kenneth Hagin is another prominent Charismatic whose featured in the magazine of the healing revival. K. Hagin, 'A Vision of the End-Time' in *Voice of Healing* (September, 1963) 10f. Hagin also went on to publish various pamphlets regarding the demonic: K. E. Hagin, *Demons and How to Deal with Them* (Tulsa: Kenneth Hagin Ministries, 1979) and K. E. Hagin, *Ministering to the Oppressed* (Tulsa: Kenneth Hagin Ministries, 1986).

[148] Baxter had been present throughout the post-War healing revival. See *Voice of Healing* (December, 1948) 8f.

was commonly a feature of early century Pentecostal revivalists such as John Lake and F F Bosworth who may well have picked it up while living in John Alexander Dowie's Zion City. Nevertheless, the post-War healing revival popularised deliverance ministry, taking it beyond the boundaries of Pentecostalism and embedding it within the emergent Charismatic Movement.

Writing in January 1955, H A Maxwell Whyte highlighted the need that existed for 'deliverance pastors' namely pastors who would function as healing evangelists within local congregations.[149] It is surely not coincidental that he was one of the first advocates of deliverance ministry to existing Christians in a manner that would later become popular in Charismatic settings. Once there was impetus for healing revivalism to be seen within the local congregation and a pastor willing to champion it, deliverance ministry was sure to become part of a regular Christian experience where it had previously been offered in the context of evangelism outside of local church settings.

The Charismatic Movement: Clement Conditions for Deliverance Ministry[150]

Writing in 1977, Colin Buchanan described exorcism as one of five 'minor incidentals' of Charismatic Worship:

> Exorcism is not necessarily, nor perhaps usually, performed in the context of worship. But charismatics have tended to associate the two... the Charismatic Movement has led to a vastly increased interest in demonology, a vastly increased diagnosing of invasion or possession by demons, and a vastly increased practice of exorcism. This may (in its more respectable practitioners) be compared to the ministry of healing.[151]

Buchanan may have been correct (at least at the time) to label exorcism as incidental to charismatic worship although the term seems a little weak.[152] Nevertheless, this 'incidental' had a 'vast' impact, at least for a while. The Charismatic Movement provided clement spiritual conditions for deliverance ministry to become a common occurrence in the churches of most mainline denominations.

---

[149] H. A. Maxwell Whyte, 'The Imperative Need of Deliverance Pastors' in *Voice of Healing* (January 1955) 9.

[150] For a sound introduction to Charismatic Deliverance Ministry see N. Scotland, *Charismatics and the New Millennium* (Guildford: Hodder and Stoughton, 2000) 129-151.

[151] C. Buchanan, *Encountering Charismatic Worship* (Bramcote: Grove, 1997) 20.

[152] I would prefer 'secondary' although as will become clear for a few years in the eighties deliverance became a *primary* characteristic of at least some sections of the Movement. Cf Wright, *Theology*, 12.

There follows an examination of deliverance ministry within the context of the Charismatic Movement. Existing studies of the emergence and development of the latter are numerous but tend to focus on key distinctives such as the Baptism of the Holy Spirit or the practice of glossolalia or divine healing. Before examining the advocacy and practice of deliverance ministry by prominent Charismatics, a close look at the development of the movement with particular reference to deliverance ministry is in order.[153]

Two Streams within the Charismatic Movement

The emergence of the Charismatic Movement is identified with the apparently sudden appearance of the *charismata* in the worship of the mainline denominational churches and particularly, in the experience of individual leaders within the same.[154] Histories of the movement usually focus on those church leaders who, at risk of reputation and livelihood, embraced and (more significantly) experienced a pneumatology previously restricted to the Pentecostal churches. Hence the birth of the movement is usually identified as taking place in Los Angeles in 1960 when Dennis Bennett, the pastor of Van Nuys Episcopalian Church experienced the Baptism in the Holy Spirit. Other denominational church leaders at the forefront of the movement include Larry Christenson (Lutheran), James Brown (Presbyterian), Tommy Tyson (Methodist), John Osteen (Baptist), Gerald Derstine (Mennonites) and Eusebius A Stephanou (Orthodox) and Kevin Ranaghan (Roman Catholic).

In truth, the Pentecostal experience had been eating into the denominations for some years before Bennett *et al's* public acceptance of it enabled mass consumption. It is beyond question that another stream of Christian leadership created a positive environment for the acceptance of the *charismata* among Christians from the mainline denominations, namely the Pentecostal healing

---

[153] This is a testing endeavour since there is no academic (or indeed popular) treatment of the emergence of the Charismatic Movement with much reference to deliverance ministry. Such analyses are understandably preoccupied with the more central characteristics of the movement. Pentecostal / Charismatic historians anxious to vindicate the movement don't tend to pay much attention to deliverance ministry probably since they have enough controversy to deal with without introducing such a contentious subject.

[154] The emergence of the baptism of the Holy Spirit and the *charismata* in the life of the mainline denominations was not quite as sudden as it is sometimes presented. There were significant precursors to the movement. See P. D. Hocken, 'Charismatic Movement' in S. M. Burgess and E. M. Van Der Maas (eds.), *The New International Dictionary of Pentecostal and Charismatic Movements* (Grand Rapids: Zondervan, 2002) 477-519 and, with particular relevance to the scene in the UK, P. Hocken, *Streams of Renewal* (Carlisle: Paternoster, 1986).

evangelists.[155] These latter were in many ways responsible for embedding within the Charismatic Movement a tendency towards a simplistic and enthusiastic dualism.

The current study reveals that significant light may be shed upon the differing emphases within the Charismatic Movement by observing the different pressures on, and commitments of, its leaders. Those with an itinerant, often independent ministry were driven by what was essentially a highly competitive market to develop a dynamic and often innovative and sensational ministry. Consequently, there was a tendency towards exaggeration and extremism. Those who remained in denominational church leadership faced in two directions at once. Whatever their commitment to the *charismata*, however impressed they were by the itinerants, they were accountable to a church hierarchy (and in many cases members of their own congregations) who were frequently antipathetic. The situation is somewhat complicated by a division within the itinerants themselves depending upon the stage and the reason for which the itinerant ministry developed. For example, in the UK Michael Harper developed his itinerant ministry and para church organisation at a very early stage of the Charismatic Renewal. His ministry was focused on propagating the Renewal primarily through the baptism of the Holy Spirit. Hence he was not inclined to welcome a glut of new ministries that appeared to focus on a marginal aspect of the renewal. However, others 'went itinerant', usually at a later stage,[156] primarily to propagate a specialist deliverance ministry; these were obviously inclined to doggedly emphasise the need for such ministry.

What follows is an investigation into a range of Charismatic deliverance ministries and the response (positive and negative) they provoked from prominent Charismatic leaders. It will become obvious that the former largely started in denominational churches then tended to leave pastoral, local church based ministry and develop an itinerant ministry once they adopted deliverance ministry. Initially attention is focused on the pathfinder of Deliverance Ministry within the emergent Charismatic Movement, Derek Prince. That is not to say that there were no studies of deliverance, or indeed practitioners of deliverance among the pastors of local churches or among the previously prominent Charismatic leadership. These however were still functioning at the level of a secondary aspect of the Movement as a whole. Attention is now given to those figures and organisations that made an influential and / or innovative contribution and thereby managed for a brief period, to elevate deliverance ministry to a primary characteristic of the Charismatic Movement.

As will become clear, Prince is the foundational figure for popular

---

[155] See above for an examination of the post-War healing revival. I have already concluded that the healing revival 'stood at the cradle' of the Charismatic Movement.

[156] Most likely because a fellowship or denomination that accepted the early emphases of the Charismatic Movement (subsequence, glossalalia and divine healing) may nevertheless have been unwilling to accept deliverance ministry.

Charismatic deliverance. Don Basham's significance lies in his success as an author; he was already a figure of some significance within Charismatic circles when he published his own book on deliverance. Prince and Basham were members of the 'Fort Lauderdale Five' who embedded deliverance within the overall schema of the Shepherding Movement. Francis MacNutt embedded deliverance within the Roman Catholic renewal movement whilst Morris Cerullo is an interesting example of a healing evangelist who flirted briefly with a heavy emphasis on deliverance (and with joining the Fort Lauderdale Five) and then moved away from these.

Early Charismatic Practitioners of Deliverance Ministry

DEREK PRINCE (1915 - 2003)

Derek Prince was in many ways the most significant Charismatic practitioner of deliverance ministry. Most of the Charismatic deliverance 'experts' of the seventies and eighties acknowledge that he heavily influenced their understanding of deliverance. His impact lies not so much in the uniqueness of his teaching (although deliverance ministry was comparatively rare in church life when he began to practise it) but in his stature as a mainline Pentecostal minister with impeccable intellectual credentials. Prince was the ablest and clearest exponent of the Pentecostal/Charismatic approach to deliverance ministry. His story is fascinating for this study in that his commitment to deliverance ministry forced him out of a denominational Pentecostal pastorate into an itinerant Charismatic ministry that catapulted him to prominence within the Charismatic Movement as a whole.

Biography

Derek Prince enjoyed a first-rate academic career. He was educated at Eton and Cambridge, emerging from the latter with a double first in Classics. He went on to serve with distinction in the Medical Corps during World War 2.[157] It was during the war, in 1941, that Prince converted to Christianity. He describes this as follows: 'I experienced a supernatural encounter with Jesus Christ that revolutionized my goals in life.' Shortly afterwards he experienced the Baptism of the Holy Spirit and a call to full-time Christian ministry. After planting a Pentecostal church in London he then went to Kenya in 1957 to lead a teacher training college.[158]

Prince believed and preached the Pentecostal 'full gospel', that is, he

---

[157] D. Prince, *They Shall Expel Demons* (Grand Rapids: Chosen Books, 1998) 31.

[158] S. D. Moore, 'Prince, Peter Derek V.' in S. M. Burgess and E. M. Van Der Maas (eds.), *The New International Dictionary of Pentecostal and Charismatic Movements* (Grand Rapids: Zondervan, 2002) 999.

proclaimed Christ as Saviour, Baptiser in the Holy Spirit, Healer and coming King. Despite an apparently successful ministry, he felt that God was challenging him with the question 'Are you satisfied? Or do you want to go further?'[159] Having responded to this question in the affirmative, Prince embarked upon what he calls 'post-graduate spiritual training'.[160] This led to several developments in his ministry[161] including a new interest in deliverance. Before turning to study Prince's discovery of deliverance ministry it should be noted that, he had already had some experiences that were conducive to it.

By way of example, Prince cites his background of struggle with depression. Despite his 'unbroken record of success' he experienced depression 'like a grey mist that shrouded my head and shoulders'. He finally came to understand that his struggle was with an *evil spirit*, specifically the 'spirit of heaviness' referred to in Isaiah 61:3. He concluded that this spirit had come to him via his father who had suffered from a similar condition.[162] Having come to this realisation Prince prayed for deliverance:

> The response was immediate. Something like a huge, heavenly vacuum cleaner came down over me and sucked away the grey mist that shrouded my head and shoulders. At the same time a pressure in the area of my chest was forcibly released and I gave a little gasp.
>
> God had answered my prayer. Suddenly everything around me seemed brighter. I felt as if a heavy burden had been lifted from my shoulders. I

---

[159] D. Prince, *Deliverance and Demonology Study Note Outline DD1* (Derek Prince Ministries) 2.

[160] D. Prince, *Deliverance and Demonology* (Ministry Cassette 6001, Derek Prince Ministries). In studying Prince I have made the only exception to my rule not to consider verbal recorded sources. My justification for this is two fold. Firstly, the style of these recordings is that of a series of lectures, presented in Prince's unusually logical and consistent manner. Secondly, the material closely follows that contained in his book *Expel* and I usually quote the tapes where they elaborate on the text therein.

[161] In 1964, Prince decided to leave his pastorate and 'moved out in faith as an itinerant Bible teacher, combining the ministries of teaching and deliverance.' Prince, *Expel*, 66. He probably felt compelled to leave his pastorate since his new doctrine of deliverance would have been unacceptable to the Assemblies of God hierarchy. The Pentecostal denominations usually asserted that Christians were secure from demonic possession, K. Warrington, 'Healing and Exorcism: The Path to Wholeness' in K Warrington (ed.), *Pentecostal Perspectives* (Carlisle: Paternoster, 1998) 173f., therefore there was no need for the kind of deliverance ministry that Prince now espoused. The dogmatic way in which the former rejected deliverance ministry to existing Christians belies the fact that it was fairly widespread in their churches – primarily as a result of the influence of the itinerant healer-evangelists.

[162] For the story of Prince's depression see Prince, *Expel*, 29-36.

was free! All my life I had been under that oppression. It felt strange to be free. But I quickly discovered that freedom was normal and oppression was abnormal.[163]

Prince also claims to have experienced a powerful deliverance that set him free from the demons that gained entry via his interest in the occult. Prior to conversion he had been an expert practitioner of yoga; apparently this deliverance took place at conversion.[164]

Belief in, and encounters with, demons were not outside Prince's experience.[165] The watershed was, as shall become clear, in his understanding of the freedom that demons have to invade the lives of Christians.

Along with Ern Baxter, Bob Mumford, Don Basham and Charles Simpson, Prince was a member of the 'Fort Lauderdale Five'.[166] This group was the initial driving force behind the shepherding or house-church movement. Basham was another prominent advocate of deliverance ministry. Prince left the movement in 1984 and repented of the authoritarian and directive style of leadership which was characteristic of the movement.[167] Prince died in September 2003.[168]

Prince's Approach to Demonology and Deliverance
Prince's writings and teaching had much to commend them. He is clear, honest, thoughtful, observant and appears genuinely motivated by a sensitivity towards the suffering of others.

When Prince experienced deliverance from the 'spirit of heaviness' he faced an immediate difficulty integrating this experience with his theological framework. Prince belonged to a Pentecostal denomination that denied outright the possibility of a Christian being demon-possessed.[169] For some time he lived

---

[163] Prince, *Expel*, 33. This occurred in 1953, Prince, *Expel*, 32. The timing is significant since deliverance was being widely practised by the (mainly Pentecostal) popular, itinerant healing evangelists concurrently.

[164] Prince, *Deliverance*, (Ministry Cassette 6005). Cf. Prince, *Expel*, 76. Prince also had experience as a missionary in Africa and was acquainted with 'African evangelists who used to describe to us their personal encounters with demons'. Prince, *Expel*, 43.

[165] Prince, *Deliverance*, (Ministry Cassette 6001).

[166] The Fort Lauderdale Five and Restorationism's interest in deliverance ministry is examined below.

[167] Moore, 'Prince', 728. Cf S. D. Moore, *The Shepherding Movement* (London: T and T Clark, 2003) 165f, 174f.

[168] I did make an initial attempt to contact Prince via his UK organisation, Derek Prince Ministries (UK). They did not reply to my first two enquiries and before I made a third, Prince's health had failed.

[169] Prince, *Expel*, 38. The Pentecostal pioneers defended themselves from the frequent accusation that they themselves were demon possessed by asserting that spirit-filled

with this tension by keeping his experience to himself.[170] However, in time Prince was forced to face up to this issue. Firstly, he was invited to assist in deliverance ministry alongside some others who were already active in this area.[171] Hot on the heels of this came a crisis in which Prince was dramatically confronted by a lady manifesting a demon during a service in which he was preaching.[172]

These latter experiences prompted Prince to take seriously his responsibility to minister deliverance. He came to the conviction that the underlying need of many (even the majority) of Christians was to be set free from the demons that had gained entrance into their person and a consequent degree of control. Without the practice of deliverance much Christian ministry is therefore superficial since it does not grapple with the real enemy, namely demons.[173] He also observes that exorcism is a consistent motif of the ministry of Jesus.[174] Therefore, there is both a need of, and a biblical mandate for, deliverance ministry.[175]

The sheer demand for this kind of ministry soon began to take its toll on Prince. He began to see that it was not practical to deliver people individually in this manner. Since the basis for deliverance was 'proper instruction out of the word of God' it was quite possible to give people this instruction in group settings and then offer them deliverance corporately. Inevitably this more public approach (and the attendant hysteria) attracted a great deal of criticism.[176] Prince countered this by shrewdly observing that dignity is a secondary consideration compared to the urgency of 'getting people free' and also that the Gospel record does not suggest that Jesus was in any way perturbed by unruly manifestations:[177]

The professing Christian Church has established a pattern of behaviour

---

believers were immune from such a condition. This contention then tended to become a tenet of the emerging Pentecostal denominations.

[170] Prince, *Expel*, 39f.

[171] Prince, *Expel*, 48f.

[172] Prince, *Expel*, 50-57.

[173] Prince, *Expel*, 59.

[174] Prince, *Expel*, 18-26, 60f.

[175] In order to establish the credibility of his approach, Prince calls for a return to 'the spiritual perspective of the New Testament'. He points Western rationalists to 'Africa and Asia [where] people have always been conscious of demons and can describe many tangible demonstrations of their intrusions into human affairs'. Prince, *Expel*, 59.

[176] Prince records one incident in particular: In 1965 he offered deliverance to about 200 people attending a Full Gospel convention. The consequent frenzy led to a 'good deal of adverse criticism'. Prince, *Expel*, 66f.

[177] As shall become clear in the next chapter, enthusiastic indignity is deeply upsetting and indeed offensive to many people. Often, this is the real reason behind purportedly theological criticism.

considered 'appropriate' for the house of God. Too often this leaves no room for the messy facts of human sin and demonic oppression. Some churchgoers are offended by the noisy and disorderly manifestations that sometimes accompany the driving out of demons. Dignity takes precedence over deliverance.

> I looked again at the ministry of Jesus and discovered various instances in which a demon or demons screamed and shouted at Him; interrupted his preaching; convulsed people when they came out, leaving them apparently dead; caused a person to wallow on the ground foaming at the mouth; and stampeded a herd of two thousand pigs into a lake. Yet Jesus was never disturbed, nor did he suppress these manifestations. He simply dealt with them as part of His total ministry to suffering humanity.[178]

Prince held to an idiosyncratic understanding of the origin and ontology of demons. He maintained (albeit tentatively) that they are the 'disembodied spirits of a pre-Adamic' humanity and that fallen angels (including Satan) are of a completely different order to demons, the latter being 'earthbound' while the former live 'in the heavenly places'.[179] Prince believed that these spirits constantly traverse the 'spiritual realm' looking for a vacancy in a human being since they need a body through which to express their evil desires.[180] Prince's experience led him to the understanding that each demon has a particular sin or affliction that they seek to express through, or bring upon the body they inhabit. For example, there are demons of arthritis, cancer, sinusitis, adultery, disappointment, masturbation, witchcraft and even tooth decay.[181]

According to Prince, demons cannot enter humans at will. However, certain conditions give them an opportunity. These are: personal or familial involvement with the occult or false religion; 'negative prenatal influences'; 'pressures in early childhood'; 'emotional shock or sustained emotional pressure'; 'sinful acts or habits'; 'laying on of hands'; and idle words.[182] A great deal of theological assumptions are involved in these seven conditions. Space restricts analysis at this point. However, it should be pointed out that only two (or possibly three) of the conditions involve wilful wrongdoing of any

---

[178] Prince, *Expel*, 68. It is worth pausing to acknowledge the quality of Prince's argument. It would indeed be churlish to object to the practice of deliverance ministry purely on the grounds that it is disorderly. The real battle is of course whether deliverance ministry is (as) necessary or appropriate as Prince advocates. Actually Prince's grievance is with the inevitable routinisation of settled congregations.

[179] Prince, *Expel*, 91-93.

[180] Prince, *Expel*, 94f, 111f. Prince, *Deliverance,* (Ministry Cassette 6003).

[181] Prince, *Expel*, 96f, 211.

[182] Prince, *Expel*, 103f.

kind on behalf of the victim. On Prince's schema most people are demonised as a result of the actions of others or through their ignorance of certain dangers.

Christian faith, consequent new birth and baptism in the Holy Spirit are no defence from such demonic invasion. As mentioned earlier, this was the theological Rubicon for Prince. Contemporary and orthodox Pentecostals denied that a Christian could be possessed by a demon[183] and Prince held this view for many years until he was forced, by his experience, to reconsider.[184] As a result of these experiences he looked closely at the biblical material concluding that the King James Version was erroneous in using the phrase 'possessed by a demon' to translate the Greek verb *daimonizo*. Prince asserts that a better, literal translation would be 'demonised', which confers a degree of control and influence without the connotation of total ownership.[185] In this way Prince opens the door to the possibility, indeed the probability, of demonic invasion of even the Christian personality.

Perhaps the most contentious aspect of Prince's understanding of this issue was his perception of the scale of the problem. Compulsions, addictions, many illnesses and emotional disorders are all attributable to this state of demonisation. In particular, Prince identifies 'restlessness' as the 'distinctive mark of the demonised.'[186] Although Prince does not explicitly make the claim, it is hard not to draw the conclusion that everyone is demonised to some extent. For example, Prince claims that one in five people need to be delivered from a demon of fear![187] Prince describes the person who is 'probably' demon-free as one 'who can maintain an attitude of serene composure in all the troubled circumstances of life. 'But there are not many such people'.[188]

Predictably, Prince was particularly strong in his warnings against involvement with the occult and false religion (the latter to include every religion other than Christianity!). He claimed that 'witchcraft is the universal, primeval religion of fallen humanity. When the human race turned from God in rebellion, the power that moved in was witchcraft. 'As the Bible says "Rebellion is as the sin of witchcraft" (1Samuel 15:23).'[189] Witchcraft, as Prince sees it, is an extremely wide category including both overt Satanism,

---

[183] Warrington, 'Healing', 173.

[184] Prince, *Expel*, 38f. Prince, *Deliverance*, (Ministry Cassette 6001). Reflecting back Prince can even identify Christians that he did not help because he did not consider it possible that they should have a demon.

[185] Prince, *Deliverance*, (Ministry Cassette 6003), Prince, *Expel*, 16f. As has been demonstrated this point was already established by Nevius at least fifty years prior to Prince (see section 2.2 above).

[186] Prince, *Deliverance*, (Ministry Cassette 6003).

[187] Prince, *Deliverance*, (Ministry Cassette 6004).

[188] Prince, *Expel*, 177. Here, Prince seems surprisingly naïve regarding human personality; as if spiritual maturity were to be achieved through emotional disengagement!

[189] Prince, *Expel*, 129. Prince indulges in outrageous eisegesis to make this point.

that which is disguised in the form of rock music or new religious movements and in any desire to control, dominate or manipulate other people.[190] Deliverance from the more overt forms of witchcraft involve a prolonged and bitter struggle.[191]

One of the principle difficulties of Prince's teaching is how one is to distinguish between sin and/or afflictions that are 'fleshly' in origin and those that indicate demonisation. Prince recognises this dilemma and acknowledges that different treatments will apply depending on the origin of the problem. Whilst recommending that Christians learn about demons and their characteristics so that their activity might be more easily identified, the key for Prince appears to be the spiritual gift of discernment. A 'spiritual' judgement must be made as to whether the root of the problem is demonic or merely carnal.[192]

Once a diagnosis of demonisation has been made Prince recommends a nine step procedure as follows: 'personally affirm your faith in Christ'; 'humble yourself', by which Prince means that one may need 'to choose between dignity and deliverance'; 'confess any known sin'; 'repent of all sins'; 'forgive other people'; 'break with the occult and all false religion'; 'prepare to be released from every curse over your life';[193] 'take your stand with God', by which Prince means acquiescing to God's will and opposing the demonic in identification with God's opposition to the demonic; and, finally, 'expel'.[194]

Prince describes the actual expulsion of the demon as an act of the will. After praying along the lines of the former eight steps, the demoniac should expel air from the lungs:

> begin to expel. That is a decision of your will, followed by an action of your muscles.

---

[190] Prince, *Expel*, 129-141. We encounter here for the first time in print a tendency (which Prince, in common with almost every advocate of deliverance ministry, and the healing evangelists before them indulged in), to exaggerate the influence and popularity of the occult. Also of interest, Prince here appears to be reacting against his past involvement in the controversial 'Shepherding' movement. Of course, deliverance ministry itself might be guilty of witchcraft under this latter category but Prince would not have seen it that way. I am grateful to my friend Dr Meic Pearse for this latter point.

[191] Prince, *Expel*, 139.

[192] Prince, *Expel*, 98f.

[193] Prince has written specifically on the issue of curses. D. Prince, *Blessing or Curse: You can choose!* (Harpenden: Word, 1990). His teaching on curses runs parallel to his teaching on deliverance as the curses seem to be avenues along which demonic powers may travel in order to oppress those cursed in some way. It should be noted that Prince's teaching in this area is, to say the least, idiosyncratic.

[194] Prince, *Expel*, 203-214.

At the same time, make way for the demon or demons to come out. Keep the exit clear! Do not go on praying or start to speak in tongues. I have discovered that movement of the lips and tongue in speech acts as a barrier to keep the demon in... Clear the way for the demon to come out.

As you begin to expel, what comes out first may just be natural human breath. But after a short while, something other than human breath will start coming out. That is your enemy! Keep the pressure on![195]

A number of possible manifestations may take place as the demon(s) leave the body. Prince's experience ranges from the unspectacular such as yawning or sighing through coughing, groaning to screaming or roaring.[196] If a subject (usually a woman!) continues to scream without achieving 'release' then it usually means that the demon 'has stopped in the narrow section of the throat and is holding on there to avoid being expelled.' In this case Prince recommends a 'forceful cough' which should be enough to dislodge the demon.[197]

Once a subject has undergone deliverance they will obviously wish to remain free of demonisation. Prince recommends a lifestyle of discipline that most orthodox Christians would aspire to.[198]

Finally, Prince examines the reasons why subjects do not achieve release from demonisation. He identifies ten possible causes: 'lack of repentance'; 'wrong motives'; 'a desire for attention'; 'failure to break with the occult'; 'failure to sever binding soulish [controlling or manipulative] relationships'; 'lack of release from a curse'; 'failure to confess a specific sin'; the demoniac is 'not separated by water baptism'; or, finally, that the demonisation in question is 'part of a larger battle'.[199] These basically add up to another set of conditions that the subject must fulfil in order to achieve deliverance. The subject must desire deliverance from correct motives, break with anything or anyone that stands in the way, and must confess every sin and be baptised. Even then, deliverance may not come if the subject is caught up in a larger, strategic spiritual struggle.

Prince leaves one with the impression that we are all surrounded by an unseen spiritual ether, which is teeming with evil spirits longing to get inside the bodies of human beings. He also has a very pessimistic view of the security

---

[195] Prince, *Expel*, 213. Cf. Prince, *Deliverance*, (Ministry Cassette 6004) which records Prince leading subjects through this process.

[196] Prince, *Expel*, 214.

[197] Prince, *Expel*, 214.

[198] Prince, *Expel*, 219-229.

[199] Prince, *Expel*, 230-237.

of Christians from demonic invasion.[200] Most orthodox Christians would find such a perspective neither biblical nor credible.

Prince's Influences

It is not easy to identify with any certainty what caused Prince to become involved in deliverance ministry. Prince himself argues that he learned 'in the school of experience'[201] and one must agree that Prince was an independent thinker, quite capable of blazing a trail of his own choosing. However, as has already been observed, his sojourn in Africa certainly had some bearing, particularly since he appeals to the African worldview in support of his belief in a spirit world.

It seems extremely likely that Prince was influenced by the healing evangelists and their emphasis upon deliverance as outlined above. Firstly, it is not reasonable to suggest that he was entirely unaware of them. Secondly, his own deliverance from a 'spirit of heaviness' took place in 1953 which coincided with the heyday of the healing evangelism. Thirdly, Prince soon began to move in same circles as the healing evangelists and their associates: he was a regular speaker with the FGBMFI (which championed deliverance) as was Oral Roberts; he struck an extremely good relationship with Ern Baxter who was previously an associate of William Branham. Whilst none of this is represents conclusive proof, it does present a good *prima facie* case.

Prince's Contribution to the Practice of Charismatic Deliverance Ministry

Prince is a key figure, perhaps *the* key figure for the Charismatic element of this study. As will become apparent, his influence seems to have extended to most of the leading Charismatic practitioners of deliverance ministry. Partly this is due to his academic credentials,[202] which made him a good source for those Charismatics looking to build credibility for their ministry of deliverance. Perhaps more significantly, Prince developed a successful public ministry with a significant emphasis on deliverance ministry in the very earliest days of the Charismatic Movement. Because of the controversy surrounding this ministry his reputation was to a large extent built upon it. Consequently, when at a later

---

[200] Prince's view is typical of the outlook that Walker refers to as the 'paranoid universe'. Walker, 'Devil', 88. Jacques Theron has attempted a critical response to Walker which is closely considered in the conclusion of this chapter. J. Theron, 'A Critical Overview of the Church's Ministry of Deliverance from Evil Spirits' *Pneuma* 18.1 (Spring, 1996) 79-92.

[201] An example of indication of undiluted enthusiasm in that Prince justifies his practice of deliverance by appeal to the evidential value of his immediate encounter with the spiritual via events and experiences. Of course Prince would be unwilling to reveal too much in the way of his influences since he wishes to present his journey into deliverance ministry as primarily a case of supernatural revelation.

[202] His British nationality seems to have leant him enhanced credibility within an American context.

stage other Charismatics began to perceive the need for deliverance ministry it was natural that they should turn to Prince for guidance.

DON BASHAM (1926-1989)

A well-known and ardent advocate of the Charismatic Movement, Don Basham's contribution to the wealth of material on deliverance ministry, entitled *Deliver Us From Evil*,[203] was published in 1972, making him one of the first leaders of the Charismatic Movement to develop a prominent deliverance ministry.[204] Basham adopts an engaging and winsome biographical approach in order to relate the story of his growing appreciation of and involvement in deliverance. The book engenders credibility since Basham constantly stresses his own uncertainty regarding his experiences particularly in the early stages).[205]

Basham's general approach is at most points similar to that of Prince so focus here is given only to a few interesting and important details, some of which may aid understanding of the origins of his interest in deliverance ministry.

Firstly, Basham and his wife, Alice, had a history of interest in the occult whilst at theological seminary,[206] which stopped when a particular session led them to conclude that they 'were in an area God did not want us to have anything to do with.'[207] One cannot help but speculate regarding his early fascination with Spiritism and his later interest in deliverance ministry.

Secondly, having sometime previously experienced great joy in his experience of baptism in the Holy Spirit, Basham found himself in a new pastorate, feeling disillusioned and stressed, wondering where that joy had gone. The Charismatic experience that Basham had seen as the turning point in his Christian experience suddenly dissipated leaving him feeling hypocritical in that he was preaching up an experience he was no longer enjoying himself.[208] This sense of guilt was compounded by his persistent attacks of fear and depression.[209] Much later on when he was already deeply involved in deliverance ministry, Basham realised that these attacks were demonic and he

---

[203] D. Basham, *Deliver Us From Evil* (London: Hodder and Stoughton, 1972).

[204] S. D. Moore, 'Basham, Don Wilson' S. M. Burgess and E. M. Van Der Maas (eds.), *The New International Dictionary of Pentecostal and Charismatic Movements* (Grand Rapids: Zondervan, 2002) 367.

[205] Moore notes that Basham was a particularly gifted writer. Moore, *Shepherding*, 35.

[206] Which does not cohere particularly well with the way in which Basham presents his time at seminary in his earlier book, *Face Up with a Miracle*. D. Basham, *Face Up with a Miracle* (Northridge: Voice Christian Publications, 1967) 25-28.

[207] Basham, *Deliver*, 134.

[208] Basham, *Deliver*, 26. With the benefit of hindsight Basham concluded that this spiritual wilderness experience was part of the way in which God was preparing him for the deliverance ministry. Basham, *Deliver*, 34.

[209] Basham, *Deliver*, 23-33.

delivered himself from a spirit of fear.[210]

Thirdly, it is clear that Basham was an introspective character, given to extensive self-examination. His writing is littered with reflections on his feelings and thoughts regarding his experiences.

Formative in Basham's emerging belief in the demonic and interest in deliverance ministry was a visit to the influential Derek Prince. Basham was clearly impressed by Prince's academic excellence and his 'crisp British accent.'[211] Prince introduced Basham to the concept of demonisation, told him of his own deliverance and drew a comparison between a 'flu' bug and a demon, each of which may enter the body of a Christian and each of which may be overcome by Christ's power which is available to those who 'appropriate' it.[212]

In *Deliver Us From Evil* Basham is keen to establish his initial scepticism regarding the demonic inherited from his liberal theological education. This serves to underline the significance of the experiences which caused him to undergo a major change in his thinking. However, it does not accord well with his previous book *Face Up With a Miracle* in which Basham outlines how he contended for his conservative theological views whilst in seminary and, tellingly, participated in deliverance ministry prior to the experiences outlined in *Deliver Us From Evil*. Furthermore, in his earlier book Basham speaks approvingly of the ministry of Oral Roberts[213] and it seems inconceivable that he would have done so if (at the time) he held liberal views on the demonic and, presumably, other related areas of theology. There is little that can be said about this other than the obvious conclusion that Basham used some poetic license in his writing in order to exaggerate the evidence of his experiences.

Basham went on to join Prince, Charles Simpson, Ern Baxter and Bob Mumford to form the controversial Fort Lauderdale group who pioneered the Shepherding/House Church Movement. At the time of writing *Deliver Us From Evil* the shepherding dimension was not at the forefront of this coming together. From Basham's perspective, he and Prince were to provide the expertise in deliverance ministry, which was rapidly gaining acceptance within Charismatic circles.[214] As a leading Charismatic figure, Basham's advocacy of deliverance ministry was an important link in its developing popularity among the movement as a whole.

THE FORT LAUDERDALE FIVE'S THEOLOGICAL ECLECTICISM

It has been well documented that the Fort Lauderdale Five were much influenced in the development of their key doctrine of 'shepherding' by

---

[210] Basham, *Deliver*, 181-184.

[211] Basham, *Deliver*, 102.

[212] Basham, *Deliver*, 104f.

[213] Basham, *Face*, 45-48.

[214] Basham, *Deliver*, 209-213.

Watchman Nee.[215] The latter is at best a peripheral figure for this study since he did not place a significant emphasis upon the ministry of deliverance. However it is interesting to note that Nee was himself influenced by the writings of Jessie Penn-Lewis[216] and certainly viewed deliverance ministry as an essential aspect of Christian ministry.[217] His writings clearly demonstrate the main themes of *War on the Saints*.[218]

It is tempting to posit a chain of influence regarding deliverance from Penn-Lewis to Prince and Basham (Mumford, Simpson and Baxter showed less interest in deliverance). However, it is unlikely that any such influence came via Nee since both Prince and Basham were practising deliverance prior to their adoption of shepherding and since Prince, along with many other Charismatics, was highly critical of Penn-Lewis. Nevertheless, and this point is of great importance, it is indicative of the way in which itinerant Charismatics began to mix up their inherited Pentecostalism with other streams of enthusiastic thought.[219] Nee's theological convictions sit much more easily within evangelical fundamentalism than with Charismatic enthusiasm.

THE FULL GOSPEL BUSINESS MEN'S FELLOWSHIP INTERNATIONAL (FGBMFI)[220]

The FGBMFI was an important Charismatic organisation that undoubtedly encouraged the popularity of deliverance ministry among Charismatics. Established by Demos Shakarian (a successful Californian dairy farmer) in 1951 it grew rapidly, organised into local chapters. 'By the mid-'60s it had more than three hundred chapters, with a total membership of 100,000... By 1988 the fellowship had more than 3,000 local chapters and had spread to 87

---

[215] A. Walker, *Restoring the Kingdom* (Guildford: Eagle, 1998) 144. Nee (1903-1972) was a significant Chinese Christian leader who wrote extensively on such subjects as church discipline and practical Christian spirituality. He was imprisoned in 1952 following the communist revolution and died twenty years later, still a prisoner. His books have become increasingly popular within Charismatic circles (which is somewhat ironic since he was a devotee of Jessie Penn-Lewis).

[216] A. I. Kinnear, *Against the Tide: The Story of Watchman Nee* (Eastbourne: Victory Press, 1973) 50, 65, 79. Cf. N. Wright, 'Does Revival Quicken or Deaden the Church?' in A. Walker and K. Aune (eds.), *On Revival* (Carlisle: Paternoster, 2003) 130. On Jessie Penn-Lewis see below (chapter 4).

[217] Kinnear, *Against*, 92.

[218] See W. Nee, *Sit Walk Stand* (Eastbourne: Kingsway, 2002) 41-64 and *Love Not the World* (Eastbourne: Kingsway, 2000) 80-87. If it were not already established that Nee had read *War on the Saints,* these two chapters would be proof enough that he had.

[219] The tendency to enthusiastic theological and ecclesiological eclecticism grows throughout the latter half of the century. See below, chapter 6.

[220] The story of Demos Shakarian and the FGBMFI is recounted in D. Shakarian, *The Happiest People on Earth* (London: Hodder and Stoughton, 1975). Cf. *Voice of Healing* (August 1953) 8-10.

countries.'[221] The name of the organisation indicates its Pentecostal roots, however, the speakers in the early days were frequently the leaders of the healing revival (Oral Roberts was the speaker at the first ever meeting). Later, the FGBMFI proved a receptive environment for the deliverance ministry of Prince and Basham among others.[222] Ziegler notes that: 'The original vision of the FGBMFI was of a nonsectarian fellowship of laity who could come together to share what God had done in their lives without any apology – even if that testimony included healing or tongues or *deliverance from demonic forces.*'[223]

From the point of view of this study the FGBMFI is an extremely significant organisation.[224] It provided a broadly Pentecostal environment, free from the denominational controls that resisted some of the more enthusiastic extremes of the itinerant healing evangelists, with added credibility due to its respectable, successful leaders and added capability due to their financial resources. When deliverance surfaced as the major theme in Prince's ministry the FGBMFI provided him with an immediate platform to communicate his message and practice his ministry. As a movement it was open to taking risks (perhaps due to the successful entrepreneurs in charge) and avoided many of the factors that cause denominational churches (even those of Pentecostal stamp) to be more cautious.

Understandably, denominational Pentecostals were sometimes threatened by the emergence of the FGBMFI and the movement was often the subject of controversy. One particular episode is worth noting. The meeting in question took place at the International Convention of the FGBMFI in 1965 at the Conrad Hilton Hotel in Chicago. Prince was speaking to an audience of around 600 people and he invited those who felt they needed deliverance to come forward; he recalls that a minimum of 200 did so. Prince himself acknowledges that a 'chaotic scene' ensued.[225]

FRANCIS MACNUTT

Francis MacNutt, a highly educated Roman Catholic priest, experienced the baptism in the Holy Spirit in August 1967 and went on to develop an influential healing ministry. Having encountered some folk who displayed bizarre and

---

[221] J. R. Ziegler, 'Full Gospel Business Men's Fellowship International (FGBMFI)' in S. M. Burgess and E. M. Van Der Maas (eds.), *The New International Dictionary of Pentecostal and Charismatic Movements* (Grand Rapids: Zondervan, 2002) 653f.

[222] Later Shakarian and the FGBMFI fell out with Basham and Prince over their Shepherding teachings. Moore, *Shepherding*, 92.

[223] Ziegler 'FGBMFI' 653. Italics added for emphasis. Cf. Shakarian, *Happiest*, 129 where the founder argues that 'Full Gospel' allows for the inclusion of testimony regarding deliverance ministry.

[224] Indeed from any point of view. Harrell describes it as 'one of the most powerful parachurch organisations in modern church history.' Harrell, *Oral*, 153.

[225] Prince, *Deliverance*, (Ministry Cassette 6001).

troubling reactions to prayers for healing, he was introduced to deliverance ministry by Barbara Shlemon, a Roman Catholic nurse. At her suggestion MacNutt listened to some of Derek Prince's tapes on the subject and subsequently familiarised himself with the ministries of Prince and Basham. Nevertheless, MacNutt pointed out to Cuneo that it was primarily as a result of firsthand encounters with the demonic that he adopted deliverance ministry:

> When you're praying for healing often enough, you inevitably come into contact with evil spirits. These spirits come out of people – bizarre, ugly manifestation. This stuff gets your attention, so eventually you say that healing and deliverance go together. Barbara [Shlemon] helped me to make sense of this, and in early 1970 I incorporated deliverance into my healing ministry.[226]

At the peak of his popularity MacNutt published a popular book on healing which included a chapter on deliverance.[227] Here he sets an agenda for Charismatic deliverance ministry within a specifically Catholic context. Roman Catholic tradition allowed for two forms of exorcism: major (or formal or solemn) exorcism for the relief of serious cases of demonic possession and which required the permission of the bishop, and minor (or informal or simple) exorcism for the relief of less serious demonic oppression. MacNutt, in common with other Catholic and Episcopalian advocates of deliverance ministry argued that Charismatic deliverance equates to a minor exorcism and therefore may be practised freely without reference to Church authorities.[228] MacNutt applied the *coup de grace* to the traditional Catholic approach by

---

[226] Cuneo, *American*, 128. Cf. F. MacNutt, *Deliverance from Evil Spirits* (Grand Rapids: Chosen, 1995) 15.

[227] F. MacNutt, *Healing* (New York: Bantam, 1997). The book was originally published in 1974. John Wimber, who wrote a foreword to a later edition commented that it had been formative upon his own healing ministry. J. Wimber, 'Foreword' in F. MacNutt, *Healing* (London: Hodder and Stoughton, 1989) 9-10. MacNutt claims that 'nearly a million copies were printed in United States'. MacNutt, *Healing*, (1989) 11.

[228] MacNutt, *Healing*, 189. Cuneo observes that the leading Roman Catholic charismatic Cardinal Suenens dealt a serious blow to Catholic Charismatic deliverance by rejecting this schema and criticising what he perceived to be an obsession with demons. Cuneo, *American*, 174f, see L. Suenens, *Renewal and the Powers of Darkness* (London: DLT, 1983) 98. Earlier in this book Suenens explicitly criticises MacNutt, 35. Later in this study attention will turn to enthusiastic sacramental exorcism. Whilst MacNutt (amongst others from a sacramental background) places an otherwise less prominent emphasis upon the sacraments, it is this equation of deliverance with minor exorcism that makes their approach one of sacramental Charismatic deliverance in contra-distinction to the enthusiastic sacramental exorcism of, most notably, Malachi Martin (on whom, see chapter 5, below).

claiming that possession is so rare that he has never encountered a single case, effectively collapsing traditional major exorcism into deliverance ministry.[229]

In 1980 MacNutt's high profile status took a tumble when he left the priesthood and broke his vow of celibacy to marry[230]; something of a scandal ensued resulting in a few years out of the limelight. By the late 1980s MacNutt was back in the frontline[231] and published a book specifically on deliverance as recently as 1995.[232]

MacNutt's approach to justifying deliverance ministry in his earlier publication almost entirely focused on his experience although he does appeal to the tradition of the church as precedent. In *Deliverance from Evil Spirits*, despite subsequent appeals to Scripture and the beliefs of non-Western cultures, MacNutt starts by identifying experience as the motive behind this ministry: 'Like all my friends who have become actively involved in casting out evil spirits, I got involved through experience, not theory.'[233]

In *Healing* MacNutt identifies four forms of healing: repentance, inner healing, physical healing and deliverance thus framing the Christian life in therapeutic categories. With regards to deliverance he keeps things reasonably simple. Demons may be discerned through the presence of inner compulsion, the host may be aware of their presence or the failure of other forms of healing may indicate a demonic presence; aware 'of the delicate nature of this ministry', MacNutt highlights the paramount need for the 'gift of discernment'.[234] Deliverance itself should be achieved via a calm, authoritative command to the demon to depart.[235] MacNutt offers a number of reasons why deliverance should only be ministered by those who have received a calling to it. The ministry itself 'should not be entered into without real prayer and discernment beforehand' and is best performed in private as a team ministry.[236] The process of the deliverance itself follows a prescribed course: pray for

---

[229] MacNutt, *Deliverance*, 67-72. Cf. 272-277, here MacNutt advocates the Baptism in the Holy Spirit to empower Charismatic deliverance in contra-distinction to the sacramental approach exemplified by Michael Martin (see below). Martin's pessimism regarding the cost of performing exorcisms is due in MacNutt's view to the attempt to perform deliverance without Charismatic empowering. MacNutt, *Deliverance*, 274.

[230] The resulting excommunication was later rescinded. S. Strang, 'MacNutt, Francis Scott' in S. M. Burgess and E. M. Van Der Maas (eds.), *The New International Dictionary of Pentecostal and Charismatic Movements* (Grand Rapids: Zondervan, 2002) 856.

[231] Cuneo, *American*, 196.

[232] MacNutt, *Deliverance*.

[233] MacNutt, *Deliverance*, 15.

[234] MacNutt, *Healing*, 198.

[235] MacNutt, *Healing*, 198f.

[236] MacNutt, *Healing*, 199f.

protection,[237] bind the spirits,[238] discern the name of the spirits,[239] invite the subject to repent from associated sin,[240] both subject and minister command the demons to leave,[241] and then the subject should be able to confirm when the demons have left.[242]

The eviction of the demons may be accompanied by unpleasant manifestations which MacNutt tries to contain by instructing 'the demons to keep quiet or to stop tormenting the person' Coughing or retching seems to be a common indication that the demons are leaving; MacNutt does not speculate as to why this should be, admitting that it is a 'mystery'.[243]

In common with other practitioners of deliverance MacNutt claims that demons usually come in groups gathering around a senior demon 'something like the taproot system around which the rest of the root system clusters.'[244] The strategy for deliverance is affected by this; sometimes it will be necessary to go straight for the 'taproot' on other occasions it may be necessary to remove some 'feeder roots' to expose the 'main root'.[245] MacNutt concludes by asserting the need for discipleship following the deliverance without which 'chances are the condition of oppression will return.'[246]

The overall impression one receives from reading *Healing* is that MacNutt viewed deliverance as a necessary evil and was understanding to those who did not share the experience which had led him to practise it. He is careful to avoid speculation and adopts a simplistic spiritual methodology avoiding the crass attempts to objectively prove the need for the ministry which are found among other advocates.

Deliverance From Evil Spirits was written around twenty years later and manages to comprehensively avoid the caution and simplicity that marked the chapter in *Healing*. In many ways it follows a well-worn path, confronting the reader with the need to respond to the urgent need of demonised people[247] – MacNutt starts by recounting a typical deliverance narrative involving

---

[237] MacNutt's Catholicism surfaces here: 'I pray that the power of the blood of Christ surround and protect every person in the room. Then I pray that Mary, the Mother of God, St Michael and the Archangel, all the angels and the saints, and all the court of heaven intercede with us for the person we are praying for. MacNutt, *Healing*, 201.

[238] MacNutt, *Healing*, 201f.

[239] The demon's name will be associated with its activity. The name may already be known to the subject or may be revealed through the gift of discernment. Failing that, the demon should instructed to reveal it name. MacNutt, *Healing*, 202f.

[240] MacNutt, *Healing*, 203.

[241] MacNutt, *Healing*, 203f.

[242] MacNutt, *Healing*, 205.

[243] MacNutt, *Healing*, 205.

[244] MacNutt, *Healing*, 206.

[245] MacNutt, *Healing*, 206.

[246] MacNutt, *Healing*, 207.

[247] MacNutt, *Deliverance*, 15.

'Roberta'[248] – before further justifying deliverance ministry via a brief examination of scripture[249] and an examination of human experience.[250]

MacNutt goes on to address how to identify the presence of a demon. He basically expands on his schema from *Healing* with two major additions. Firstly, he describes some physical symptoms to look out for;[251] secondly he warns the reader regarding the danger of mistaking Multiple Personality Disorder (MPD) for demonisation which might have grave consequences.[252] Accepting that most physical symptoms of demonic oppression are equivocal,[253] MacNutt's emphasis is still very much on the spiritual gift of 'discerning spirits' which enables the recipient to 'come closer to certainty.'[254] Cuneo includes a colourful report of how this worked in practice when he paid a visit to MacNutt's healing centre in Jacksonville:

> Upon arriving, I was ushered into a waiting room in the ministry's main building… Within minutes three women came into the room on the pretext of introducing themselves and engaging me in small talk. But this was no ordinary small talk. One woman stared intently into my eyes, another slowly circled me two or three times, and the third stood off to the side with upturned nostrils…

> Later over lunch, I mentioned this odd welcome to MacNutt and asked whether I was being scrutinized for indwelling demons. 'Of course you were,' he said, laughing. 'We have eleven salaried people on our staff, and most of them are charismatic Episcopalian women with strong gifts for discerning evil spirits. They can smell them, feel them, sometimes sense them spatially. Sometimes they'll even say to me, "Francis, there's something on you," and they'll pray over me.' 'And how did I come out in the inspection?' 'You came out fine. You're clean.'[255]

MacNutt goes on to identify four categories of evil spirit (although he

---

[248] MacNutt, *Deliverance*, 18-20.

[249] MacNutt, *Deliverance*, 31-40.

[250] MacNutt, *Deliverance*, 48-66. This amounts to an attack upon Western post-Enlightenment rationalism.

[251] MacNutt, *Deliverance*, 77-79.

[252] MacNutt, *Deliverance*, 79-81.

[253] 'we are merely using our minds to argue from an effect… to the possible cause.' MacNutt, *Deliverance*, 81.

[254] MacNutt, *Deliverance*, 81. MacNutt notes that those with this gift recognise physical symptoms that indicate the presence of a demon. MacNutt, *Deliverance*, 82. One cannot help but think of Oral Roberts and William Branham who claimed to detect the presence of demons via a sensation in their hands.

[255] Cuneo, *American*, 196f.

recognises there are more) that one might encounter: spirits of the occult,[256] spirits of sin,[257] spirits of trauma (about two-thirds of deliverances relate to these),[258] and ancestral (familiar) spirits.[259] Later in the book he spends time identifying the different deliverance procedures for these various kinds of spirits.[260]

The state of demonisation may occur as a result of all the usual means (repeated sin, trauma, occult involvement, trans-generational transmission) but may also result from a curse. Drawing upon Derek Prince's experience in this field, MacNutt goes into some depth outlining the various forms of curse which may bring about demonic oppression. One may become cursed through one's family tree,[261] from the direct action of an occult practitioner,[262] or we may bring a curse upon ourselves through idolatry, failure to honour parents, 'oppressing people, especially the weak' or through 'illicit or unnatural sex'.[263] Any curse, whatever its origin, will require specific deliverance ministry. Human judgements may at times function as curses and may also require a particular form of deliverance.[264] Finally, MacNutt identifies the possibility of specific spiritual, psychological and sexual ties that may need to be broken.[265]

MacNutt outlines the best way to prepare for deliverance ministry[266] and how to assemble a balanced ministry team[267] before offering extensive advice regarding, and various formats for, the form of the ministry itself dependent to some extent upon the type of demon one encounters.[268]

The most significant addition to the material found in Healing is the

---

[256] MacNutt, *Deliverance*, 88.

[257] MacNutt, *Deliverance*, 88-90.

[258] MacNutt, *Deliverance*, 90-92.

[259] MacNutt, *Deliverance*, 92-94

[260] MacNutt, *Deliverance*, 182-240.

[261] MacNutt, *Deliverance*, 108-110.

[262] MacNutt alleges that Christian leaders are frequently the target of occult groups in this regard. MacNutt, *Deliverance*, 110. He believes that his horse died as a result of a curse directed by a local witch's coven. He now includes the family pets in daily prayers for protection from these curses. MacNutt, *Deliverance*, 115.

[263] MacNutt, *Deliverance*, 118.

[264] MacNutt, *Deliverance*, 120-125.

[265] MacNutt, *Deliverance*, 127-129. MacNutt attributes to Tommy Tyson the idea that illicit sex generates a permanent bond (or 'soul tie') between the parties involved which will need to be broken subsequently. MacNutt, *Deliverance*, 129. Tyson was a charismatic Methodist pastor/evangelist who also served 'as director of spiritual life at the newly founded Oral Roberts University'. S. Strang, 'Tyson, Tommy' in S. M. Burgess and E. M. Van Der Maas (eds.), *The New International Dictionary of Pentecostal and Charismatic Movements* (Grand Rapids: Zondervan, 2002) 1155. The removal of soul ties is a persistent secondary feature of Charismatic deliverance.

[266] MacNutt, *Deliverance*, 147.

[267] MacNutt, *Deliverance*, 152-156.

[268] MacNutt, *Deliverance*, 167-240.

inclusion of a chapter on Satanic Ritual Abuse (SRA).[269] MacNutt has been much influenced by the work of James Friesen[270] (see below) and accepts the widespread need to treat victims of SRA and the frequently resulting Multiple Personality Disorder (MPD). MacNutt gives brief guidelines with regard to the treatment of this condition and directs the reader to study Friesen for themselves. He finishes this chapter alleging that those who publicly question the existence of SRA may be Satanists themselves attempting to cover their tracks.[271]

MacNutt advocates the use of 'blessed objects' during deliverance ministry. In particular he recommends the use of consecrated oil, water and salt.[272] The book closes with a brief chapter on deliverance of places and objects.[273] The latter could even include a personal computer. Having experienced numerous problems with her PC a contact of MacNutt called for professional help:

> The support man from Microsoft called my problem 'strange' and 'weird', and told me it was at a level deeper than the software and that he couldn't help me. I clung to Colossians 2:15... "Even if this computer screen remains white," I said, "Jesus triumphed over you by the cross!" And I bound spirits and praised God. And five hours later the text returned (for no apparent reason) and every glitch disappeared.[274]

Francis MacNutt was of great significance to the early Charismatic Movement; his healing ministry was highly regarded and he played a key role in establishing the Renewal amongst Roman Catholics. Hence his adoption of deliverance ministry, however reluctantly, was a major coup for those striving to raise its profile in Charismatic circles. He was particularly influential in introducing deliverance to Catholic Charismatics.[275]

If his early ministry was marked a reluctant willingness to engage in the necessary evil of deliverance, twenty years later one can sense a deep enthusiasm for deliverance ministry and considerable broadening of his perception of the need for this ministry. In the intervening twenty years deliverance ministry itself underwent a number of 'fad-like' mutations (curses, soul ties, inner vows, SRA and MPD, and SLSW) with various techniques emerging to deal with each; MacNutt incorporated them all into his ministry as they have came along.

---

[269] MacNutt, *Deliverance*, 223-235.

[270] MacNutt, *Deliverance*, 80, 233.

[271] MacNutt, *Deliverance*, 234.

[272] The salt may be sprinkled around a troubled location or consumed with food. MacNutt, *Deliverance*, 241-247.

[273] MacNutt, *Deliverance*, 265-268.

[274] MacNutt, *Deliverance*, 266.

[275] Cuneo, *American*, 174.

At first glance, MacNutt does not resemble an enthusiast. Firstly, he was extremely well educated.[276] Secondly, he readily acknowledges human sources. He identifies how he was influenced by Agnes Sanford, Jo Kimmel, Tommy Tyson and Oral Roberts regarding his healing ministry and to Barbara Shlemon, Derek Prince and Don Basham as regards deliverance.[277] Thirdly, though his reliance on experience is self-conscious, he is aware of the difficulties this presents in convincing others; indeed, in his earlier writing he is almost apologetic for having to address the issue of deliverance[278] and recognises that his own experiences 'may seem problematic if not downright medieval'.[279] Like other enthusiasts from a sacramental background, MacNutt does not place much emphasis upon the imminent eschatology typical of enthusiasts generally.[280] Nevertheless, MacNutt shows undoubted evidence of tendency toward enthusiasm. This is most obvious in his appeal to experience of the supernatural (noted above) which led to his involvement with deliverance ministry. As has been demonstrated, at times MacNutt's impulse to perceive spiritual causes for even the most trivial of events is very pronounced.

MORRIS CERULLO

Morris Cerullo, an ordained Pentecostal minister, was involved with the post-War healing revival, later the FGBMFI and came close to joining up with the Fort Lauderdale Five. Cerullo is an intriguing figure who sometimes appears at the fringe of the emergence of widespread deliverance ministry among Pentecostals / Charismatics. In one sense he is an unremarkable, if durable, healing evangelist with a tendency towards Word-Faith teaching. His significance for this study lies in his contacts with several people who are of much greater significance with regards to deliverance and, secondarily, because his own ministry, straddling the healing revival and the Charismatic Movement clearly featured an emphasis on deliverance.[281]

---

[276] Strang, 'MacNutt', 856.

[277] MacNutt, *Healing*, 7-9.

[278] MacNutt, *Healing*, 189.

[279] MacNutt, *Healing*, 209. Elsewhere, MacNutt accepts that it is impossible to construct objective proofs from experience. MacNutt, *Deliverance*, 48, 75 and 92.

[280] Cf. the introductory material in chapter 5 below.

[281] Cerullo's approach to deliverance, in common with other healing evangelists and the early Pentecostals was triumphalistic and straightforward even equating deliverance with Christian conversion. He appears to be uneasy with the emerging Charismatic deliverance ministries. M. Cerullo, *The Back Side of Satan* (Carol Stream, Illinois: Creation House, 1973) 5, 7, 194, 197-204. In common with the latter however, Cerullo accepted the widespread need for deliverance. Cerullo, *Backside*, xii (but cf. 201). Interestingly *Backside* makes reference to Kurt Koch who would certainly have held serious doubts about Cerullo and may well have considered him in need of deliverance himself. Cerullo, *Backside*, 18.

Cerullo's organisation, World Evangelisation, developed an anti-occult ministry in the early 1970s including the introduction of 'the world's first anti-occult mobile unit' in January 1972.[282] Cerullo hired two ex-Satanists, Mike Warnke and (when he left in early 1972) then the less well-known, but even more controversial, Hershel Horatio Smith. In 1973 Cerullo published his own book regarding the occult, *The Back Side of Satan*, which contained a brief version of Warnke's story.[283] Cerullo's anti-occult team at this time included Dave Balsiger who was to co-author Warnke's *The Satan Seller*, also in 1973, shortly after they both left Cerullo's organisation. In 1974, Cerullo's replacement ex-occultist, Hershel Smith, published his own lurid story in *The Devil and Mr Smith*. Smith's ministry was short lived; he 'vanished from the scene soon after his book was published.'[284] Cerullo, cooled his interest in anti-occult ministry in late 1973. According to Hertenstein and Trott he was 'worried about the popularity of the devil.'[285] Assuming that assessment is correct, it seems that Cerullo has a track record of being drawn to but later pulling away from the more controversial aspects of Charismatic spirituality. Another example can be found in his near-involvement with the shepherding movement.[286]

FRANK AND IDA HAMMOND

Written in 1973, against a background of increasing Evangelical obsession with all things Satanic, the Hammond's short and colourful book *Pigs in the Parlour* sold hundreds of thousands of copies during the seventies and eighties and made a significant impact upon the Charismatic Movement as a whole. Its title refers to the authors' belief that demons ('pigs') are all too often taking up comfortable residence in a place they don't belong – the lives of Christian believers ('the parlour').

> What would you do if a herd of filthy pigs came into your parlour and began to make themselves at home? Would you invite such a thing?...
> You would drive them out as quickly and unceremoniously as possible!
> And this is to be our attitude toward demon spirits. As soon as they are

---

[282] Cerullo, *Backside*, 56.

[283] Cerullo, *Backside*, 165-174.

[284] M. Hertenstein & J. Trott, *Selling Satan* (Chicago: Cornerstone, 1993) 165. Hertenstein and Trott claim that the co-author of Hershel Smith's book, one Dave Hunt, held reservations regarding the historicity of the Smith's testimony. Hertenstein, *Selling*, 165.

[285] Hertenstein, *Selling*, 165. Cf. Cerullo, *Backside*, 201.

[286] Although his emphasis upon prosperity teachings and exaggerated claims regarding miraculous healings have recently brought him into disrepute among evangelicals in the UK.

discovered they are to be driven out.[287]

The Hammonds got involved in deliverance ministry as a result of reading a pamphlet by Derek Prince at a time when a pastor friend was struggling with persistent headaches.[288] They discerned that the root of the illness was demonic and attempted to expel a demon. After a couple of sessions of deliverance ministry their friend was completely free of pain. They also quote with approval a case of deliverance involving Kenneth Hagin and the informed reader will perceive themes of the word-faith teaching associated with Hagin in the theology of the Hammonds.[289]

The Hammonds taught that demons may, and frequently do, enter the life of believers through sin, the rough and tumble of life, through convincing a person that they are turning out like their parents,[290] or through involvement in 'religious error.'[291] Demons may be detected spiritually through the gift of discernment or through mundane observation – they are often the cause of recurrent emotional or mental disturbance, uncontrolled speech and sexuality, addictions and sickness.[292] They assert that demons may gain 'entrance' to a child or even a foetus who will then need deliverance.[293] Like Merill Unger, the Hammonds believe that demons may only invade the soul and body; the spirit is secure from their attack.[294] Apparently, objects and houses are sometimes the focus of demonic activity; such objects should be destroyed and plagued houses 'should be cleansed by the authority of the name of Jesus'.[295]

Once a demon has been identified it must be expelled via deliverance ministry and this may take a number of forms. Demons may be dislodged by self-deliverance,[296] by individual deliverance whereby a single person delivers a demonised individual or by group deliverance where several demonised

---

[287] Hammond, *Pigs*, 3.

[288] Hammond, *Pigs*, 91-95.

[289] Hammond, *Pigs*, 62 and, for example, 35.

[290] Here the Hammonds have developed the ubiquitous teaching that demonic oppression may be inherited through the generations in a slightly different direction. Hammond, *Pigs*, 25f.

[291] Hammond, *Pigs*, 29f.

[292] Hammond, *Pigs*, 28f.

[293] Hammond, *Pigs*, 65. The authors go on to relate details of how they ministered deliverance to a three month old baby.

[294] Hammond, *Pigs*, 136-138. Cf. M. F. Unger *What Demons can do to Saints* (Chicago: Moody, 1991) 76-98.

[295] Hammond, *Pigs*, 141-143. According to the Hammonds, demons are particularly attracted to owl and frog decorations since these are 'unclean and abominable creatures ... of darkness'. Hammond, *Pigs*, 142. Overcoming stiff opposition, this is probably the worst example of misinterpretation of scripture to be found their book. Cf. Wright, *Theology*, 107.

[296] Hammond, *Pigs*, 57-59.

persons may be delivered at once.[297] It is even possible to perform deliverance by proxy where one individual stands in for the demonised party who is absent from the proceedings.[298] In every case the deliverance is performed in the authority of the name of Jesus.[299]

Various strategies are suggested to facilitate the moment of expulsion. The Hammonds believe that demons leave through the mouth and nose and that it is sometimes helpful to 'prime the pump' by asking the subject to breathe out forcefully or cough a few times. This is normally enough to get the ball rolling.[300] Secondly, Bible passages and songs that make reference to the blood of Jesus are 'packed with power'. The Hammonds relate one case where a demon begged not to be spoken to of 'the blood', 'because it is so red, because it is so warm, because it is alive, and it covers everything'.[301] Sometimes deliverance can only occur as the practitioner identifies a ruling spirit and expels it first. The Hammonds' observe demons rarely operate as individuals; instead they work in groups and the ruling spirit is the one that first gained access to the life of the subject. Each demon in such a group is identified by its special nature. From their experience of the workings of the demonic the Hammonds have drawn up an extensive list of demons' names classified into groups along with that of the likely ruling spirit, that they claim to have encountered. For example, a ruling spirit of 'withdrawal' may be accompanied by 'pouting', 'daydreaming' and 'fantasy' demons.[302] Demons may give a false or foreign name to avoid exposing their true character.[303] It is helpful for the subject to know the names of the evicted demons, particularly the ruling demon, in order that he or she may be prepared to resist those demons in future and 'maintain his [or her] deliverance'.[304]

---

[297] Hammond, *Pigs*, 53-56.

[298] Hammond, *Pigs*, 61-63. The Hammonds go on to point out that this form of deliverance should only be carried out 'when the Holy Spirit specifically directs'. Hammond, *Pigs*, 63.

[299] Hammond, *Pigs*, 53, 57, 105.

[300] Hammond, *Pigs*, 51, 108.

[301] Hammond, *Pigs*, 109. This is a good example of the frequent practise of building theology on the 'testimony' of demons. Furthermore, it demonstrates the proclivity for extreme Charismatics to adopt views most akin to magic regarding the 'power of the blood'.

[302] Hammond, *Pigs*, 113-121. The list offered by the Hammonds thus closely resembles an English language thesaurus. The obvious point is that in pressing demon nature/names so hard the Hammonds are obliged to argue that these have been developed alongside the English language since other languages may not have words that correspond to the fine distinctions between the demon names they identify. This may seem a pedantic criticism but it is significant in identifying the parochial naivety of the Hammonds' understanding.

[303] The implication being that demons always have English names?

[304] Hammond, *Pigs*, 111f.

During the deliverance ministry itself, it is to be expected that the demon will manifest itself physically through the demonised subject. The commoner manifestations include rapid movement of the tongue in and out of the mouth, a hissing noise via the nostrils, snake-like writhing on the floor, numbing or tingling in the hands, screaming, rhythmic body movements, pain and laughing. Since demons usually leave via the mouth, the moment of deliverance is often accompanied by coughing or even vomiting up blobs of phlegm.[305]

The need for deliverance ministry is exacerbated by the difficulty of retaining one's freedom from demons. The Hammonds outline a testing set of criteria for achieving this: 'Put on the Whole Armour of God', 'Confess Positively', 'Stay in the Scripture', 'Crucify the Flesh', 'Develop a Life of Continuous Praise and Prayer', 'Maintain a Life of Fellowship and Spiritual Ministry', and 'Commit Yourself Totally to Christ.'[306]

> Doing these things will insure that your 'house' (life) is filled after having been cleansed [delivered]. No demon will be able to return much less bring any others in with him. If a spirit should trick you and regain entrance, see that he is cast out as soon as possible... If other areas of demon activity in your life are subsequently brought to light, seek deliverance. Jesus has made possible complete deliverance. Walk in daily deliverance. Do not settle for anything less.[307]

Clearly the Hammonds envisage that deliverance ministry is to be the ongoing experience of the Christian.[308] They, in common with most of the more extreme varities of deliverance practitioners, appear to have replaced (or at least supplemented) the orthodox Christian emphases on repentance, discipline and the aid of the Holy Spirit as the antidote to sin, with deliverance ministry. The former emphases are now relegated to strategies to avoid (or at least minimise) further demonisation.

The most remarkable section of *Pigs in the Parlour* is that which identifies

---

[305] Hammond, *Pigs*, 52.

[306] Hammond, *Pigs*, 35-37. This lifestyle would be beyond most, if not all, spiritually mature Christians let alone the average recipient of deliverance ministry. Most Christians while wishing to affirm the value of committing oneself 'totally to Christ' would not immediately contemplate the possibility of demon invasion if this high standard was not perfectly achieved.

[307] Hammond, *Pigs*, 37. Less extreme advocates of deliverance ministry tend only to associate demonisation with persistent sin; the Hammonds imply that a demon could gain entrance through an uncharacteristic slip.

[308] They claim that they have never met a Christian who was not in need of deliverance. Hammond, *Pigs*, 12.

the causes of, and prescribes the cure for, schizophrenia.[309] The Hammonds estimate that this condition is found among a quarter of those they minister to.[310] There are very serious consequences to attributing the cause of such a mental illness to the work of demons. The Hammonds effectively imply that they there is no role for psychiatry – instead the treatment of mental/emotional disorders appears to primarily (if not exclusively) require deliverance ministry. Interestingly, the lengthy process of deliverance ministry for schizophrenics advocated by the Hammonds appears to be almost a prototype for the approach adopted a few years later by some Christian psychiatrists to treat Multiple Personality Disorder.

As usual for practitioners of deliverance ministry, the Hammonds invest the practice with eschatological significance.[311] However, it is of great interest to note that contra evangelical fundamentalists such as Unger and Koch[312] who exemplify a premillenialist view that sees deliverance ministry as a response to the moral and spiritual decline of society, the Hammonds are postmillenialist and consequently they view deliverance ministry as an aggressive strategy to be employed in order that the Church may achieve its Christ-ordained potential.

> Before the church can fulfil that which the Lord has prophesied concerning His victorious church (Matt 16:18) it must take the offensive against the devil. The message and practice of spiritual warfare is spreading rapidly today throughout the church. The devil is being resisted and he is forced to flee. For the first time we are seeing the backside of the devil. It is a beautiful sight.[313]

Hence, while postmillenialists view deliverance as an appropriate reaction to persistent and uncontrolled sin, the Hammonds have a mandate proactively to root out demons to advance the victorious kingdom. This presentation of deliverance ministry as the means to the end of an all-conquering Church was

---

[309] Hammond, *Pigs*, 123-133. The Hammonds claim that 'Some authorities in the field of mental illness estimate there may be as many as fifty million schizophrenics in the United States'. Hammond, *Pigs*, 123.

[310] Space precludes a thorough analysis of the special and apparently 'infallible' revelation that was granted to Ida Hammond, but suffice to say that it appears to be the product of a fertile imagination. One can only guess what a trained psychiatrist would make of it. For example the founding principle for the Hammonds understanding of this condition is that it involves a 'split personality'. This is a popular misconception of schizophrenia that is quite inaccurate. A little knowledge can be dangerous!

[311] Hammond, *Pigs*, 145-153. Their view of the eschatological significance of deliverance ministry was developed as a result of one of Frank's dreams.

[312] Regarding Merrill Unger and Kurt Koch, see below, Chapter 4, for a full analysis and list of publications.

[313] Hammond, *Pigs*, 150f.

extremely seductive within the heady atmosphere of the Charismatic Movement at the time.[314]

It is only too easy to criticise a book like *Pigs in the Parlour*. In the cold light of academic analysis much of it appears to be arrant, and potentially dangerous, nonsense.[315] However, its sheer popularity demands that it be engaged seriously.[316] It represents the high point of American deliverance ministry. Here are Christian leaders achieving profile precisely for their deliverance ministry rather than what had previously been the case, namely, high profile Christian leaders adopting deliverance ministry in order to reinvigorate their ministry. After this time, those specialising in deliverance ministry were forced to go to even greater extremes as in the case of Bill Subritzsky,[317] whilst more mainstream Charismatics such as John Richards and Michael Green attempted to provide more balanced teaching on what was becoming a point of increasing controversy within and (for some) embarrassment for the Charismatic Movement.[318] Increasingly, leading Charismatics felt impelled to adopt a position with regard to deliverance ministry, often publishing their own contributions to the debate.

Studies of Deliverance by Significant Charismatic Figures

In the early 1970s burgeoning interest in deliverance ministry, particularly among Charismatics, inevitably caught the attention of the secular media. At this time renewed interest in all things spiritual, particularly in the popular media, made exorcism the focus of much attention. Conversely, at first, the mainline churches seemed loath to address the issue perhaps due to the potential for division over what was fast becoming a contentious subject.[319]

---

[314] Where an emphasis upon deliverance ministry coincided with a firm postmillenialism the scope for the former increased beyond the category of a private pastoral affair to a vital component of a methodology for church growth. Historically this development took place within the Charismatic Movement around 1975 through 1985 in particular through the Shepherding Movement which combined these two emphases. With all this in mind the arrival on the scene of Strategic Level Spiritual Warfare should be of no great surprise, indeed it seems almost inevitable.

[315] Andrew Walker describes it as 'totally unbelievable'. A. Walker, *Enemy Territory* (London: Hodder and Stoughton, 1987) 33.

[316] A point that could be made many times over regarding academic engagement with popular spirituality. Many popular Christian books are not to be found in theological libraries and are to all intents and purposes ignored by academic courses.

[317] On Subritzky, see below.

[318] On Richards and Green see below.

[319] This policy of non-engagement was hastily abandoned when stories of deliverance going badly wrong began to emerge in the media.

Enthusiastic exorcism / deliverance began to make all the wrong headlines when a number of cases went badly awry. The most famous of these is the notorious 'Barnsley Case'. In this instance a man named Michael Taylor underwent an all-night session of deliverance ministry. Inside thirty minutes of his return home the following morning he gruesomely murdered his wife.[320] Howard notes two other cases where deliverance ministry has gone badly wrong including one case involving 'internal ministry'.[321] The latter is a distasteful subject involving a belief that demons may lodge in the genitalia and require anointing with communion wine in order that they may be removed.[322]

In the meantime deliverance ministry was causing friction amongst Pentecostals and Charismatics with some noted leaders championing this new emphasis while others were in outright opposition. It would not be unreasonable to view this fissure as the first serious example of what would come to be a repeated phenomenon within the Charismatic Movement. The Movement, based as it was on the defining experience of Baptism in the Holy Spirit, has subsequently proved vulnerable to being redefined around new experiences.[323] When these emerge to sufficient prominence leading Charismatics often feel it necessary to either support or oppose the new experience or teaching. An examination of the public responses to the growing popularity of deliverance, published or otherwise, by leading Charismatic and Pentecostal figures, is examined below.

One might be forgiven for thinking that some of these books are of exactly the same genre of those examined above since they appear to be manuals for deliverance ministry. However, the key difference is that these books were published as a response to the controversy stirred up by the advocates of this new Charismatic phenomenon. They represent varying attempts by the existing leaders of the Charismatic Movement to exert some leadership over the growing controversy.

MICHAEL HARPER

Michael Harper was the darling of the early British Charismatics. This was in no small part due to his impressive Evangelical credentials; he worked, for six years, at All Souls, Langham Place, arguably the Mecca of British Evangelicalism.[324] During this time he received the baptism of the Holy Spirit,

---

[320] R. Howard, *Charismania* (London: Mowbray, 1997) 81-83.

[321] Howard, *Charismania*, 87-107.

[322] Howard, *Charismania*, 102f.

[323] I. Stackhouse, *The Gospel Driven Church* (Milton Keynes: Paternoster, 2004). Poloma describes Pentecostalism as 'a movement constantly in need of the refreshing waters of religious experience.' M. Poloma, 'The Millenarianism of the Pentecostal Movement' in S. Hunt (ed.), *Christian Millenarianism* (London: Hurst, 2001) 186.

[324] For a brief biography see P. D. Hocken 'Harper, Michael Claude' in S. M. Burgess and E. M. Van Der Maas (eds.), *The New International Dictionary of Pentecostal and Charismatic Movements* (Grand Rapids: Zondervan, 2002) 689f.

speaking in tongues for the first time in August 1963. The following year he left All Souls to pioneer a new organisation which he called The Fountain Trust. Six years later he wrote a short book entitled Spiritual Warfare[325] which outlined his own approach to exorcism within the wider context of a traditional and militant view of Christian discipleship.

Whilst Harper was clearly an advocate and indeed practitioner of the ministry of casting out demons it should be noted that he was keen to set a middle course between those who deny the applicability of such a ministry in the modern age and those 'demon chasers' who were inclined to a naïve spiritual dualism that sees a demon lurking behind every human ill. Indeed, and somewhat radically for a leading Charismatic at the time, he rejected the term 'deliverance ministry' along with any sense that there could be a specialist ministry in this area. Despite his fairly deep misgivings, Harper still felt his book needed to be written since he believed that the church was at that time dangerously exposed due to its tendency to ignore her diabolic enemy.[326] To his credit Harper saw the potential dangers of deliverance ministry at an early stage and warned against them prior to the emergence of the cases such as those that occurred in Barnsley three years after the publication of *Spiritual Warfare*. Harper's influences included Merrill Unger and Kurt Koch (reflecting his evangelical heritage) and David du Plessis who also had concerns about specialist deliverance ministries.[327]

Harper opened his book with a brief report of a deliverance[328] that he observed in 1965 at an event organised by his own Fountain Trust at which Charismatic pioneer Dennis Bennett was ministering.[329] This account is of great interest since it underlines the point that deliverance ministry was a normal if secondary characteristic of earliest Charismatic practice.[330] Spiritual Warfare is punctuated with similar accounts, however, Harper presented them as relatively simple affairs usually involving a simple rebuke to the demon to effect an eviction.[331]

---

[325] M. Harper, *Spiritual Warfare* (London: Hodder and Stoughton, 1970).

[326] Harper, *Spiritual*, 14f., 16.

[327] D. DuPlessis, 'Foreword' in W. R. McAlister, *The Dilemma: Deliverance or Discipline* (Plainfield: Logos, 1976) vii-ix. These concerns are echoed by John Thomas in a thorough treatment of the 'origins of illness in New Testament thought'. J. C. Thomas, *The Devil, Disease and Deliverance* (London: Sheffield Academic Press, 1998) 317.

[328] Although Harper rejected the term I will continue to use it here for simplicity since what he describes is identical to what would usually be called 'deliverance'.

[329] Harper, *Spiritual*, 11f.

[330] Two years later Harper invited Robert Pettitpierre (on whom see chapter 5 below) to exorcise his house after he began to experience 'night feelings of gloom and fear.' Harper, *Spiritual*, 103.

[331] Harper, *Spiritual*, 11f., 109-116.

Harper believed that the missionary movement 'brought the church once more into conflict with entrenched evil'[332] and that recent years had seen the re-emergence of open satanic activity in traditionally 'Christian' nations. He noted the rise of witchcraft, divination, deviant religious sects (particularly the eastern NRM Soka Gakkai), spiritualism and the erosion of morality as evidence in a chapter bearing the colourful title 'The Devil's Pentecost'.[333] He went on to quote Merrill Unger to the effect that this rise in satanic activity is just what one would expect as the second coming of Christ draws near.[334]

Harper made the commonplace point that demon possession is an inappropriate term to describe the victim of demonic activity[335] and used a simple metaphor to illustrate his understanding of how demons can affect the lives of those they afflict. Just as warfare can take the form of an assault, siege or an invasion, so demons may launch an individual temptation to sin, so besiege a person in a given area of their life that they lead them into what Harper termed 'bondage' and finally, the demon(s) may actually invade the life of the believer leading to a state of demonisation.[336] Moreover, demons may afflict a subject physically, motivate theological confusion and cause some (though not all) psychological disorders.[337]

Harper understood the eviction of demons to be a ministry rather than an office and so it may, in principle be administered by any Christian person; he was opposed to the idea of 'specialist' deliverance ministers or centres.[338] In this context he approvingly quoted David du Plessis 'Don't go around looking for demons. But if you find them, *tread on them!*'[339] Coming from a 'pre-Exeter report' Anglican context he observed that according to Canon Law the bishop's permission was required prior to proceeding with an exorcism. He suggested that a 'general permission to carry on this ministry' should be sought since the bishop may not take kindly to incessant and occasionally urgent requests of this kind, 'and if the truth be known, some do not believe in the existence of evil spirits anyway!'[340]

Although he held that any person of good standing in a local congregation should, with the approval of the church leaders, be permitted to carry out deliverance ministry,[341] Harper believed that certain qualities are necessary if one is to 'exercise... this ministry successfully':[342] moral purity will facilitate

---

[332] Harper, *Spiritual*, 39.
[333] Harper, *Spiritual*, 40-50.
[334] Harper, *Spiritual*, 42. On Unger see below, chapter 4.
[335] Harper, *Spiritual*, 106-107.
[336] Harper, *Spiritual*, 105f.
[337] Harper, *Spiritual*, 90-99.
[338] Harper, *Spiritual*, 60-62.
[339] Harper, *Spiritual*, 61.
[340] Harper, *Spiritual*, 60
[341] Harper, *Spiritual*, 61.
[342] Harper, *Spiritual*, 62.

discernment with regard to the presence of demons and the consequent need for deliverance;[343] the power and gifts of the Holy Spirit are important;[344] and knowledge of the Scriptures.[345]

In resisting and, in more serious cases, evicting demons Harper was concerned that the ministry is properly prepared for. He recommended a time of prayer and speaking in tongues.[346] The ministry itself should begin with a full and frank repentance[347] prior to the deliverance itself which should take the form of joining with the subject in resisting the devil in cases of demonic assault,[348] binding and loosing in the case of demonic bondage[349] and 'casting out'[350] in the case of demonic occupation.[351] In the latter case Harper was in favour of keeping things simple; although the demon's name would probably emerge as the area of the subject's personality afflicted by the demon became apparent, there is no need for discussion to take place with the demon.[352] Harper did not advocate protracted deliverances, criticised the focus on physical manifestations and warned that laying on of hands is inappropriate until the demon is evicted.[353] The eviction should be completed with a simple command to the demon: 'I command you to go where the Lord Jesus sends you, and never return to this person. I place you under the authority of him "who is far above all."'[354]

Finally, Harper recommended that the subject be properly cared for after the deliverance ministry. He asserted that the spiritual vacuum created by the

---

[343] Harper, *Spiritual*, 62-64.

[344] Harper, Spiritual, 75-79. Harper noted that the 'word of knowledge' 'is particularly useful when trying to help people who have had damaging experiences in early childhood which they cannot themselves remember, and which they have repressed.' Harper, *Spiritual*, 76f.

[345] Harper, *Spiritual*, 67f.

[346] Harper, *Spiritual*, 108f. This reflects the early Charismatic emphasis, inherited from Pentecostalism, that the Baptism in the Holy Spirit was at least usually evidenced by glossalalia. Hence, Harper placed an emphasis upon the value of this gift during deliverance ministry that is much more marginal in the writing and practice of later Charismatics.

[347] Harper, *Spiritual*, 109f.

[348] Harper, *Spiritual*, 110f.

[349] Harper, *Spiritual*, 111-113.

[350] Harper asserted that 'exorcism' was not a biblical term and should be rejected in favour of 'casting out' a literal translation of the Greek term *ekballo* which is frequently used in the New Testament to describe the eviction of demons. Harper, *Spiritual*, 113.

[351] Harper, *Spiritual*, 113-116.

[352] Harper, *Spiritual*, 114.

[353] Although he did not make the point, this warning was probably based on the concern that physical contact of this kind could allow the demon to transfer from the subject to the minister.

[354] Harper, *Spiritual*, 116.

absence of the demon is filled via the baptism in the Holy Spirit[355] and given the psychological repercussions of the ministry, prayer for healing of the memories may be required.[356] The subject will need to adopt normal Christian spirituality including self-discipline, faith and praise.[357]

Harper concluded his book with a significant reflection on *The Screwtape Letters* observing that Screwtape may now be considering how to deal with Harper's book. Whilst he acknowledged that one strategy would be to 'get the book laughed out of court', he also identified the alternative threat of using it to motivate an obsessive interest in the demonic.[358]

Harper's book represents an admirably prompt attempt to cautiously affirm, redefine and finally marginalise the burgeoning deliverance ministries of the time. As a champion of Charismatic Renewal, Harper, unlike Basham among others, was unwilling to relativise the baptism in the Holy Spirit to a first stage experience to be followed by others such as deliverance. Harper intended to put deliverance in its proper place within the traditional schema of the Charismatic Renewal. His reasons for so doing might not have been purely theological since he had a vested interest in keeping the Renewal true to its roots. Effectively, Harper wanted to resist the Renewal's descent into Charismatic faddism; his attempts were at best only partially successful.[359]

MICHAEL GREEN

Michael Green's contribution to the issue of deliverance ministry was published in 1981 and entitled *I Believe in Satan's Downfall*.[360] His aim appears to have been, on the one hand, to refute liberal theologians who were aggressively arguing that belief in demons should be dispensed with (and that deliverance ministry was therefore not only unnecessary but potentially dangerous), and on the other to present a more moderate approach to deliverance ministry than was being pedalled by many of his Charismatic contemporaries. Accordingly, he devotes approximately the first half of his book to a justification for belief in Satan and a comprehensive explanation of his activities and strategy. He then goes on to address the issues of occultism, counterfeit religion and demonisation. Finally, he looks at the decisive defeat of Satan in the atonement and its application to Christian living. His work rests upon engagement with respected theologians and scholarly exegesis of

---

[355] Harper, *Spiritual*, 116f.

[356] This is not the tying of deliverance and 'healing of the memories' (made popular by John Sandford on whom see below) that it appears to be at first glance. Harper was only suggesting this healing for the memory of the deliverance itself.

[357] Harper, *Spiritual*, 118f.

[358] Harper, *Spiritual*, 121.

[359] There is every reason to expect that Harper's views on Spiritual Warfare will have modified subsequent to his conversion to Orthodoxy. Unsurprisingly however he has not written anything further on the subject.

[360] M. Green, *I Believe in Satan's Downfall* (London: Hodder and Stoughton, 1981).

Scripture.

In his discussion of 'the Ministry of Christians to the Demonised', Green issues a clear rebuke to those Charismatic leaders who were urging Christians to take up cudgels against prolific invading demon spirits:

> The Church Father, Tertullian, maintained that any Christian who did not know how to exorcise deserved to be put to death! But that certainly does not mean that every Christian ought to be involved in this kind of ministry. All can: not all should. And never look for it! If God means to use you in this ministry he will make it so painfully obvious that you can scarcely avoid it without gross disobedience.[361]

He then argues that there is a need for exorcism only in the case of demonic possession. Since Christians cannot be possessed in this manner, deliverance ministry is used where the subject is afflicted by an evil influence beyond their control.' The former ministry should only be undertaken by 'authorised priests with the express permission of the bishop in the name of the church.' The latter can be undertaken by any mature Christian at any time.[362]

After listing the usual possible symptoms of demonic presence,[363] and giving guidelines for preparing for the deliverance ministry,[364] Green makes extensive suggestions for the ministry itself, stating that it is 'extraordinarily difficult to generalise because the circumstances in which cases of the demonic present themselves differ so much, and in any event a great deal of flexibility is obviously necessary.'[365] His approach represents an amalgam of Charismatic, Evangelical and Anglo-Catholic doctrine and praxis. His central thrust emphasises thorough confession followed by a claim for protection and power in the name of Jesus; the demon should then be evicted, also in the name of Jesus. This latter stage may need to be repeated. Green also affirms the use of prayer in tongues, quotation of Scripture, the use of signs and symbols (such as the mark of the cross, holy oil and holy water as well as more impromptu symbolic actions), and celebration of the Eucharist. He asserts that the deliverance team must be 'sensitive to what God is saying during the proceedings, which may be quite long'; an object may need to be destroyed. Eventually the demon(s) will have to leave 'because Jesus is Lord.' The whole process may be exhausting for everyone involved but there is no danger for those 'living close to Christ.' Finally, Green points out that the person

---

[361] Green, *I Believe*, 132.

[362] Green, *I Believe*, 132. Green equates exorcism with Roman Catholic 'solemn exorcism' and deliverance with 'minor exorcism'.

[363] Green, *I Believe*, 134-137.

[364] Green, *I Believe*, 137-139.

[365] Green, *I Believe*, 139.

exorcised will need subsequent pastoral care.[366]

Green's writing on deliverance ministry is brief and inevitably leaves many questions unanswered, such as, 'How do demons enter their subject?' or 'How can one maintain deliverance?' However, one suspects that he would prefer a certain amount of ambiguity to indulging in the kind of speculation and prescription that is so commonplace in the writings of more less cautious Charismatics.

JOHN RICHARDS

In 1974 John Richards, long time secretary to the Anglican Study Group on exorcism, published a book entitled *But Deliver Us From Evil*.[367] Richards is perhaps best described as a thoughtful and cautious Charismatic. His book is well thought out, contains a great deal of research and engages with alternative views. His work is highly commended by Michael Green.[368]

Having examined the Occult Revival in some depth, Richards turns his attention to the question of demon possession, preferring a three-tier model of demonic activity, namely, demonic influence, demonic oppression and demonic attack. He does, however, allow for 'the apparent take-over of a person by an alien personality or intelligence' calling it 'mediumship' or 'possession'.[369] He assures the reader that in accepting the reality of such demonic activity they need not become 'a spiritual or psychological flat-earther':

> One fear among many about using 'demonic' language or thinking in terms of 'possession' is that to do so means aligning oneself utterly with those who have long been familiar, even enthusiastic about such things. Most of the 'baggage', whether apocalyptic, medieval, Roman or Pentecostal, can and should be left behind.[370]

Richards is at great pains to dampen down excess enthusiasm for deliverance ministry. Warnings about becoming preoccupied with the demonic resound throughout his book. Nevertheless he claims that there is no need to fear the effects of a misguided exorcism.[371]

Richards goes on to make a case for the reality of demonic personality and activity. He quotes psychiatrists and medics to the effect that some (not all) cases of epilepsy and mental illness are demonic in origin and require exorcism as a cure. He then outlines a sophisticated argument from experience:

---

[366] Green, *I Believe*, 139-147.

[367] J. Richards, *But Deliver Us From Evil* (London: Darton, Longman and Todd, 1980).

[368] Green, *Believe*, 114, 134.

[369] Richards, *Deliver*, 91f.

[370] Richards, *Deliver*, 92.

[371] Richards, *Deliver*, 105.

If there has been *one*, just one *real* case of demonic possession in history the theologian must have an understanding of God's world in which such a thing is possible. Neither he, nor the scientist or the doctor can select from reality only those things which harmonise most easily with current thought and terminology.[372]

This argument is clever because it feels somewhat arrogant to assert that there has *never* been a case of demonic possession in all of human history.[373] Having inserted the thin end of the wedge, he pushes through the thicker end arguing that experience of exorcism frequently requires modification of theoretical theological frameworks.[374]

Having established a need for it, Richards goes on to prescribe the proper manner of understanding and performing this ministry. He stresses the exorcism must take place within the wider context of healing and demonstrates considerable insight in recognising that 'the danger of even considering the deliverance ministry is that it may be taken outside of the context of the *whole* Gospel and seen as the panacea for all ills.'[375] He views exorcism as the short, sharp shock that achieves the expulsion of the demon; the ongoing deliverance of the subject to God requires a much deeper level of support and care provided by the clergy and the whole Christian community.[376]

Richards advocates the formulation of a case history for every subject that should indicate how the demonised state was arrived at. The need for a case history militates against the appropriateness of mass exorcisms.[377] Referring to this case history the minister should make a diagnosis based on rational consideration of the evidence. Divine guidance through the gift of discernment of spirits should always take a secondary place to this rational approach.[378] A spiritual diagnosis should be made which recognises that the subject is a unity of 'spirit, mind and body – in which all aspects of the person share in the suffering of any particular part.'[379] Hence all cases of demonic affliction will have a spiritual aspect that should be diagnosed alongside medical and

---

[372] Richards, *Deliver*, 217.

[373] The weakness of course being that one could use a parallel argument to defend the existence of a number of implausible paranormal events. Furthermore, and persuasively, a post-modern response might be to stress the distance between the objective experience and the subjective interpretation. Given this distance, how could one be sure that a genuine possession *had* occurred?

[374] Richards, *Deliver*, 115-118.

[375] Richards, *Deliver*, 120.

[376] Richards, *Deliver*, 121. Hence the role of the exorcist should not be a prominent one.

[377] Richards, *Deliver*, 121-124.

[378] Richards, *Deliver*, 124. Having said that, Richards then interprets some of his case evidence to the effect that people just 'know' when a demon is the root cause of problems. Richards, *Deliver*, 142f.

[379] Richards, *Deliver*, 126.

psychological aspects.[380] Richards then devotes several pages to a discussion of the terminology associated with demonic influence before asserting that a Christian may be influenced by a demon. He goes on to make the case that demonisation is usually the result of self-conscious involvement with the occult or gross sin[381] before relating 23 case histories which include the usual mix of outlandish manifestations including the case of a priest who undertook an exorcism without attendant faith and promptly dropped dead.[382]

Richards delineates the significance of Christian exorcism in line with some wider theological and ecclesiological themes:

> The casting out of demons is the work of God through his Church and a sign of the coming of his Kingdom, the doing of his will, and the deliverance from evil for which every member so faithfully prays; it is God's action, not ours because the Kingdom, the Power and the Glory belong to him not us.[383]

He goes on to deny a range of alternative interpretations of Christian exorcism including cosmic or psychological conflict, the struggle between the flesh and regenerate nature, the 'externalisation of basic drives and impulses in order that they may be recognised and renounced', the desperate action of a dying Church, an attempt to return to the Apostolic Church and 'a defence against spiritual armies that are about to overrun us.'[384] These denials represent Richards' desire to reclaim the significance of exorcism for the conservative middle ground of the Church from the extremes of theological liberalism, radical pre or postmillenialism, triumphalism, defeatism and Freudian/Jungian

---

[380] Richards, *Deliver*, 127. This holistic anthropology, now widely accepted by pastoral counsellors, allows for a much more balanced view of the human condition including that of demonisation. More insightful advocates of deliverance ministry usually adopt a similar anthropological model even if they do not make it explicit.

[381] Richards, *Deliver*, 129-134. However, he also accepts the possibility of demonic transmission across generations and that others may be troubled by a demon associated with a particular location rather than a particular person. Richards, *Deliver*, 122f.

[382] Richards, *Deliver*, 143. An uncharitable analyst of this section of case evidence might well make the point that, having claimed that Pentecostal, Roman and Medieval baggage can and should be left behind, Richards goes on to recycle a great deal of it. The evidence is drawn from the work of Kurt Koch (on whom see chapter 4, below) and Don Basham among others. Richards, *Deliver*, 136-154. The spectacular and indeed disastrous nature of some of the histories militates against his previous assertion that even unnecessary exorcism does no harm. Richards, *Deliver*, 105. Furthermore, in the light of the tragic Barnsley case which took place in the same year as *But Deliver Us From Evil* was published, Richards general optimism about this ministry seems somewhat negligent.

[383] Richards, *Deliver*, 161.

[384] Richards, *Deliver*, 161.

psychology.

Richards explains that exorcism may take the form of prayer to God or a direct instruction to the demon. He equates these two forms with Roman Catholic minor and major exorcism respectively. In turn they address the problem of demonic 'obsession' and demonic 'possession'. He insists that it matters little what formula is used for a major exorcism; the question is one of authority rather than form. The former resides in the person of Jesus Christ. Nevertheless, Richards suggests that a major exorcism should comprise three components. Firstly, the demon should be directed to 'harm no one'. Richards quotes anecdotal evidence to the effect that demons may cause physical injury or possibly even death if this direction is not made. Secondly the demon should be commanded 'to come out'. It is important to bless the person thus exorcised so that the resulting vacuum is occupied by the Holy Spirit. Finally, the demon should be directed 'to go somewhere else'. This should take the form of a charge to go 'where God wants them [the demons] to be', rather than a 'presumptuous' attempt to send them to the 'Pit' or the 'Abyss'.[385]

Richards accepts that it is useful to ascertain the name of the demon so that the order to leave is clear and also to ensure that when it has departed it is replaced with its 'opposite in the aftercare of the person.'[386] He also accepts validity of 'binding' a demon until such time as it can be properly exorcised.[387] He warns that touching the recipient of exorcism is unwise since 'there may be a danger of some temporary evil transference'.[388] He goes on to teach that demons may afflict the Christian[389] before outlining the need for avoidance of the occult and ongoing support to ensure that deliverance is maintained.[390]

According to Richards, 'it will be from people in whom the Spirit dwells that God will call out his ministers [of exorcism]'.[391] He is keen to locate the practice of Christian exorcism, at least potentially, within the whole body of Christ[392] and is therefore resistant to the Anglican restriction on its practice to 'specialists'.[393] The Christian exorcist will continue to recognise humbly that it is the Holy Spirit who evicts demons and will maintain a godly lifestyle. Proper

---

[385] Richards, *Deliver*, 165-167.

[386] Richards, *Deliver*, 168.

[387] Richards, *Deliver*, 169f.

[388] Richards, *Deliver*, 171.

[389] Richards, *Deliver*, 172f.

[390] Richards, *Deliver*, 174-177.

[391] Richards, *Deliver*, 181. He makes clear that this does not necessarily restrict the ministry to 'Charismatics'. However, he does not make clear to whom it does restrict the practice of exorcism. The majority of his case material is drawn from Charismatic and Pentecostal experience and this speaks for itself.

[392] Richards, *Deliver*, 177-190.

[393] Richards, *Deliver*, 179. He attempts to interpret the situation to the effect that the Church of England was moving away from this approach. Actually in 1975 the commitment to exorcism as a 'specialist' ministry was reaffirmed by the General Synod.

aftercare is an essential component of the ministry and this will inevitably involve the professional clergy.[394]

After an examination of the demonisation of places, Richards' study of the deliverance ministry concludes with a few brief comments including a prediction that medicine and psychiatry will come to be thankful for spiritual insights into their work,[395] and a plea to the denominational Churches that they take the burgeoning Pentecostal movement more seriously.[396]

But Deliver us from Evil is undoubtedly the work of a sincere and competent pastoral theologian. It is a genuine attempt to wed competing theologies and ecclesiologies of exorcism. Richards' tone is moderate and his desire to prune these various approaches of their 'baggage' is laudable. However, it is important to note that Richards swallows the camel of the experiences of his Pentecostal, Charismatic, Evangelical and Roman Catholic sources apparently uncritically.

In his effort to be positive and identify common ground, Richards fails to grapple with the serious differences between various theologies of exorcism. For example, there can be little doubt Kurt Koch would take a dim view of Don Basham's ministry of exorcism. Nevertheless, Richards quotes them both, leaving their differences unexamined; this renders his analysis somewhat superficial. Reading between the lines it is clear that Richards' work rests primarily on Pentecostal/Charismatic foundations; nevertheless, he plays these down in order that his approach may remain inoffensive to, and workable in the context of a broad Church.

LÉON-JOSEPH SUENENS (1904-1996)

Eminent and highly respected, Cardinal Suenens was a key figure, if not the key figure, within the Roman Catholic Renewal. In 1983 his contribution to the debate regarding Charismatic deliverance ministry was translated into English and published entitled *Renewal and the Powers of Darkness*. In short, Suenens is opposed to the practice of 'Charismatic deliverance ministry', preferring to maintain the traditional Roman rite of exorcism which may only be practised by an ordained priest acting with the approval of the bishop.

Suenens holds to an orthodox demonology but alleges that the advocates of Charismatic deliverance present 'scenes... [that] are distorted visions of reality.'[397] He argues that the 'Devil's most deadly weapon is not the grip that he may have on man, but sin itself'[398] and our emphasis should be on resisting temptation rather than on 'phenomena which may be purely

---

[394] Richards, *Deliver*, 172-191.

[395] Richards, *Deliver*, 215.

[396] Richards, *Deliver*, 220.

[397] Suenens, *Renewal*, 31.

[398] Suenens, *Renewal* 31, cf. 45.

psychopathological.'[399] He specifically criticises common practice such as obtaining the names of demons, attributing illness to demonic activity, offering deliverance to children and belief in an organised demonic hierarchy.[400] He specifically fingers MacNutt, 'one of the authors who, in my view, have excessively popularized in the Catholic Charismatic Renewal the subject of demonic influences'.[401]

Suenens goes to the heart of the matter when he offers the following penetrating observation of the experiential basis for Charismatic deliverance:

> In the final analysis, this domain [the framing of theology, in this case Satanology/demonology] has been entrusted to the Magisterium, who alone has received from the Master the charism of ultimate discernment. To reject this teaching in favour of one's own personal experience would be incompatible with the Catholic faith. This point is important.
>
> When reservations are made about the manner in which the expelling of demons is practiced, one comes up against the objections of those involved. They maintain that they have 'witnessed' the casting out of demons, and that there can be no doubt about the very great spiritual fruit of these deliverances.[402]

Suenens goes on to argue that according to strict rules of logic that it is impossible to be certain about the cause of this 'very great spiritual fruit'. As a Roman Catholic his ready made solution to the enthusiastic tyranny of personal spiritual experience is to appeal to the authority of the Church over the authority of the individual.[403]

Suenens recommended that the Roman Catholic Church should refute the Charismatic's presumed freedom to practice deliverance as a 'minor' exorcism and reassert that it is in the lap of the Church to establish correct guidelines for the practice of exorcism and deliverance;[404] furthermore, he emphasised that 'it is of the utmost importance to reserve to the bishop or his mandatory every form of exorcism that seeks to identify the Devil or the devils and to enter into dialogue with them by way of a direct summons, adjuration or command, with

---

[399] Suenens, *Renewal*, 32 cf. 34.

[400] Suenens, *Renewal*, 62-64.

[401] Suenens, *Renewal*, 35.

[402] Suenens, *Renewal*, 77f.

[403] Suenens, *Renewal*, 78-81.

[404] For this reason he urges the Church to update its liturgy of exorcism and to issue guidelines regarding the distinction between exorcism and deliverance ministry. Suenens, *Renewal*, 94-101.

a view to their expulsion.'[405]

Suenens is the clearest (though by no means the only) example of a major figure within the Renewal Movement launching a full-frontal attack upon the new emphasis on deliverance ministry. His attack rests upon an affirmation of a more orthodox theological view that temptation is the greatest weapon in the devil's armoury and his reassertion of the Church's authority over the individual and his or her personal religious experience.[406]

MICHAEL SCANLAN (1931-)

Franciscan priest Michael Scanlan was and remains a leading Catholic Charismatic[407] with a commitment to transforming pastoral care in the context of Christian community. In 1974 he published a short book advocating the practice of inner healing within such a community setting;[408] six years later he co-authored *Deliverance From Evil Spirits* with Randall Cirner[409] contending for a similar approach to deliverance ministry based upon 'the more than ten years experience that we have both had in pastoral care and in praying with people for deliverance.'[410] This community emphasis carries an implicit (and occasionally explicit) criticism of deliverance ministries as practiced by itinerant 'experts' and results in a comparatively sober approach.

Scanlan and Cirner begin by making a case for the existence of evil spirits primarily by describing their various destructive strategies, namely temptation, opposition and bondage. In certain cases any of these attacks may need deliverance ministry which may be effected at four levels depending upon the severity of the attack: self deliverance, fraternal deliverance, pastoral deliverance and finally in extreme cases 'special ministry' will be required. In common with other episcopal practitioners of deliverance, Scanlan, argues that deliverance is the equivalent of minor or informal exorcism and he recommends that in cases of possession requiring solemn exorcism that the

---

[405] Suenens, *Renewal*, 97.

[406] It is evident with hindsight that the logic of Charismatic experience usually militates against traditional hierarchical ecclesiology. In this sense Suenens' attempt to shoehorn Renewal into traditional Catholicism was an unlikely endeavour. Suenens clearly felt that the movement could be focused upon personal spiritual awakening within traditional ecclesiastical categories and this is certainly possible. However, heightened religious experience is not a static affair as the history of Renewal indicates; it seems that it cannot be maintained easily apart from continuous reinvention and redirection. Suenens' criticism of deliverance ministry was in fact a fundamental criticism of religious enthusiasm from a traditional Roman Catholic perspective.

[407] P. D. Hocken, 'Scanlan, Michael' in S. M. Burgess and E. M. Van Der Maas (eds.), *The New International Dictionary of Pentecostal and Charismatic Movements* (Grand Rapids: Zondervan, 2002) 1041.

[408] M. Scanlan, *Inner Healing* (New York: Paulist, 1974).

[409] M. Scanlan and R. Cirner, *Deliverance From Evil Spirits* (Cincinnati: Servant, 1980).

[410] Scanlan, *Deliverance*, 1.

person be referred for professional and specialist ministerial care. Ultimately suspected cases of possession should be referred to the bishop. One detects a serious distinction here between Scanlan and MacNutt. Where MacNutt viewed demonic manifestation such as the emergence of a demonic personality as the precipitating factor for his own deliverance ministry, Scanlan sees such dramatic symptoms as evidence that a case is beyond the scope of deliverance ministry:

> We do not deal with exorcism of possessed people. Neither do we deal with the relatively small number of cases of unusually dramatic manifestations of spiritual bondage which do not involve possession.

> Solemn exorcism should be used only in cases of possession. There are cases where Satan is able to take over the personality of the affected person and is able to frustrate the person's exercise of free will...

> If a person has sufficient control over himself to repent, renounce spirits, and command them to leave, we can take the initiative and use deliverance successfully. if the person cannot do this because he cannot say the words, goes into a trance, or gives way to a new personality, then we would stop deliverance and pursue other remedies.[411]

Having limited the applicability of deliverance to relatively mild forms of demonic problems, Scanlon outlines a seven stage schema for deliverance ministry:

1. *Preparation* including repentance 'from all serious sin'[412] that might be granting a demons a right to oppress.[413]
2. *Introduction* in which the minister of deliverance introducing everyone, explains what will take place, says prayers and liberally sprinkles holy water. [414]
3. *Listening and Discerning*, here the team listen both to the subject and to the Holy Spirit to discern what if any spirits need to be dealt with.[415]

---

[411] Scanlan, *Deliverance*, 69.

[412] Scanlan, *Deliverance*, 80.

[413] Scanlan, *Deliverance*, 78.

[414] Scanlan, *Deliverance*, 83. In a later section Scanlon briefly asserts the value of both the sacraments and sacramentals (blessed water and oil – he does not mention salt) Scanlan, *Deliverance*, 107-109.

[415] Scanlan, *Deliverance*, 83, cf. 95f. Scanlon is at pains to underline how discernment combines natural listening with supernatural guidance. One cannot help but detect a criticism of MacNutt's strictly supernatural approach here.

Scanlan notes that a 'personality foreign to the person speaking'[416] may emerge (which seems at odds with his previous assertion that such a development would occasion a referral for possible exorcism).

4. *Repentance* to include anything that has emerged during the course of the previous stage.[417]
5. *Deliverance* during which individual or groups of spirits should be renounced by name by the subject and the leader of the team. 'This stage ends when there is a spiritual sense that the spirits have been cast out.'[418]
6. 'Healing and Blessing' to fill in the 'void' left behind after deliverance. This stage may also require some inner healing.[419]
7. Pastoral Guidance including a clear plan for further pastoral care and a person appointed to oversee the care.[420]

In a closing chapter, Scanlan argues that both deliverance and inner healing have differing and necessary roles to play[421] and has his approach endorsed by a practising psychologist[422] before making some significant comments regarding 'physical manifestations'.[423] In relating his experience of the most common of these 'restlessness (squirming, a desire to leave the room), drowsiness (yawning, mental lethargy), nausea and sometimes facial and bodily contortions'[424] there is a complete absence of the normal emphasis upon outlandish manifestations. In fact Scanlan argues that dramatic manifestations are less in evidence where the subject has the 'strength of character' to avoid externalising internal spiritual developments, where there is a high level of love and trust between the subject and the ministry team and where there is no unnecessary emphasis upon the expectation of such manifestations.[425] Far from exploiting the apologetic value of demonic manifestations Scanlon views them as largely unnecessary human responses to the beneficial internal spiritual benefits of deliverance. This is unique amongst advocates of deliverance.

To conclude, Scanlan outlines an approach to deliverance that is embedded in his wider and heartfelt commitment to community based pastoral care. Far from sensationalising demonic activity in a bid to make a case for the validity of deliverance ministry,[426] he argues that the existence of demons is best known

---

[416] Scanlan, *Deliverance*, 83.
[417] Scanlan, *Deliverance*, 85f.
[418] Scanlan, *Deliverance*, 87.
[419] Scanlan, *Deliverance*, 87-89.
[420] Scanlan, *Deliverance*, 89-91.
[421] Scanlan, *Deliverance*, 109-111.
[422] Scanlan, *Deliverance*, 111f.
[423] Scanlan, *Deliverance*, 112-114.
[424] Scanlan, *Deliverance*, 112f.
[425] Scanlan, *Deliverance*, 113f.
[426] Scanlan similarly downplays the evidential significance of Charismatic healing; he refuses to describe the healings he goes on to relate as miracles 'because natural medical

to us through revelation. Scanlan's impulse is towards an unsensational deliverance ministry embedded within communal pastoral care; he exemplifies a gentle and informed mystical form of deliverance firmly focused on a mature and genuine compassion.

NICKY CRUZ

Nicky Cruz rose to prominence as an unlikely convert of David Wilkerson; the story was told in the best-selling *The Cross and the Switchblade*. In 1973 he published *Satan on the Loose*[427] which contains a good deal of personal experience with the demonic,[428] then a little biblical demonology,[429] before highlighting the rise of the occult[430] and then finally outlining his own approach to deliverance ministry.

Cruz takes a fairly conservative angle on demon possession asserting that it is not possible for a Christian to be in such a condition.[431] Furthermore, he dislikes the practice of speaking of habits or vices in demonic terms (demon of smoking or alcohol) preferring to see these as fleshly problems that should be positively dealt with through the 'combination of our will and His [God's] power.'[432] Nevertheless, he does believe that Christians may be oppressed by the devil where they capitulate to temptation.[433]

Where Christian faith is absent, Cruz believes that demon possession is a real possibility, especially if a person gets involved in the occult. Such possession will require deliverance and Cruz relates the story of Julio who experienced such deliverance at a prayer meeting at the hands of two ladies experienced in such ministry.[434]

Satan on the Loose is typical of much Charismatic literature of its time, highlighting the dangers of the occult and the need for deliverance ministry where demons have possessed an individual. However, on two key points (the security of the Christian from demonic possession and the roles of demon) Cruz actually undermines the need for widespread deliverance ministry within the Christian community, instead arguing for a fairly typical evangelical approach to sanctification.

---

explanations could be given for all.' Scanlan, *Inner*, 5. Nevertheless Scanlan is obviously a keen advocate of charismatic healing.

[427] N. Cruz, *Satan on the Loose* (London: Oliphants 1973).

[428] Cruz, *Satan*, 9-35.

[429] Cruz, *Satan*, 70-84.

[430] Cruz, *Satan*, 100-117.

[431] Cruz, *Satan*, 120.

[432] Cruz, *Satan*, 121.

[433] Cruz, *Satan*, 120.

[434] Cruz, *Satan*, 128-139.

Late Century Charismatic Deliverance Ministry (1980 to 2000)

By 1980 the first flush of fervour for Charismatic deliverance had passed and new fads[435] began to stir up further controversy within Charismatic circles – one might be forgiven for expecting deliverance ministry to slide backwards towards its natural status as a secondary characteristic of the enthusiastic Charismatic Movement. Whilst this is certainly the case in a general sense it oversimplifies the development of the movement as a whole.

As the Charismatic Movement progressed from one fad to another the Movement became increasingly fragmented. The initial uniting experience was of course baptism in the Holy Spirit and it was this shared experience that brought notable unity to the movement, unity that successfully traversed and eroded deep denominational divides. Fires burn out and fierce fires burn out more quickly, and subsequent fads basically represent an attempt to reignite the glowing embers of previous fires. Unfortunately, each new fad creates a division within the Movement as a whole meaning that a good portion of Charismatics fail to accept any given stage of the cyclical faddist progression. Meanwhile an ever diminishing group of Charismatics progress from fad to fad incorporating them into these into a constantly evolving theological *pot pourri*. This latter group, augmented by new recruits attracted by the renewed enthusiastic excitement, would continue to emphasise deliverance ministry as a primary characteristic but one that would be incorporated into the developing Charismatic schema. A further group, perhaps the largest, comprise those on the road to routinisation; these don't join either side of the argument but allow each fad to pass them by.

Consequently, the Charismatic Movement increasingly may be characterised by three different types: 1) those who have become stalled somewhere along the process of enthusiastic evolution (faddism) and are to some extent defined not only by what they are in favour of but also by what they oppose. A good example is the FGBMFI which is in favour of the Baptism of the Holy Spirit, deliverance ministry and took an active part in championing these experiences but then objected to the shepherding movement and was no less active in its opposition. These groups may rejoin the progress of the Movement at a later stage or remain static defined by opposition to fads they have not accepted. 2) Those who have currently accepted every stage of Charismatic faddism and attempt to include all of these within their schema. New fads will usually

---

[435] This term is used thoughtfully and to great effect by Stackhouse. Stackhouse *Gospel* 8-11. Much earlier, in reference to evangelical revivalistic enthusiasm, Knox observed that 'revivalism has shown a law of diminishing returns; each new wave, as it recedes, registers less of a high-water mark – Moody and Sankey, Torrey-Alexander, Aimée Macpherson. And all these, it is unnecessary to add, were imports from the United States of America.' Knox, *Enthusiasm*, 578, cf. (in regard to the enthusiasm of early Methodism) 542, also, 549, 565f. The parallel with the tidal nature of the enthusiasm of the Charismatic Movement is striking.

emerge from within this group. The 'third wave', which resists the name 'Charismatic' but in reality accepts every major aspect of the movement (and has been responsible for propagating a few fads of its own), provides an excellent example of this. 3) Those whose Charismatic standing is sliding into routinisation. This last group may pay lip service to various Charismatic phenomena but will have a decreasing interest in experiencing them first hand and will instead show an increasing interest in presenting a more rational, down to earth, less experiential spirituality. A good example within the British scene is Spring Harvest.

Most practitioners of Charismatic deliverance post 1980 are to be understood as belonging among the first and second groups. Hence they often reinterpret the significance of deliverance ministry in the light of subsequent enthusiastic fads. Another reason for persistent interest in deliverance ministry is where it plays a useful role when incorporated in a wider ministry that is of personal interest to a particular practitioner. Of course all of those studied below demonstrate hallmarks of enthusiasm most pronounced in their immanent spirituality and, in many cases, the telltale sign of imminent eschatology.

BILL SUBRITZKY

New Zealander Bill Subritzky is to this day an extremely gifted and popular evangelist and conference speaker; his profile is largely based upon the usual Charismatic credentials including a vigorous deliverance ministry. His own best-selling contribution to this ministry was published in 1985 and entitled *Demons Defeated*. His evangelistic ministry is typically Charismatic although his approach to deliverance perhaps goes to new extremes; he has had a particular influence over the Charismatic scene in the UK.[436] Unsurprisingly Subritzky acknowledges the profound influence of Derek Prince.[437]

Demons Defeated does not include a serious attempt to present the reader with an explanation as to how demons interact with the human personality. Subritzky points out that much sin is due to lack of self-control rather than to demonic activity; however, this stands in tension with much of the rest of the material to be found in the book.[438] He takes his anthropology from I Thessalonians, namely that humans are spirit, soul and body, but fails to apply this concept in any meaningful way to the rest of his teaching.[439]

Like his forerunners in this ministry, Subritzky sees the influence of demons behind sin and asserts that 'behind every sin there is a spirit, and if we continue

---

[436] Walker credits him with 'the greatest impact upon Anglican and now independent charismatic church exorcisms in Great Britain in the late 1980s and early 1990s. Walker, 'Devil', *91*.

[437] W. Subritzky, *Demons Defeated* (Tonbridge: Sovereign, 1985) 10f., 76 and 92f.

[438] Subritzky, *Demons*, 56, cf. 69.

[439] Subritzky, *Demons*, 97.

with the sin then we open ourselves to a spirit.'[440] Demons commonly enter humans through trauma, contact with a dead person or through the eye or ear 'gate'. In fact there are so many opportunities for demons to enter that it would be remarkable if any given person was not carrying several.[441]

Multiple Personality Disorders are always caused by demon activity, as is any perverse sexual activity including oral sex, compulsive masturbation and homosexuality.[442] He argues that sexual activity is a possible avenue for demonic infestation as 'strong spirits or demons of lust and perverted sex can pass from one body to another during the act of sexual intercourse.'[443] Addictions and many physical disorders, particularly allergies, are caused by resident demons.[444] Subritzky descends to the ridiculous when he claims to have delivered a young man from a 'seagull' demon that had been causing difficulty in his marriage. Apparently it had entered him when he had listened to a demonically inspired song entitled 'Jonathan Livingstone Seagull.'[445]

Subritzky's experience of deliverance ministry is, to say the least, remarkable. He claims to have 'seen' and even 'smelt' demons.[446] Sometimes Subritzky has seen the 'little piggy eyes of the demon' in the eyes of the person being delivered.[447] Where the demon being evicted is one of 'sexual uncleanness', his subject often coughs up white foam sometimes 'by the bucketful.'[448]

Subritzky has constructed a detailed analysis of the organisation of demonic forces including an 'Unholy Trinity' of the Spirits of Jezebel (feminism),[449]

---

[440] Subritzky, *Demons*, 69.

[441] Subritzky, *Demons*, 65-82.

[442] Subritzky, *Demons*, 72, 102, 103f. Subritzky believes that AIDS is the punishment Paul predicted for male homosexual practice in Romans 1. Subritzky, *Demons*, 103.

[443] Subritzky, *Demons*, 14.

[444] Subritzky, *Demons*, 104f., 106f.

[445] Subritzky, *Demons*, 117f.

[446] Subritzky, *Demons*, 25, 60, 134. Usually this 'seeing' is 'in the spirit' (whatever that means), though on one occasion it was apparently literal.

[447] Subritzky, *Demons*, 133.

[448] Subritzky, *Demons*, 134.

[449] Subritzky here touches upon an important undercurrent in Charismatic demonology – the Jezebel spirit. Many Charismatics understand this to be an evil spirit that usually causes a woman to become overly assertive, to seek a leadership and therefore usurp the positions ordained for men. Obviously, this belief functions within groups that hold to conservative gender roles. Recently, John Paul Jackson has written a book explaining how to deal with the Jezebel spirit which, despite his protestations to the contrary, is misogynistic, ethereal and deeply pessimistic. J. P. Jackson, *Unmasking the Jezebel Spirit* (Eastbourne: Kingsway, 2001). Intriguingly, Knox identifies 'female emancipation' as a key feature of enthusiasm and recognises the significance of key female leaders. Teaching regarding the Jezebel spirit may well be viewed as a conservative male reaction to this feature of enthusiasm; another example is found in the

Anti-Christ and Death and Hell.[450] These spirits have demon children that visit various problems upon those they afflict. Among his stranger ideas, perhaps the strangest, is that one may differentiate between angels and demons in that the former have bodies and notably wings.[451]

Much of Subritzky's teaching rests upon idiosyncratic and literal interpretations of the bible. He remains an Anglican and this is evidenced in his inclusion of set prayers to deal with specific instances of demonisation and his confidence in the occasional efficacy of blessed water.[452]

Subritzky's ministry as a successful itinerant healing evangelist persists to this day. He continues to speak in churches, public halls and, tellingly, in FGBMFI meetings. The durability of his ministry which has remained largely unchanged since the late eighties is remarkable, however, his popularity is not what it once was.

PETER HORROBIN AND ELLEL GRANGE

Peter Horrobin's ministry and the healing deliverance centre that he established in 1986 (Ellel Grange) are probably the most visible and significant example of Charismatic deliverance ministry in the UK. Furthermore, Ellel Grange achieved a degree of notoriety in 1992 when it featured in a *Dispatches* television documentary. Despite the persistent controversy surrounding 'Ellel Ministries' further centres have been established not only in the UK but also in Australia, South Africa and Canada. The total number of full-time staff numbered 180 as of 2003.[453]

Horrobin's approach to ministry is outlined in two books: Healing through Deliverance Volume 1: The Foundation of Deliverance Ministry and Healing Through Deliverance Volume 2: The Practice of Deliverance Ministry.[454] In the forewords, no less a figure than Derek Prince writes 'I have come to believe that deliverance from demons, is at this time, the most urgently needed ministry in the Body of Christ. This book provides the answer. I heartily commend it to you.'[455]

---

strong and conservative role assigned to women by the Shepherding Movement (which of course included a strong emphasis upon Charismatic deliverance).

[450] Subritzky, *Demons*, 18, 29-41.

[451] Subritzky, *Demons*, 63f. Presumably one is supposed to make this judgement when one 'sees' the angel or demon 'in the spirit'.

[452] Subritzky, *Demons*, 181f., 235-248. Here Subritzky strays into methods more appropriate for sacramental exorcism – a good example of the tendency among late-century deliverance practitioners to theological and ecclesial eclecticism.

[453] P. Horrobin, *Healing Through Deliverance Volume 1: The Foundation of Deliverance Ministry* (Grand Rapids: Chosen, 2003), 320.

[454] Horrobin, *Volume 1* and P. Horrobin, *Healing Through Deliverance Volume 2: The Practice of Deliverance Ministry* (Grand Rapids: Chosen, 2003). These books were first published in 1991.

[455] Horrobin, *Volume 1*, 12.

The foundation of Horrobin's understanding is that normal Christian ministry should include preaching, healing and deliverance.[456] Healing is, in fact, the overriding concept in Horrobin's understanding of salvation via Christian faith:

> the most important healing any of us can ever experience is to receive Jesus into our lives as Saviour and Lord. The very word *salvation* in the Greek of the New Testament means 'wholeness and healing,' and it is translated in various ways according to the context. Salvation is healing, and healing is part of the ministry of salvation.[457]

Having established (to his own satisfaction at least) that deliverance ministry is of primary importance, Horrobin leads the reader of *Volume 1* in a detailed analysis of various New Testament passages in which he detects a deliverance emphasis. Horrobin's hermeneutic is governed by the assumption that any reference to healing contains an implicit reference to deliverance[458] and he frequently adopts innovative, idiosyncratic and ingenious interpretations to find reference to deliverance or wider spiritual warfare themes where there seems to be none.[459] Whilst this is commonplace among advocates of deliverance ministry, Horrobin provides a particularly inventive example.

Horrobin's approach to deliverance has clearly been influenced by Derek Prince, but also by the Sandfords.[460] This is interesting in so far as he is writing prior to the Sandfords' book on healing and deliverance. Whilst he does not mention them by name, he repeats many of their key phrases ('bitter root', 'inner vows', 'inner healing') and much of their emphasis upon marital and parental relationships.[461] Nevertheless he clearly criticises their view that inner healing largely obviates the need for deliverance – a view which they were to amend in a later publication (see below).[462] Elsewhere, in a long list of possible reasons why deliverance ministry might fail to evict a demon Horrobin writes the single word 'passivity' with no further explanation.[463] This, along with Horrobin's constant repetition of the concept of 'ground', indicates familiarity with *War on the Saints* (on which see below).

In common with most practitioners of deliverance, Horrobin believes that there are vast numbers[464] of demons all of whom long to be enclosed by a

---

[456] Horrobin, *Volume 1*, 192.

[457] Horrobin, *Volume 1*, 35.

[458] Horrobin, *Volume 1*, 269.

[459] By way of example see Horrobin, *Volume 1*, 99, 136, 156-159, 275.

[460] Derek Prince has already been considered above. On the Sandfords see below.

[461] Horrobin, *Volume 2*, 48, 49, 121, 134, 139, 180 and 192.

[462] Horrobin, *Volume 2*, 124, 245.

[463] Horrobin, *Volume 2*, 256. *War on the Saints* is included in the bibliography.

[464] See Horrobin, *Volume 1*, 79 for Horrobin's tentative attempt to calculate the quantity of demons in existence.

physical body, preferably human.[465] Taking a tri-partite anthropology,[466] Horrobin outlines the vulnerability of humans to demonic infestation. Demons may oppress their victim's spirit, body (through sickness) and soul. According to Horrobin, the latter is comprised of the mind, the emotions and the will and each of these may become sickened, possibly because of a demonic presence.[467] Horrobin recognises that 'man is an integral whole' and consequently 'if he is sick in one area, other areas may be affected.'[468] This involved anthropological model provides endless opportunities for Horrobin's therapeutic approach to Christian discipleship. Whilst Horrobin does not argue that deliverance will be required in every case, he does assert that a healing ministry without a deliverance component will 'probably be less than 20 per cent of what it could and should be.'[469] True to this conviction and, no doubt, his experience of criticism, the tone of Horrobin's writing is often aggressive when addressing those who do not share his views on the need for widespread deliverance.[470]

Horrobin understands demons to work within a legal framework; people become demonised as and when they offer demons legal right to oppress them primarily through capitulation to sinful patterns of behaviour but also through a myriad of other means.[471] An important part of deliverance ministry is to remove this legal right through repentance (where sin is the 'entry point') or through the severing of curses and 'soul ties'.[472] Consequent to Horrobin's understanding of the legal rights of demons to act in this way is his belief that deliverance ministry is only to be offered to Christians since non-Christians cannot remove this legal right and therefore they will only be re-demonised if they are delivered. Demons will, once they have taken up residence, seek to attract others to their host and it is usual to find groups of demons inhabiting a

---

[465] Horrobin, *Volume 1*, 86.

[466] Horrobin, *Volume 1*, 32-34.

[467] Horrobin, *Volume 1*, 34-44.

[468] Horrobin, *Volume 1*, 44.

[469] Horrobin, *Volume 1*, 26.

[470] Horrobin, *Volume 1*, 106, 138, 173, 273 and 295. Whilst Horrobin does not mention it explicitly, it is clear that he has read Wright's *Theology of the Dark Side* and makes two specific criticisms of it. Horrobin, *Volume 1*, 21, 95.

[471] Horrobin writes over one hundred pages explaining the different ways in which people become demonised. These include demonisation via the family line, through sexual, occult or religious sin, ungodly soul ties, personal upset, trauma, the death of others, curses, addictions, fears and fatigue. He makes clear that this is not an exhaustive list. Horrobin, *Volume 2*, 85-207.

[472] Soul ties are basically improper relationships caused by illicit sex, misuse of authority etc. Horrobin argues that these operate like tubes through which demons may cross from person to person. Horrobin, *Volume 2*, 119-135, 229. Horrobin's view of how curses operate is very similar to, and clearly influenced by, that of Derek Prince. Horrobin, *Volume 2*, 185.

victim under the authority of a lead demon or 'strong man'.[473]

New Christians should undergo a thorough counselling procedure including, where necessary, deliverance ministry to rid them of any demons that have legal right to trouble them. Whilst he does not assert that every non-Christian is demonised it is hard to draw any other conclusion from his assessment of the wide ranging manner in which people become subject to such a condition. Horrobin argues that the sooner these demons are evicted the better since demons that are able to remain undetected in the life of a Christian are harder to evict at a later stage.

One discovers in Horrobin's approach an unusually developed sacramental emphasis. He advocates the use of consecrated oil 'to extend that anointing to the flesh',[474] and elsewhere observes that 'people have come up out of the waters [of baptism] to be immediately delivered of the powers of darkness which could not stand the consequences of their obedience and the cleansing powers of the consecrated waters.'[475] Sometimes this spills over into activity that resembles the occult practices he is so opposed to:

> We have also found, in some very heavy deliverance ministries, that if we give the person receiving ministry consecrated water to drink, the effect on the demonic can be dramatic and immediate. By 'consecrated water' I mean water that has been prayed over so that it may be filled with the Holy Spirit. There is a power impartation when that is done, similar to the power impartation that takes place when a person receives the laying on of hands.

> We first discovered this when a person we were praying with asked for a glass of water. I went to the kitchen to get one, but on the way back the Lord spoke to me very clearly and told me to bless the water by the laying on of hands. I did so, took it to the room and gave it to the person to drink. She took one sip, spat it out and the demon speaking out through her said, 'Get me some proper water!' We got some water that we did not pray over. She was then able to drink the whole glass without any problem.

> She said that the water actually tasted different, and because it was unconsecrated the demons had no problem with allowing the water to enter her stomach. But a member of the team then laid her hands on the lady's stomach and consecrated the water that was now inside. There was

---

[473] Horrobin, *Volume 1*, 91.

[474] Horrobin, *Volume 2*, 242.

[475] Horrobin, *Volume 2*, 176f.

an immediate reaction, as if the water was boiling in her stomach, and she went into immediate deliverance. This experience was part of the learning program God was putting us through at the time – not a technique recommended for future ministry.[476]

Horrobin also believes that objects such as jewellery and even places and buildings can have demons attached. He advocates the destruction of any items suspected of holding a 'demonic influence' and the 'exorcism' of buildings, particularly church buildings to consecrate them for spiritual use and to remove any evil attachments. He often holds a 'communion service in the house as part of the rededication of the property'.[477]

Horrobin is by no means unintelligent (he is a graduate of Oxford University) and his argumentation is compelling once one swallows the camel of accepting the factuality of his experiences of the demonic as he presents them. The books, like so many in the field, create, for the critical reader, a sense of cognitive dissonance as one grapples with the sheer certainty with which Horrobin blithely presents the reader with a parade of outlandish demonic encounters. He is not unaware that he must persuade the reader to accept his experiences as factual in order to make his case:

> Where theology and experience are at such variance with each other, one must either have the courage to (1) investigate the experiences that others relate and, if necessary, reassess one's theological position as a result or (2) dismiss the experiences of others as deception and heresy and remain in an entrenched position, not daring to face up to the real world outside...

> The whole issue [at this point Horrobin is discussing the key question as to whether a Christian may be in a demonised condition] cannot be discussed at the level of finding proof texts to justify one's viewpoint. For try as you may, and others before me have looked very hard, you cannot come up with any text that uncompromisingly wins the point for either side of the discussion.

> Neither can you, however, find a text that proves one way or the other that Christians can get cancer. Experience, however, indicates very strongly that Christians can, and do, get cancer. Everyone reading this

---

[476] Horrobin, *Volume 2*, 177.
[477] Horrobin, *Volume 2*, 201.

book will know of Christians who have died from the disease.[478]

This (rather weak) argument amounts to an attempt to coerce the sceptic into accepting the veracity of Horrobin's experiences with the demonic, as he presents them, leading to a fundamental theological shift. This is a classic example of enthusiastic apologetics for a spiritually immanent, experience driven hermeneutic, and (as is usually the case) the enthusiast makes little concession to the experience of his opponents.[479]

It must be conceded that if Horrobin's experiences are true as he presents them then the sceptical observer would be forced into some fairly radical rethinking. However, one particular case reported by Horrobin leaves the door open to some suspicion:

> I remember praying for one person who deeply needed healing from spirits of infirmity that affected him and, as a result, everyone around him. Superficially, he did want to be healed (from the symptoms), but the presence of the Holy Spirit upon him was stirring up the enemy and he immediately said, *in a voice that sounded like his but that was definitely not him speaking*, 'Don't ever pray for me like that again!' When confronted, the enemy had used all that man's religious tradition to put an end to any praying that would expose and unseat the demonic strongholds that controlled his health.[480]

It seems that in this case Horrobin's detection of the demonic is based largely on his expectation that it will be present.[481] It is important to notice the operation of enthusiasm which builds a belief upon experiences which are themselves products of that belief thus creating a viewpoint that is impervious to reasoned external penetration. Horrobin's emphasis upon the priority of experience over reason is also embodied in his assertion that the presence of demons and the consequent need for deliverance is to be identified by direct revelation from God (the so-called gift of discernment of spirits) rather than purely through consultation with books.[482]

In conclusion, it is clear that Horrobin has collapsed Christian spirituality into a therapeutic meta-category. Justification and sanctification are viewed as stages within a process of healing. Whilst this is arguably orthodox it allows

---

[478] Horrobin, *Volume 1*, 286.

[479] 'if a person is unwilling to believe that he could be demonised, then healing is rarely possible, because the person is giving the demons a right to be there through unbelief.' Horrobin, *Volume 2*, 27.

[480] Horrobin, *Volume 1*, 173. Italics added for emphasis.

[481] One is entitled to wonder how many more of Horrobin's experiences are this dubious.

[482] Horrobin, *Volume 2*, 55, cf. 24, 109, 187 and 224.

Horrobin to place great emphasis upon deliverance ministry as an integral part of the therapeutic process. Horrobin's controversial deliverance ministry is a classic case of religious enthusiasm. By his own admission his biblical case is not compelling;[483] despite his extensive and creative survey of biblical material he concedes that it is his experiences that govern his interpretation and he pressures the reader to accept them at face value.

JOHN, PAULA AND MARK SANDFORD

The Sandford family rose to prominence within Charismatic circles in the early to mid 1980s largely as a result of the publication of their popular book, *The Transformation of the Inner Man.*[484] They followed this with several other books including *Healing the Wounded Spirit*[485] and *A Comprehensive Guide to Deliverance and Inner Healing.*[486] Their approach is innovative in that they incorporate deliverance ministry into a Freudian/Jungian psychotherapeutic model of Christian discipleship and sanctification which they termed *inner healing.* They inherited this ministry from their 'first mentor and friend' Agnes Sanford, 'the major pioneer in ministry for the healing of memories, which for her was all one with the forgiveness of sins'.[487]

The Transformation of the Inner Man hardly mentions deliverance, and when it does so, marginalises its significance within the counselling process:

We have not spoken of demons or deliverance anywhere else in this book (or in the previous two), because we do not want to give Satan any glory. *We know that if a counsellor transforms a person's inner house of character in Jesus, whatever demon inhabits, if any, must flee, having no longer a house to dwell in.* Seldom do Paula and I have to do an exorcism directly. We know that the devil and all his hosts were once for all defeated and disarmed... Therefore, we seldom have to speak directly to demons to defeat them... So though we occasionally do exorcisms we very infrequently say anything about Satan, and concentrate on teaching how to bring people to Jesus on the cross. *That is the only lasting form of exorcism,* for the devil's forces will return after exorcism to a house not dealt with... The cross gives glory to Jesus, whereas too much direct attack upon Satan gives him the attention he craves. *We accomplish the*

---

[483] On the contrary, it is actually untenable.

[484] J. and P. Sandford, *The Transformation of the Inner Man* (Tulsa: Victory House, 1982).

[485] J. and P. Sandford, *Healing the Wounded Spirit* (New Jersey: Logos, 1985).

[486] J. Sandford and M. Sandford, *A Comprehensive Guide to Deliverance and Inner Healing* (Grand Rapids: Chosen, 1992).

[487] P. D. Hocken, 'Sanford, Agnes Mary' in S. M. Burgess and E. M. Van Der Maas (eds.), *The New International Dictionary of Pentecostal and Charismatic Movements* (Grand Rapids: Zondervan, 2002) 1039.

same end – deliverance – but we celebrate only the power of Jesus.[488]

Despite this, deliverance features quite prominently throughout their later publications though largely as a component part of their emphasis on inner healing. The effect of their later position is to embed deliverance and their understanding of demonisation within an increasingly idiosyncratic psychotherapeutic pastoral model and methodology. The basic anthropology adopted by the Sandfords (inherited from Agnes Sanford) is that every person has a pre-existent, inner spirit that has a separate consciousness from that of the soul (normal human consciousness). That spirit (sometimes the 'inner man' or the 'inner child') can develop a number of diseases (often dating back to early childhood or even *in utero* trauma); most mental or emotional conditions are rooted in these spiritual disorders. The human spirit may also be afflicted by demonic spirits that require deliverance but only as part of the wider goal of restoring the spirit to full health. The Sandfords are keen to emphasise the dangers of indiscriminate exorcism,[489] for example, a depressive spirit should never be exorcised, neither should someone suffering paranoid schizophrenia except where the request comes from a qualified psychiatrist. Interestingly the Sandfords believe that even where a demon is present one should not rush to deliverance ministry – 'there is a time to deal with it and a time to leave it alone'.[490]

According to the Sandfords, demonisation should be detected via the spiritual gift of discernment of spirits. They understand this to be 'our spirit's ability to feel what is in the other, to sense and identify defilement. We may possess that gift purely from God, but it grows by experience'.[491] Later, they broaden their definition of this spiritual gift to include other, more practical methods of diagnosis:

> When demons are the factor, it is usually easily discerned by those who are gifted by the Holy Spirit. The telling mark is the change in the people. Not only do they think and talk in ways foreign to themselves... they have about them a presence which is not their own. The timbre of their voice betrays something else acting in them... people influenced or controlled by demons (not necessarily inhabited), enter a level of stridency or irrationality. One can almost see the demonic leaking out the corners of their mouths. They sometimes come up with ideas and

---

[488] Sandford, *Transformation*, 300. Italics added for emphasis.

[489] The Sandfords quote Jeremiah 6:14 to the effect that quick-fix exorcisms proclaim peace where there is no peace. Sandford, *Healing*, 172. Ironically Prince uses the same passage to establish the need for widespread exorcism. Prince, *Deliverance* (ministry tape 6001).

[490] Sandford, *Healing* 89, cf. 466.

[491] Sandford, *Healing*, 205

information you know they could not have thought of or known without help. It often happens that spiritually sensitive Christians discern the presence of something demonic by feelings of nausea, or a sense of twistedness and oppression which causes pain or pressure in the chest or head.[492]

The Sandfords have a fairly typical understanding of how demons seize opportunities to afflict people, particularly emphasising the dangers of the occult[493] and resentment against God. The legal motif is also present: 'repentance removes the ground for Satan's attack.'[494]

The act of deliverance is simple and the process of demonic expulsion is clear:

> In many cases, no name is needed. An exorcist simply commands a demon to leave, and he must. Such attitudes as lust, pride, fear etc., are not demons who have that name. They are aspects of our flesh. It is actually confession of that sinful attitude which brings release. Since the Devil requries a foothold in us, when that attitude is washed away in the blood of Jesus, Satan's hold in that area is broken, and thus his energy or presence is expelled from that area. We need only, by the guidance of the Holy Spirit, lead people to specific, detailed confession. When enough of Satan's lodging places are destroyed, he must leave. That is why, after people have named a number of such attitudes as though they were demons, a person finally feels released. It was basically the power of confession and forgiveness which caused whatever exorcisms may have happened.[495]

It is worth quoting this section in full since it represents a comparatively thoughtful presentation of the process of Charismatic deliverance ministry without compromising the effectiveness of other Charismatic approaches. It allows for the effectiveness of typical Charismatic deliverance whilst reinterpreting the actual process which is taking place.[496]

In 1992 John and Mark Sandford published *A Comprehensive Guide to Deliverance and Inner Healing*. In it they plead for and explicate an approach

---

[492] Sandford, *Healing*, 216.

[493] Sandford, *Deliverance*, 307-342.

[494] Sandford, *Deliverance*, 111, 156, 308.

[495] Sandford, *Healing*, 338. It is at least questionable whether this understanding of the process of exorcism should really be called exorcism at all. It is primarily a description of the breaking of demon inflamed habitual sin through the biblical pattern of confession and repentance.

[496] Cf. Sandford, *Deliverance*, 127-157 where a highly flexible approach to deliverance is persuasively summed up in the assertion that the practitioner is a healer rather than a mechanic.

to pastoral care that includes both of these practices arguing that neither can be consistently effective, and may become counter productive, in isolation.[497]

To establish their credentials they note that John and his wife Pauline had 'been involved in deliverance ministry since 1958 and the beginning of the charismatic renewal... [they] suppose... [they] have done as many deliverances as anyone in the body of Christ, except perhaps Derek Prince or Bill Zubritzky (sic).'[498] They imply that deliverance ministry emerged and was pervasive within the Pentecostal movement (which is an optimistic simplification from their perspective) but was not immediately accepted by early Charismatics. The Sandfords argue that this was due to the blue collar emotionalism of the Pentecostals and the white collar rationalism of the Charismatics respectively.[499] God finally broke the Charismatic rationalism via an eruption of deliverance ministry:

> [We] believe God used the influx of demonic demonstrations and deliverance ministry to force us to see how much we were ruled by our logical systems and unconscious biases, rather than the Holy Spirit... For a while, then, a sector of the Church lurched into foolishness. Vomit buckets appeared in prayer and counselling rooms. People were going to have to 'upchuck' their demons.[500]

There is clear evidence of enthusiastic spiritual immanentism here in terms of reading the purpose of God behind the eruption of deliverance ministry in Charismatic circles. Furthermore, here the deliverance ministry in not a product of anti-rationalism (although that is implicit) so much as vice-versa. Of course, suspicion of reason is implicit in the whole argument. The Sandfords note with relief that the Church now takes a more balanced approach investigating solutions other than deliverance ministry but still open to its necessity in some situations. Discernment is more careful and the ministry is performed without the anticipation of uncontrolled manifestations. '*Most importantly*, some in the Body of Christ have learned how to combine deliverance and inner healing.'[501]

Having outlined four levels of demonic activity (infestation; inhabitation; obsession and possession), the Sandfords go on to define inner healing as 'evangelising unbelieving hearts.'[502] They define this process as 'the

---

[497] Sandford, *Deliverance*, 20.

[498] Sandford, *Deliverance*, 21. One cannot but feel that this claim is one that they would have been extremely loathe to make ten years earlier.

[499] Interestingly this is the exact opposite of Walker's claim that it was the early Pentecostals' 'working class common sense' that kept them from obsession with deliverance ministry. Walker, 'Devil', 90.

[500] Sandford, *Deliverance*, 25f.

[501] Sandford, *Deliverance*, 26. Italics added for emphasis.

[502] Sandford, *Deliverance*, 50f.

application of the blood and cross and resurrection life of our Lord Jesus Christ to these stubborn dimensions of believers' hearts that have so far refused the redemption their minds and spirits requested when they invited Jesus in'.[503] Here, the Sandfords clearly reveal the essential confusion of their anthropology. In *Healing the Wounded Spirit* it was the spirit that needed healing, here it is the heart – the spirit seems to be put straight on conversion. Given the lengthy examination of the need for the healing of the spirit in their previous work this is a remarkable inconsistency, which makes their work extremely slippery as regards analysis. For all their obviously genuine concern to help people and their flexible and gentle approach to deliverance ministry within the overall category of inner healing, the Sandfords are prone to indulge in theological eccentricity. Numerous examples of this include their belief in an 'incubus' spirit, 'a type of demon that attacks its host by molesting her sexually'[504] and their experience with a cat working as a warlock's familiar.[505]

In conclusion, the Sandfords' attitude to deliverance ministry has changed between the early 1980s when they were loathe to place any emphasis upon it, to the early 1990s when they claimed that deliverance had been a regular part of their counselling procedure. They advocate a flexible approach to deliverance including it within the wider schema of their sanctification. Their understanding of sanctification as inner healing is somewhat more contentious but is perhaps the prime example of deliverance ministry being incorporated in a therapeutic pastoral method. Despite their generally good use of common sense and the not so occasional points at which their reflection is genuinely enlightening, the Sandfords cannot resist the attraction of enthusiastic spiritual immanentism and suspicion of reason. Furthermore, their writing is seasoned with idiosyncratic interpretations of their pastoral experience.

REBECCA BROWN [506]

In 1986 Rebecca Brown published a truly hair-raising account of the deliverance of an ex Satanist (referred to as Elaine) entitled *He Came to Set the Captives Free*.[507] The account of Elaine's career in Satanism and witchcraft is shocking and indeed might be described as pornographic; at times the account descends into the absurd such as her tales of encounters with wer-creatures and materialised demons[508] and the need for those involved in deliverance ministry

---

[503] Sandford, *Deliverance*, 51.

[504] Sandford, *Deliverance*, 154.

[505] Sandford, *Deliverance*, 236f.

[506] Rebecca Brown might have been reasonably included in section 4.3.1 below since she relates the tale of an escapee from Satanism which bears many resemblances to the stories of Doreen Irvine and Mike Warnke. However, she uses this story as a means of outlining her extreme approach to deliverance ministry and furthermore she is at least sympathetic to a Charismatic approach.

[507] R. Brown, *He Came to Set the Captives Free* (Chino: Chick, 1986).

[508] Brown, *Captives*, 65, 223-230.

to eat red meat.[509]

Brown believes in a world wide Satanic conspiracy called 'The Brotherhood' which has deeply penetrated society's power structures and also the Church.[510] The implications of this highly paranoid worldview is that the Christian may only trust God, even their fellow Christian is only to be trusted with extreme caution.[511] Brown presents deliverance ministry as a lurid and fearful encounter with powerful demonic forces in which the Christian can only hope to be successful when living in radical and sacrificial communion with God to the point that they may accurately discern God's voice giving them step by step instructions.[512] The possibility of making mistakes in the process of deliverance due to misunderstanding God's intentions is very real and the implications very serious.[513] References to Jessie Penn-Lewis and Watchman Nee are liberally sprinkled throughout[514]; whilst one can be sure that neither of these two writers would have any sympathy with Brown's approach it does indicate the vulnerability of highly self-analytical spiritualities towards radical misdirection.

The implications of any Christian taking Brown seriously are very grave. It could certainly cause them to become extremely anti-social and might lead them towards harmful even dangerous extremes of behaviour. Given the way in which Mike Warnke's testimony has been discredited,[515] *Captives* may be consigned to the category of harmless if unedifying fiction were it not for the worrying fact that many Christians are influenced by such material.

THE THIRD WAVE, STRATEGIC LEVEL SPIRITUAL WARFARE (SLSW) AND CHARISMATIC DELIVERANCE MINISTRY

In the early 1980s a new, broadly Charismatic group surfaced referring to themselves as the 'Third Wave' (TW). These usually come from evangelical backgrounds and perceive themselves to be sympathetic to, yet distinct from, the Charismatic Renewal. Wagner identifies 'casting out demons' as a basic characteristic of the TW.[516] Whilst this is technically correct, it is important to understand that deliverance ministry was only one component in the TW's stress upon warfare with evil spirits, this stress itself being a key part of an overriding missiological methodology.

---

[509] Brown, *Captives*, 184-186.

[510] Brown, *Captives*, 30-40, 62f. and 233.

[511] Brown, *Captives*, 233-245.

[512] Brown, *Captives*, 91-104, 200-219.

[513] Brown, *Captives*, 219.

[514] Brown, *Captives*, 110, 118, 135, 209-211, 217 and 219. On Penn-Lewis see below.

[515] See section 4.3.1 below.

[516] C. P. Wagner, 'Third Wave' in S. M. Burgess and E. M. Van Der Maas (eds.), *The New International Dictionary of Pentecostal and Charismatic Movements* (Grand Rapids: Zondervan, 2002) 1141.

John Wimber
John Wimber achieved an international profile within Charismatic circles during the 1980s; under his leadership the Vineyard Movement has grown into a significant association of churches, primarily in the US, although it also has a sizeable presence in the UK. Wimber developed a doctrine of the Kingdom of God, founded on the systematic theology of George Eldon Ladd,[517] which emphasised the 'power encounter'[518]; deliverance ministry was incorporated as a key component of this wider category. Wimber's ministry was characterised by these power encounters which often, but not always, took the form of encounters with demons at work in the lives of individuals.[519]

Wimber's approach to deliverance ministry (he preferred to use the more general term 'healing') is essentially a straightforward version of that of his Charismatic predecessors.[520] Simply, he asserted that demons are a reality and that many people (Christians and non-Christians alike) are under their influence (or 'demonised'). Wimber took the usual view that demons gain entry through capitulation to sin or being the victim of sin, down generational lines and via curses or traumas.[521] These demons, which bring about certain specific problems, may be cast out through a power encounter in which Christ evicts them. A godly lifestyle renders the Christian immune from subsequent attack:

---

[517] J. Wimber and K. Springer, *Power Evangelism* (London: Hodder and Stoughton, 1985) 9.

[518] Wimber, *Evangelism*, 28-43. Wimber constructed a naively dualist conception of two opposing Kingdoms – that of God and Satan. He collapsed the 'flesh' or as the NIV translates it 'the sinful nature' into the latter kingdom thus making sanctification primarily an issue of power encounter. J. Wimber, *Kingdom of God* (Placentia: Vineyard Ministries, 1985) 17. Martyn Percy observes that 'for Wimber, the Kingdom of God is a kingdom of power announced then practised – which overthrows the controlling power of Satan.' M. Percy, *Words, Wonders and Power* (London: SPCK, 1996) 18.

[519] Wimber's friend and erstwhile colleague, Peter Wagner, has applied the concept of the power encounter at a socio-corporate level and thus developed the concept of 'strategic level spiritual warfare'. See C. P. Wagner, 'Territorial Spirits' in C. P. Wagner and F. D. Pennoyer (eds.), *Wrestling with Dark Angels* (Speldhurst: Monarch, 1990) 83-125; C. P. Wagner, 'Spiritual Warfare' in C. P. Wagner (ed.), *Territorial Spirits* (Chichester, Sovereign, 1991) 3-27 and the relevant section immediately below. I have deliberately not emphasised SLSW in this study since it represents a significant departure from deliverance ministry even if it is founded on a pseudo-logical extension of the latter's application.

[520] It is worth noting that Wimber was familiar with the writings of early-century healing evangelists such as John G Lake, William Branham, the Bosworth brothers and Alexander Dowie. Whilst he doubted their theological credentials he accepted their basic integrity. J. Wimber, 'Power Evangelism' in C. P. Wagner and F. D. Pennoyer (eds.), *Wrestling with Dark Angels* (Tunbridge Wells: Monarch, 1990)

[521] J. Wimber and K. Springer, *Power Healing* (London: Hodder and Stoughton, 1986) 130-132.

What every Christian needs to know about spiritual warfare is that while Satan is strong... We have nothing to fear from Satan or demons, as long as we live faithfully and righteously, never backing down when challenged by evil.[522]

Wimber did not prescribe a methodology for dealing with the demonic. What he did commit to paper is fairly simple and ignores many of the abstruse ideas which are prevalent in the more colourful and fanciful Charismatics. He appears to have been less interested in the technique of achieving deliverance than in presenting such ministry as valid, essential even. This, allied to his theology of spiritual warfare, in which Christ is the inevitable victor, gives the impression that Wimber saw this type of power encounter as a quick, dramatic, crisis event in which Christ will certainly emerge victorious.[523] His trust in Christ rather than 'magical' techniques may be commendable; however, Wimber's approach is comparatively simplistic (possibly due to an understandable desire not to recount the self-glorifying and sensational stories found in much of the Charismatic literature) so his writings are of debatable value to someone wishing to find guidance as to how to proceed with deliverance ministry.

Whilst Wimber's approach to deliverance may not differ notably from that of other Charismatics, there is a key divergence in his judgement on the ministry's significance. Within his wider schema of power evangelism and power encounter, Wimber views deliverance as more than just pastorally desirable. Instead, he holds it (alongside other supernatural phenomena) to be essential inductive evidence of God's presence. Wimber's dualistic emphasis on power (which has been robustly critiqued by Martyn Percy[524]) includes an emphasis upon conflict; this conflict is focused on Satan who functions as a

---

[522] Wimber, *Healing*, 117, cf. 132-136.

[523] Wimber relates one encounter with a demon early in his ministry that took a long time to resolve. He comments: 'In the end I think that the demon left because I wore him out, certainly not because I was skilled at casting out evil spirits. (Since that time I have learned much about this type of encounter. If I had know then what I know now, I am convinced the episode would not have taken longer than an hour.)' Wimber, *Evangelism*, 28. In a footnote, Wimber, recognising that his example leaves unanswered the key question of what things he has learned during the course of his ministry that now makes him by implication 'skilled at casting out evil spirits', directs the reader to the bibliography for further reading regarding deliverance ministry. The bibliography itself contains very little on this subject and certainly nothing by the popular Charismatic writers. This bears out the conclusion that Wimber was not very interested in the technique of deliverance ministry.

[524] Percy, *Words*. To balance to Percy's very critical investigation see John White's more sympathetic (though lightweight) treatment: White, *When*.

scapegoat for failure[525] (necessary since Wimber's stress on God's power to effect positive outcomes would otherwise be vulnerable to contrary conditions) and 'places a great weight on the agents of power: demons or exorcists.'[526] Consequently, deliverance in Vineyard circles is practised in much the same way as one would find in other Charismatic settings, however far from being one Charismatic fad among many, for Wimber and his followers it is an essential element of church life that supports and is supported by the theology and *de facto* sociology of the Vineyard movement.[527]

Peter Wagner

Peter Wagner, until 1991 a close associate of John Wimber, is best known as the champion of what has become known as Strategic Level Spritual Warfare (SLSW). This may be defined as the amplification of Wimber's understanding of the 'power-encounter' in line with Wagner's missiological concerns and ambitions; SLSW seeks to effect power-encounters that will effect entire people groups by disempowering 'strategic level' territorial spirits that hold sway over social groups or the geographical locations with which they are identified.[528]

Whilst this study is not concerned with this broadening of what might properly be called 'Charismatic Deliverance', it should be noted that the latter is firmly and necessarily embedded within the schema of Wagner and other SLSW theorists and practitioners. Consequently, SLSW has done much to popularise deliverance as the basic building block of a broader approach to spiritual warfare and evangelism.[529]

---

[525] Wimber famously accused Satan of murdering David Watson when the latter failed to recover from cancer. Percy, *Words*, 55; cf. D. Watson, *Fear no Evil* (London: Hodder and Stoughton, 1984).

[526] Percy, *Words*, 93. It is therefore important for Wimber to present himself as a successful exorcist in an analogous manner to that of post-War healing revivalists.

[527] 'Wimber's anecdotes about healings and deliverance playa crucial part in affirming the body of believers.' Percy, *Words*, 108.

[528] SLSW is employed by various evangelists, most notably, Carlos Annacondia and Ed Silvoso. The most effective critique has been offered by Chuck Lowe, C. Lowe, *Territorial Spirits and World Evangelisation?* (Sevenoaks: OMF International, 1998). The popularity of SLSW has been greatly enhanced by the fiction of Frank Peretti: F. Peretti, *This Present Darkness* (Eastbourne: Monarch, 1986); *Piercing the Darkness* (Eastbourne: Monarch, 1989).

[529] The other prominent exponents of SLSW include Charles Kraft, Timothy Warner, Cindy Jacobs and Ed Murphy. For a brief description of the historical development of SLSW see C. Arnold, *3 Crucial Questions about Spiritual Warfare* (Grand Rapids: Baker, 1997) 143ff. Clinton Arnold may be described as a critical friend of SLSW, advocating a more moderate approach than that of Wagner *et al*. Despite popular misunderstanding to the contrary Walter Wink is not an exponent of SLSW; his own approach may appear similar but rests on very different epistemological foundations.

Clinton Arnold

The way in which SLSW has advanced the cause of deliverance ministry is best demonstrated by a brief examination of the contribution of Clinton Arnold. Arnold is without question the most thoughtful contributor to the field of SLSW and consequently, that part of his work which focuses of deliverance ministry is of great interest.

Arnold addresses head on the question of whether a Christian can be possessed. After some excellent (if brief) historical analysis of recent deliverance ministry,[530] he takes the well-worn approach of arguing that the term 'possessed' is unhelpful;[531] he favours an understanding that allows for demonic invasion, control even, without the connotations of ownership associated with 'possession'.[532] He outlines in some depth a nuanced approach to the vulnerability of the Christian to demonic incursion.[533]

Arguing from a scholarly understanding of the scriptures, Arnold argues that Jesus' exorcisms are paradigmatic for Christians since they were performed by the agency of the Holy Spirit which is available to the Christian today.[534] Thereafter he makes a convincing case that the early church practised exorcism in a manner not dissimilar from modern day deliverance.[535] Sparing a moment to contend with Powlison's aversion to the practise,[536] Arnold outlines his own straightforward 'self-help' approach to deliverance which advises the sufferer to be in close relationship with God before evicting the demon(s) by identifying what caused the vulnerability to demonic attack, stir up fortitude to contend with this attack, inform yourself of your status and authority in Christ, repent of whatever it is that caused vulnerability and ask God for fortitude where there is a sense that the demonic attack is being allowed by Him. At this point a strong and direct command to the demon may be necessary to effect deliverance. Finally, the sufferer should commit to a local church fellowship and glean prayer support.[537]

Arnold goes on to identify numerous excesses that have plagued the field of deliverance ministry.[538] If his recommendations for effective deliverance ministry are a blend of the most thoughtful and sensitive Charismatic practice, his analysis of what not to do is both perceptive and telling and is indicative of

---

See chapter 6, below. Cf W. Wink, *Engaging the Powers* (Minneapolis: Fortress, 1992) 3-10.

[530] Arnold, *Questions*, 75-78.

[531] Arnold, *Questions*, 78-80.

[532] Arnold, *Questions*, 80f.

[533] Arnold, *Questions*, 81-101.

[534] Arnold, *Questions*, 103-106.

[535] Arnold, *Questions*, 107-112.

[536] Arnold, Questions, 114f.

[537] Arnold, *Questions*, 115-129.

[538] Arnold, *Questions*, 129-138.

his knowledge of the field and his excellent judgement. Among many safeguards he warns against using deliverance to usurp the primary need for discipleship.[539] He also firmly rejects 'belief in an Internationally Networked Satanic Cult Conspiracy' as well as naïve acceptance of SRA and consequent MPD on the basis of 'recovered memories'.[540]

Clinton Arnold represents the positive conclusion of twentieth century Charismatic deliverance in so far as he has outlined a methodology which is typically and energetically Charismatic but avoids the commonplace extremes that often serve to discredit the practice. His critical engagement with the Charismatic Movement in general and the Third Wave in particular has resulted in a mature approach. Nevertheless, Arnold's schema emerged somewhat late in the day; enthusiastic obsession with deliverance had largely burnt itself out in any case.

The Contribution of the Third Wave Movement to Charismatic Deliverance
The Third Wave's concept of 'power evangelism', the 'power encounter' and SLSW breathed new life into Charismatic deliverance in the early 1980s. As a whole the movement served to galvanise the ebbing Charismatic Movement in the direction of mission, incorporating existing Charismatic spirituality into an evangelistic agenda. Hence deliverance took on new significance as a powerful and convincing demonstration of the inbreaking Kingdom.

One of the strengths of the Third Wave Movement is its willingness to engage with thoughtful, academic (usually evangelical) individuals. This has led to the production of some approaches to Charismatic Deliverance that avoid many of the pitfalls of more naively enthusiastic approaches.

Conclusion: Charismatic Deliverance in the Twentieth Century

Charismatic Deliverance and Enthusiasm

In the light of the evidence considered in this chapter, it can with some confidence be concluded that Charismatic deliverance ministry is an innately enthusiastic practice. A failure to appreciate the backdrop of enthusiasm when analysing Charismatic deliverance will inevitable lead to a failure to appreciate its development, significance and function. A clear example of this failure may be seen in a paper by Jacques Theron.[541] In seeking to rebut Andrew Walker's

---

[539] Arnold, *Questions*, 130f.

[540] Arnold, *Questions*, 133-136.

[541] Theron, 'Critical', 79-92. This is not an attempt to simply savage Theron; rather this critique is a necessary example of the importance of understanding that Christian enthusiasm is the necessary (but not sufficient) cause for Christian exorcism / deliverance.

observation that exorcism / deliverance functions within and feeds a cognitive 'paranoid universe',[542] Theron makes a series of points that fall to the ground when one is aware of the pervasive enthusiastic milieu that lies behind the practice of exorcism / deliverance:

- First, Theron highlights the diversity of the Charismatic Movement and argues that this diversity conveys immunity from a single charge such as that brought by Walker.[543] This argument is weak at first glance since Walker is addressing a specific mindset that common sense would affirm is a necessary prerequisite for emphasis upon exorcism / deliverance in any case. It is weaker still when the evidence is examined as is demonstrated above.[544] It is demolished once one becomes aware that exorcism / deliverance is always the fruit of a Christian enthusiasm which is essentially dualistic and therefore conducive to the development of such a 'paranoid universe'.[545]
- Second, Theron argues that exorcism / deliverance is motivated by experience rather than 'an unhealthy interest in the Evil One or by studying the demonic.'[546] Much might now be said in response to this however, the underlying point is that this is merely more evidence of the presence of Christian enthusiasm and certainly cannot be used as defence against Walker's criticism since experience is itself equivocal and his argument might equally be used by every Christian enthusiast for every form of extreme practice.
- Third, Theron observes that Charismatic practitioners of exorcism / deliverance tend to move away from a rationalistic Western world view towards a 'Postmodern worldview'.[547] If he were to understand that enthusiasm is the primary motivator of Charismatic deliverance then such an analysis would become unnecessary. Any talk of worldviews (and one suspects that Theron is largely referring to the Third Wave here) is illusory. The primary motivation for exorcism / deliverance is Christian enthusiasm; adoption of a less rationalistic worldview is in all likelihood merely more evidence for this fundamental contention.

This critique of Theron's failure to rightly understand Charismatic

---

[542] Walker, 'Devil', 88.

[543] Theron, 'Critical', 82.

[544] See chapter 3.

[545] Some of Theron's other comments regarding Charismatics developing their understanding of deliverance ministry in line with the tradition of their denomination are entirely irrelevant once one understands that enthusiasm rather than denominational allegiance is the motivating force behind exorcism / deliverance.

[546] Theron, 'Critical', 82.

[547] Theron, 'Critical', 83f.

deliverance due to his ignorance of a major causal factor (namely enthusiasm) could be expanded upon, however, the underlying point is already made. Failure to understand the significance of the enthusiastic environment out of which Charismatic deliverance springs, will lead to misunderstandings regarding the practice itself.

Deliverance and the Logic of Itineracy

The defining mark of Charismatic Renewal was the crisis experience of 'Baptism in the Holy Spirit.' Many claims were made regarding the personal, psychological and spiritual benefits of such an experience which (with the benefit of hindsight) now appear exaggerated leaving many Charismatics frustrated after their initial excitement faded. As a result Charismatics were ready to adopt Deliverance Ministry as a further step towards the promised land of personal *shalom*.[548] Charismatic spirituality was the brand of Christian enthusiasm most conducive to the practice of deliverance ministry and therefore it was widely exercised within the movement and frequently with an intensity bordering on hysteria. This in itself, along with evidences of its misuse either through ignorance or worse outright abuse, was enough to produce a powerful reaction against deliverance among the more sober minded within and without the ranks of the Charismatic Movement. Others sought to bring a more balanced perspective whilst still allowing for the practice of exorcism/deliverance. The progress of deliverance ministry continued, although somewhat arrested since the heady days of its peak popularity.

Some discussion regarding the tidal faddism of the Charismatic Movement has already taken place with reference to Stackhouse's *The Gospel Driven Church*.[549] It is now possible to throw some further light on the mechanics of this. Almost all of the fads Stackhouse identifies were actually marginal interests and activities inherited by the Charismatic Movement from their Pentecostal / salvation healing revivalist forebears. From its earliest stages the Charismatic Movement tended to throw up prominent itinerant leaders[550] often because their new found enthusiasm could not be accommodated within the cooler atmosphere of the local church but also because the leaders themselves saw the potential of the Movement to progress beyond Renewal to the evangelical Nirvana – Revival. The more capable among them rose to international prominence which in turn proved the inspiration for other similar though usually smaller scale ministries.

---

[548] In effect the idealism of the Charismatic Movement was a key component in its vulnerability to novelty. In establishing unrealistic expectations among its adherents it left them forever hankering after a final, decisive pneumatic experience.

[549] Stackhouse, *Gospel*.

[550] Wacker speaks of the 'special glamour' of itinerant Charismatic ministry. Wacker, *Heaven*, 147.

Specialist itinerant ministers have a vested interested in continuing to elevate the need for, and glorifying the effects of, their ministry; this was as true of the early Charismatic leaders who emphasised the Baptism of the Holy Spirit as it would be of later figures who emphasised what was initially a secondary aspect of the Renewal such as deliverance ministry. Of course this over emphasis is ultimately self-defeating since none of these aspects of enthusiastic spirituality, (however authentic within the wider Christian tradition) can possibly bear the weight of expectations generated and consequently a vacuum begins to emerge as increasing numbers grow disappointed or even disillusioned within the particular ministry in question.

The vested interest of the itinerants explains why the recurrent fads appear with so much fanfare and hype and also why each fad often attracts the ire of the previous generation of Charismatic leaders who placed their theological and ministerial eggs in a different basket. Each new fad appears to have a slightly shorter lifecycle as the progress of their over hyped emergence, obsessive practice and the slower and quieter course of their fading into the background grows more hackneyed and the Charismatic constituency grows more cynical.[551] Hence it is quite arguable that enthusiastic faddism is driven to a great extent by the practical implications of itinerancy.

The Tides of Enthusiasm

Tidal faddism was a primary, perhaps the primary, characteristic of Charismatic Christian faith in the twentieth century. Whilst such fads have, historically been slower moving, modern communications and the increased pace of life have enabled a much faster ebb and flow of fervent enthusiasm particularly in the latter four decades of the last century.

Charismatic Deliverance Ministry, an enduring secondary characteristic of Charismatic Christianity, briefly flared into prominence during the 1970s before gently receding into the background; nevertheless, Charismatic deliverance ministry still has its campaigners. Towards the end of the century it was incorporated into a subsequent fad for a much larger category, namely, Strategic Level Spiritual Warfare, or it was mutated or became routinised

---

[551] It is arguable that the so-called 'Toronto Blessing' represents the zenith and nadir of faddism. The zenith in that it is undoubtedly the most hyped of the fads; the nadir in that its failure to deliver the hoped for revival has perhaps left the majority of Charismatics so disenchanted that they are not liable to be drawn towards the next fad. This is borne out by the failure of the next fad involving the spontaneous appearance of gold fillings, to get very far off the ground. It should be noted that neither the Toronto blessing nor the supposedly miraculous appearance of gold teeth are truly new phenomena. The 'manifestations' associated with the former have a long history within the Pentecostal / Charismatic Movement and the latter was certainly claimed to have taken place amongst the farrago of supernatural phenomena supposedly centred around the eccentric ministry of A. A. Allen.

within more traditional categories of Christian spirituality. These latter developments are examined in chapter 6 below.

CHAPTER 4

Evangelical Fundamentalist Deliverance Ministry

During the last century, a form of deliverance ministry (parallel to that practised by Charismatics) emerged among groups that might be fairly termed Evangelical Fundamentalists (EF).[1] Evangelical Fundamentalists often frown on the emotionalism and sensationalism of their Charismatic counterparts and assume an air of intellectual superiority; nevertheless, they share many of the same characteristics, most importantly, biblicism, ethical rigorism and, frequently, enthusiasm.

EF is certainly a different, though related, brand of Christian enthusiasm to that found among Charismatics. EF is defined by a paradigmatic pessimistic premillenialism which creates an assumption of opposition to everything that lies without.[2] Their opposition to Charismatic enthusiasm and particularly its emotionally demonstrative nature is originally due to the split between themselves and the early Pentecostals as will be examined below; by mid century, this opposition sits comfortably within a wider pessimism and negativity to culture both secular and Christian. Hence, whereas Charismatic enthusiasm is primarily marked by non-rational, experiential faith which tends

---

[1] 'Fundamentalism' is, of course, a contentious and ambiguous term. It is used here to highlight the 'oppositional' nature of the Evangelicals among whom Evangelical deliverance emerged in self-conscious distinction from Charismatic deliverance. (Partridge asserts that 'oppositionalism' is the 'fundamental theological feature of modern [religious] fundamentalisms.' C. H. Partridge, 'Pagan Fundamentalism?' in C. H. Partridge (ed.), *Fundamentalisms* (Carlisle: Paternoster, 2001) 156). For a general discussion regarding the term 'fundamentalist' see H. A. Harris, 'How Helpful Is The Term Fundamentalist?' in *Fundamentalisms* (Carlisle: Paternoster, 2001) 3-18.

[2] Koch's *Day X* can be fairly described as a thoroughgoing demonisation of secular culture and those aspects of Christian culture of which he disapproves. Of course this pessimistic approach provides the platform for the premillenialist's hope of the second coming. K. Koch, *Day X* (Grand Rapids: Kregel, 1971) 103f. The classic publication of this genre is Hal Lindsey's *The Late Great Planet Earth* which sold millions of copies throughout the world. H. Lindsey, *The Late Great Planet Earth* (London: Lakeland, 1971). Both of these books, despite or perhaps because of their stridency (which is typical of the genre) appear faintly ridiculous with hindsight. For a brief introduction to EF premillenialism see O. Lindermayer, 'Europe as Antichrist: North American Pre-Millenarianism' in S. Hunt (ed.), *Christian Millenarianism* (London: Hurst, 2001) 39-49.

towards triumphalism, EF enthusiasm is primarily marked by sectarian eschatology tending towards pessimism. For all their desire to be seen as more rational and less emotional than their Charismatic *bêtes-noir*, EF interest in exorcism is built upon the same enthusiastic experiential foundations as that of Charismatics

The emergence of EF deliverance might appear to indicate that EFs were convinced by their Charismatic contemporaries and adopted the latter's methods. This certainly took place to a degree,[3] but it is not the whole story.

Sectarianism may be defined as a corporate tendency to argue and form separate factions defined by the positions taken in the argument which caused the split. Knox demonstrates sectarianism is a primary characteristic of enthusiastim.[4] The initial emergence of EF deliverance ministry begins with the story of a typical and dramatic enthusiastic schism that generated the first major exponent of deliverance ministry of the century. In this case the sectarianism becomes the motivating factor in a theology of deliverance.

The Emergence of EF Deliverance Ministry

Evan Roberts, Jessie Penn-Lewis, the Welsh Revival[5] and Emerging Pentecostalism

Evan Roberts is widely recognised to have been the central figure in the Welsh

---

[3] Cross-pollenation was commonplace. Reflecting on my own childhood growing up in Pentecostal churches in the UK in the 70s and 80s, it is clear that Pentecostals of the time had been deeply infected with EF culture and in many ways conformed more closely to the latter than to their Charismatic enthusiastic roots.

[4] Knox, *Enthusiasm*, 1, 12f. Cf. Middlemiss, *Interpreting*, 11-13. See Wacker, *Heaven*, 177-196 for a fascinating account of enthusiastic conflict in early Pentecostalism.

[5] Surprisingly there is little in the way of academic analysis of the Revival so one is largely forced to piece together one's reconstruction from the devotional literature. J. Edwin Orr carried out the best research; he made a career out of studying such phenomena. Sadly his material is now out of print. Ian Randall has published a useful summary of the revival in a short paper though primarily for devotional purposes, I. Randall, 'When the Spirit Comes in Power' in *Out of Control* (Milton Keynes: Authentica, 2004). Eifion Evans' book *The Welsh Revival of 1904* remains the most comprehensive of the devotional volumes. E. Evans, *The Welsh Revival of 1904* (London: Evangelical Press, 1969). Smith has recently offered a more concise account. M. Smith, *When the Fire Fell* (Nevada: Preparedness Publications, 1996). Celebrating the centenary of the revival Kevin Adams has published a brief history which includes a good deal of useful primary materials, K. Adams, *A Diary of Revival* (Farnham: CWR, 2004); alongside this is a record of the revival in pictures, K. Adams and E. Jones, *A Pictorial History of Revival* (Farnham: CWR, 2004). Other works including 'spiritual' biographies are too numerous to mention however some will be quoted in the following study. It is amazing that a rigorous academic survey has not been undertaken.

Revival.[6] Prior to the Revival Roberts had a lively spiritual life (which became increasingly intense) and an active interest in revival.[7] After a crisis experience at a conference in Blaennanerch in September 1904,[8] he began to plan a preaching tour of Wales.[9] He came to believe that 100,000 souls would be won for Christ via a coming revival.[10] By late October, Roberts felt led to postpone his studies in order to return to his home town of Loughor and preach to the young people.[11]

In the space of a week it became obvious that something dramatic was happening.[12] Roberts himself was in no doubt that these were the first fruits of a grand revival. Crowds thronged to the little parish church in Loughor to hear Roberts speak and pray, to sing enthusiastically and, in many instances, to make public profession of Christian faith. The meetings lasted for hours on end.[13]

This was the first chapter in Roberts' brief, dazzling career as a revivalist. Roberts began an itinerant ministry in Glamorgan that met with great success.[14] During the first two months (November and December 1904) the Welsh Revival was estimated to have claimed approximately 32,000 converts.[15] Roberts was not the only renowned revivalist reaping a rich harvest in Wales during this time, but he was certainly the most high profile, at least in the early stages.[16]

Inevitably Roberts' ministry began to be scrutinised, particularly by those who felt antagonistic towards his increasingly enthusiastic approach. Roberts appears to have been deeply upset by this criticism and this combined with the inevitable affects of his unadvisedly hectic schedule led to a gradual breakdown in his health and increasingly unpredictable behaviour (which in turn fostered

---

[6] Randall, 'Spirit', 81.

[7] 'Roberts had always had a great passion for revival... after an extraordinary mystical experience [he] was in the habit of waking nightly at 1am for communion with God.' Smith, *Fire*, 41.

[8] 'Roberts was deeply affected by a prayer by Seth Joshua, in which he included the words, "Lord, bend us." Roberts was led to pray, in deep anguish of Spirit, 'Bend me.' Randall, 'Spirit', 81, Adams gives a helpful diary of Roberts' movements around the time of the Blaenannerch Conference. Adams, *Diary*, 50.

[9] D. M. Phillips, *Evan Roberts, The Great Welsh Revivalist and His Work* (London: Marshall Brothers, 1906) 121f.

[10] Phillips, *Roberts*, 137. Cf Smith, *Fire*, 45; Randall, 'Spirit', 82; Adams, *Diary*, 72.

[11] Evans, *Welsh*, 74.

[12] Adams, *Diary*, 87f.

[13] Smith, *Fire*, 49-57.

[14] Smith, *Fire*, 69f.

[15] Evans, *Welsh*, 129.

[16] Adams, *Diary*, 122f.

more criticism).[17]

Jessie Penn-Lewis was already a well-known figure in 1905. Her colourful international ministry was initially energised by a deep spiritual experience as a result of which she 'came to a fuller understanding of Romans 6:6-11'.[18] She was an ardent advocate of early 'higher life' (Keswick) teaching on sanctification, namely that both the believer's justification and sanctification were achieved in the atonement, the former being appropriated through conversion, the latter through submission to, and experience of, the Holy Spirit. She was the driving force behind the establishment of the 'Welsh Keswick' in 1903.[19]

Mrs Penn-Lewis was in touch with many of the evangelists and ministers associated with the Revival.[20] Her contact with figures such as Seth Joshua and Emlyn Davies was often motivated by pastoral concern although she needed to keep abreast of events as she was writing a regular column on the Revival.[21] As early as January 1905 she attempted to meet with Evan Roberts however he declined the invitation.[22]

Penn-Lewis finally succeeded in meeting Roberts in the summer of the same year and it appears that she made an impression on him. Jones notes that 'Evan began to speak rather like Jessie about entering into the sufferings of the cross.'[23] Roberts' friendship with the Penn-Lewises developed fast and when he finally broke down in Spring 1906 he retreated to Great Glen, their family home.[24]

Regarding this period of convalescence Evans notes 'Evan Roberts had retired [in 1906] 'for a time of rest and recuperation' to the home of Mr and

---

[17] Randall, 'Spirit', 83. Quite apart, although possibly resulting from, his mounting exhaustion, the question of Roberts' mental stability began to be raised more persistently as time went by.

[18] Evans, *Welsh*, 29f. Cf B. P. Jones, *The Trials and Triumphs of Mrs Jessie Penn-Lewis* (North Brunswick: Bridge-Logos, 1997) 24-26, It appears that her emphasis upon (her understanding of) the atonement became rather all-consuming and led to the breakdown of her involvement with both the Keswick Convention and its Welsh equivalent. Evans, *Welsh*, 30f., 51f., 168. Cf. Jones, *Trials*, 66f., 147, 195, 197, 201f.

[19] Evans, *Welsh*, 31, Randall, 'Spirit',79. Adams highlights the impetus the Welsh Keswick gave to the revival, Adams, *Diary*, 56, 63.

[20] Jones, *Trials*, 119-130.

[21] Jones, *Trials*, 119.

[22] Jones indicates that at this stage Penn-Lewis was attempting to meet Roberts, along with her fellow Keswick leaders, to discuss 'how he could be linked up with their movement in order to safeguard the revival.' Jones suggests that Roberts' decision to decline the invitation may be because he learned of their plan. Jones, *Trials*, 157.

[23] Jones, *Trials*, 158. He publicly adopted her teachings in Easter 1906. Jones, *Trials*, 160.

[24] Jones, *Trials*, 160.

Mrs Penn-Lewis near Leicester.''[25] He goes on to quote Garrard's biography of Penn-Lewis:

> His recovery, however, was slow and intermittent, lasting many months, and during the long period of convalescence, he began to open his mind to his hostess on many experiences of supernatural forces witnessed during the Revival. Since her own mighty enduement of power for service, Mrs Penn-Lewis had learned the path of the Cross, and seen the dangers attendant upon souls who, having experienced such a breaking-through into the supernatural realm, do not know identification with Christ in his death as the place of safety from the wiles and assaults of the devil... This God-given knowledge and experience, together with the insight into the devices of the enemy gained by Mr Roberts in his experiences during the Revival, are conserved to the Church of God in *War on the Saints*.[26]

Roberts went on to become a virtual recluse, devoting himself to a life of private prayer. Sadly he seems never to have fully recovered from his breakdown and his public ministry was never again front-page news despite several abortive attempts to relaunch it.

Roberts' convictions regarding spiritual conflict apparently crystallised during his self-imposed exile in collaboration with Jessie Penn-Lewis. It is tempting to portray Roberts as a vulnerable and complicated character that came under the domineering and controlling influence of Penn-Lewis. Whilst there is certainly some truth in this, the reality is somewhat less simplistic.

War on the Saints (1912)

War on the Saints was published in 1912, the result of 'six years of prayerful testing of the truth here given, and three years of toil in the placing of these truths in writing, in the face of unceasing attacks from the unseen realm.'[27] It carried a somewhat enigmatic foreword from Roberts, 'As a key to a lock so is the truth in this book to NEED...'[28]

War on the Saints is an extremely peculiar book. Its immediate backdrop is

---

[25] Evans, *Welsh*, 178f. It appeared to some that Penn-Lewis exerted an unhealthy, degree of influence over Evan Roberts, particularly in the light of the fact that the latter's health was fragile following a nervous breakdown. Evans, *Welsh*, 172f.

[26] M. N. Garrard, *Mrs Penn-Lewis, a Memoir*, quoted by Evans, *Welsh*, 179.

[27] J. Penn-Lewis and E. Roberts, *War on the Saints* (Leicester: Excelsior, 1912) Foreword. Were there no further evidence available, this language would be enough to alert us to the presence of enthusiasm.

[28] Penn-Lewis, *War*, Foreword.

the authors' conviction that the Baptism in the Holy Spirit,[29] whilst beneficial to the Christian life, opens the unwary recipient to intimate contact with the spiritual realm and therefore to the malevolent activity of evil spirits.[30] Consequently they believed that many of the participants in the Welsh Revival and hence the burgeoning Pentecostal Movement were suffering from the effects of demonic activity. The wider context is the authors' imminent, dispensational premillenialism.[31] Both these streams of thought are found within this key passage:

> The power of God which broke forth in Wales, with all the marks of the days of Pentecost, has been checked and kept back from going on to its fullest purpose, by the same influx of evil spirits as met the Lord Christ on earth, and the Apostles of the early Church; with the difference that the inroad of the powers of darkness found the Christians of the twentieth century, with few exceptions, unable to recognize, and deal with them. Evil spirit possession has followed, and checked every similar revival throughout the centuries since Pentecost, and evil spirit possession must now be understood, and dealt with, if the Church is to advance to maturity; and understood, not only in the degree of possession recorded in the gospels, but in the special forms of manifestations suited to the close of the dispensation, *under the guise of the counterfeit of the Holy Spirit*, yet having some of the characteristic marks in bodily symptoms, as in the gospel records, when all who saw the manifestation knew it was the work

---

[29] Which was a characteristic doctrine of the Welsh Revival.

[30] Actually, the argument runs along the lines that the evil spirit(s), already present, 'break forth into activity, and hide their 'manifestations' under cover of the true workings of the Spirit of God, dwelling within the inner shrine of the spirit.' Penn-Lewis, *War*, 55. This doctrine highlights the reservations the authors held in hindsight regarding the Welsh Revival with its over-riding emphasis on the baptism of the Holy Spirit. Cf R. F. Lovelace, *Dynamics of Spiritual Life* (Exeter: Paternoster, 1979) 135. Lovelace believes that it was the spread of 'spiritualism and the occult during the 1904-05 revival' which led to the publication of *War on the Saints*. This analysis misses the point. It is not that the writers believed that spiritualism and the occult had permeated the revival so much as the revival and the ongoing Pentecostal Movement with their eager and *naïve* spirituality opened the door to demonic forces. In that sense, from Penn-Lewis' perspective, the revival resembled spiritualism and the occult. For more background, a detailed Penn-Lewis bibliography and comprehensive records of responses to *War on the Saints* see *De Oorlog Tegen de Heiligen* (Amsterdam: CHEV, 2005) 483-722.

[31] It is apparent from several passages in *War on the Saints* that Penn-Lewis (and Roberts) felt that the Church's triumph over demonic forces via the spiritual warfare they were advocating was the precursor to Christ's return and subsequent Millennial rule. Penn-Lewis, *War*, 2, 10 and (particularly) 30.

of the spirits of Satan.[32]

Having made the case that the awakening of the Western Church has 'unveiled the reality of Satanic powers in active opposition to God and his people', *War on the Saints* calls upon believers to join the struggle against the powers of wickedness.[33]

The relationship between demonology, consequent approaches to exorcism and eschatology is a recurring theme throughout the literature published by exponents of deliverance. Whilst enthusiastic exponents of deliverance do not all hold to premillenial eschatology (like Penn-Lewis) it is true to say that some kind of imminent eschatology almost always forms part of their worldview.[34] Deliverance is therefore usually integrated into a wider concept of a dualistic struggle between God and Satan; it is imbued with great significance where it is interpreted as a significant part of the final stages of that struggle.

Penn-Lewis taught that Satan's strategies differ according to the context. The strategy of the evil spirits at the time of the Welsh Revival was to counterfeit the work of the Holy Spirit in order to discredit the Revival and hence undermine its progress.[35] She identifies what she terms 'passivity' as a great danger for the believer; it gives Satan great freedom to deceive and oppress:

> The primary cause of deception and possession in surrendered believers may be condensed into one word, passivity; that is, a cessation of the active exercise of the will in control over spirit, soul and body, or either as may be the cause.[36]

It is particularly revealing that she was so concerned to warn of the dangers of passivity. Holiness teaching was a major facet of the Welsh Revival and its main emphasis was that sanctification, like justification, is to be received by faith; the believer is encouraged to *passively* receive the gift of sanctification through faith, often through a spiritual crisis. In the light of this, *War on the Saints* is in clear opposition to the mainstream Holiness teaching of the day.[37]

---

[32] Penn-Lewis, *War*, 45.

[33] Penn-Lewis, *War*, 31.

[34] Knox observes that imminent eschatology is a consistent feature of enthusiasm so it is no great surprise to encounter it as a common concomitant of deliverance / exorcism. Knox, *Enthusiasm*, 4.

[35] Penn-Lewis, *War*, 45. Decades later Koch identifies this counterfeiting among 'extremists' as one of Satan's main tactics to discredit revivals. He uses the Welsh Revival as a case in point although his understanding of its history is defective. K. Koch, *World without Chance?* (Grand Rapids: Kregel, 1974) 94.

[36] Penn-Lewis, *War*, 69.

[37] Penn-Lewis's controversial views on the atonement were already in tension with mainstream Holiness at this point.

Penn-Lewis systematically outlines a model of justification that requires the believer's radical and active co-operation with the Holy Spirit.[38] This entails the engagement of the whole personality to avoid sin and deception; the latter will otherwise lead to Satanic oppression.[39]

Other aspects of the Christian teaching and praxis of her contemporaries also fell under Penn-Lewis's critical gaze. Worship should not be addressed to the Holy Spirit directly[40]; spiritual manifestations are often questioned and may at worst be demonic[41]; 'tarrying' for the Holy Spirit 'has opened the door so frequently to Satanic manifestations from the unseen world'[42]; glossolalia may actually be the 'counterfeit "gift of tongues"'.[43] All these activities (and many others – indeed just about anything which Penn-Lewis dislikes or disagrees with) are either the product of, or leave believers open to, demonic deception. Believers who are deceived in such a way are ineffective and may even lose their salvation.[44]

The road to deliverance from demonic oppression is a long one. Penn-Lewis terms this process 'fighting through.'[45] The oppression is always due to some form of capitulation to evil spirits: '[they] can never interfere with the faculties of brain or body, unless sufficient ground for possession has been obtained by them.'[46] Freedom cannot be achieved unless the believer acknowledges this 'ground' and changes both thinking and behaviour:

> The Scriptural ground for obtaining deliverance is the truth concerning Christ's full victory at Calvary, through which every believer can be delivered from the power of both sin and Satan, but in actual fact the victory won at Calvary can only be applied as there is conformity to divine laws.[47]

Futhermore:

> Assuming, then, that the believer has discovered that he is the victim of the deceptions of deceiving spirits, what are the subjective steps in the path to freedom? Briefly, (1) acknowledgement of deception; (2) refusal

---

[38] Penn-Lewis, *War*, 70f.

[39] Penn-Lewis, *War*, 57, 66f, 71, 94.

[40] Penn-Lewis, *War*, 52.

[41] Penn-Lewis, *War*, 60f., 110.

[42] Penn-Lewis, *War*, 63f.

[43] Penn-Lewis, *War*, 165f. In October 1907, in a letter to Alexander Boddy, she wrote that she was 'pained and grieved' that glossolalia was 'being attributed to the Holy Ghost.' W. K. Kay, *Pentecostals in Britain* (Carlisle: Paternoster, 2000) 13.

[44] Penn-Lewis, *War*, 16.

[45] Penn-Lewis, *War*, 191.

[46] Penn-Lewis, *War*, 154.

[47] Penn-Lewis, *War*, 182.

of ground; (3) stedfast fight against all that possession means; (4) being on guard against all excuses; (5) the detection of all the effects of possession; and (6) a discerning of the result of these actions. For the believer must learn to read the signs of dis-possession, as well as the symptoms of possession, lest he be deceived again by the Adversary.[48]

Cutting through the ambiguous language, it seems clear that Penn-Lewis envisages 'fighting through' as a lengthy business entailing a great deal of effort from the believer. Moreover, there is a distinct possibility that deliverance may prove to be only temporary if the believer slips back into the behaviour or beliefs that were the original 'ground' for possession. This appears to be a rather pessimistic view of the Christian position. If the Christian is so vulnerable to Satanic oppression and there is no strategy that can offer any lasting security then turns Christian spirituality into a lifelong daily fight against evil spirits. Nigel Wright correctly questions this approach:

If the danger of deception is so great, it is only the mature and discerning (and perhaps not even they?) who are in a position to withstand. We are left with a rather hopeless picture of the church... After all, if to be baptised in the Holy Spirit renders a person vulnerable to invisible and supernatural invasion by the enemy, what hope is there for any of us? Where is the sense of security in openness to the Father? Where is the comfort given by Jesus to the effect the 'nothing will harm you'?[49]

It seems clear that Penn-Lewis, and presumably Evan Roberts too, had come to the conclusion that the Welsh Revival had become very seriously compromised by demonic infiltration. On one level their book amounts to an attempt to expose those aspects of the Revival of which the authors disapproved. On another it is a classic and literal example of demonising the opposition. A telling criticism of *War on the Saints* is that it perceives the deceptive activity of Satan to be immediate rather than ultimate.[50] Hence anyone who holds, or worse still teaches, a doctrine that Penn-Lewis judges to be errant, is not merely deceived (and therefore in need of correction), but may well be demonised (and therefore in need of deliverance).[51] Walker asserts that preoccupation with the

---

[48] Penn-Lewis, *War*, 183.

[49] Wright, *Theology*, 105f.

[50] The insight that Satan's main strategy for attacking believers lies in deception, particularly during times of spiritual fervour is nevertheless most helpful. It is a point that sits comfortable with Neil Anderson's understanding of a 'truth encounter'. On this see Chapter 6.

[51] As a result of this approach Penn-Lewis ends up implying that vast swathes of those involved in the Welsh Revival were demonised.

demonic of this kind produces what he calls a 'paranoid universe'.[52]

War on the Saints is, as previously mentioned, a peculiar book. It has many positive insights into the mistakes made during a time of Revival. Nevertheless, the solution it presents appears to leave the believer in a position of permanent vulnerability. It seems that the Welsh Revival was the source of a great deal of teaching and praxis that Penn-Lewis and Roberts thought to be not only dubious but demonically inspired. Much of the teaching that they were so opposed to had crystallised into the Pentecostal Movement. More light may be shed upon this by a brief examination of the parallel situation in Germany (see below).

THE INFLUENCE OF PENN-LEWIS AND WAR ON THE SAINTS

Jessie Penn-Lewis was a formidable woman; her influence should certainly not be underestimated. She was certainly an influential figure on many leading twentieth century, enthusiastic Non-Charismatics such as Watchman Nee. She was among the foremost in her opposition to the Azusa Street Revival, emergent Pentecostalism and particularly glossolalia though she generally remained on good terms with her antagonists.

The influence of *War on the Saints* is more difficult to assess. The fact that it stirred up opposition among the Pentecostal churches is understandable in the light of its contents and was, at least partially due to its demonisation of ecstatic manifestations rather than its views on deliverance. Penn-Lewis' views on spiritual warfare certainly met with some acceptance among missionaries ministering in animist cultures largely via her popular journal *The Overcomer* and for some years she remained an influential figure within enthusiastic (non-Charismatic) Evangelicalism in the West. She was certainly partially responsible for the widespread demonisation of Charismatics by non-Charismatic Evangelicals, though she was by no means the only person to draw and propagate this conclusion.

EF deliverance ministry did not emerge until mid century, pioneered by Kurt Koch and Merrill Unger (largely it seems as a result of the influence of overseas missionaries) and came of age in the seventies parallel to the Charismatic form of the same ministry. Despite the obvious similarities, between the understanding expressed *War on the Saints* and late century deliverance ministries, it is unlikely that Penn-Lewis was a primary influence on either type (since they emerged parallel to each other it is more likely the result of external influences upon very similar but nevertheless discrete expressions of enthusiastic Christianity). Nevertheless, almost all of the EF, and many Charismatic practitioners[53] of deliverance refer to *War on the Saints*, in their writings and among the former group she is often praised fulsomely. Actually, her influence among EF deliverance ministers is more apparent in

---

[52] Walker, 'Devil', 88.

[53] The irony of Charismatic practitioners of deliverance quoting Penn-Lewis is delicious.

their antagonism to, indeed demonisation of Charismatic forms of enthusiasm than it is in their deliverance ministry.

The Emergence of Continental Pentecostalism and Consequent Response

In the early years of the twentieth century revivalistic fervour was spreading throughout Europe. Hollenweger identifies the initial incursion of Pentecostalism into Europe with T B Barratt, a Methodist minister from Norway who became an ardent Pentecostal after a visit to the Azusa Street mission in November 1906.[54] Upon his arrival back in Oslo, he led his own church into Pentecostalism which in turn provided a springboard for the movement to penetrate Western Europe as a whole.[55]

The new Pentecostal movement spread through Western Europe like wildfire. It split the Holiness constituency in half; some embraced Pentecostalism, many others like Penn-Lewis, repulsed by the dramatic manifestations, vehemently rejected it, often attributing its success to the work of evil spirits.[56] In Germany, Pentecostalism proved particularly divisive.[57] In 1907 various German church leaders met together in Barmen to debate the new movement. It became clear that opinion was divided. In papers written prior to the conference itself, Pastor Paul, an active promoter of Pentecostalism, encouraged others to seek the gift of tongues, while Dollmeyer renounced his previously positive view of the Azusa Street revival believing that he had been deceived.[58] Dollmeyer 'alleged that in order to delay the final victory, Satan had sent demonic spirits to infiltrate God's host. It was an angel of Satan who was presently offering false gifts... Satan had got in among the saints.'[59] The overall sympathy of the leaders appears to have been with Dollmeyer but attempts were made to hold the two groups together. The conference concluded with an agreement to spend six months in 'silent consideration'.[60]

This attempt to avoid a major fracture within German Evangelicalism did not succeed. The following year (1908) the leaders of German Pentecostalism

---

[54] Hollenweger, *Pentecostals*, 63. Cf. G. B. McGee, 'To the Regions Beyond: The Global Expansion of Pentecostalism' in V. Synan (ed.), *The Century of the Holy Spirit* (Nashville: Thomas Nelson, 2001) 71. There were probably many Pentecostal ambassadors pouring into Western Europe of whom Barratt came to be the most high profile.

[55] McGee, 'Regions', 75f.

[56] Bebbington notes that Pentecostalism, despite 'having similar origins, occupying much common ground... [was nevertheless] totally repudiated by the larger body.' D. Bebbington, *Evangelicalism in Modern Britain* (London: Routledge, 1989) 198.

[57] Hollenweger, *Pentecostals*, 221-228.

[58] Jones, *Trials*, 171-174.

[59] Jones, *Trials*, 174.

[60] Jones, *Trials*, 175.

held their own conference in Hamburg to promote the new movement.[61] The movement continued to grow as did fervent opposition. On September 15, 1909 the Gnadau Union (the dominant union of evangelical Christians) issued the Berlin Declaration. The most significant section read as follows:

> The so-called Pentecostal Movement is not from above but from below; it has many phenomena in common with spiritualism. Demons are active in it. Led by Satan with artfulness, they mix lies and truth in order to seduce God's children. There are many cases where it is evident that the so-called 'people gifted by the Spirit' are possessed.[62]

Unsurprisingly, this statement caused a drastic split between those German Evangelicals who supported the new Pentecostal movement, and those who opposed it. The repercussions of this split were far reaching both geographically and chronologically.[63]

What is of interest to this current study is the fact that Pentecostalism was not merely opposed, but demonised, in what appears to be something of a parallel to the approach adopted by Penn-Lewis. The fact that German Evangelicalism was largely removed from the sphere of academic theology and hence was characterised by theological ignorance and naiveté, partially accounts for the extremity of the Declaration. Finis comments 'Extreme demonological concepts bordering on pure superstition distorted the debate massively... Were it not for the lack of theological understanding, much damage could have been prevented.'[64]

Evaluation of Reaction to Emergent Pentecostalism

Emergent Pentecostalism (or proto-Pentecostalism as we might term the Welsh Revival) was usually accompanied by a variety of phenomena most notably glossolalia, but also typically including prophecy, healing and physical manifestations such as shrieking, falling down, crying, laughing and so on. Early opponents of Pentecostalism often attributed these to the work of deceiving spirits,[65] whilst advocates of the movement usually viewed them as

---

[61] Jones, *Trials*, 176.

[62] *The Berlin Declaration*, 1909, translated by T. Finis, in T. Finis, 'A Quest for Holiness' (Unpublished MTh thesis, London, 1998) Appendix 1.

[63] Finis, *Quest*, 1. Cf. Hollenweger, *Pentecostals*, 228.

[64] Finis, *Quest*, 124. Hollenweger recounts the publication by two German evangelical leaders of the case of a young girl who had apparently become possessed by an evil spirit during Pentecostal services. Later, this case was seen to be spurious. Hollenweger, *Pentecostals*, 225-228.

[65] Whilst *The Berlin Declaration* (in Finis, *Quest*, Appendix 2) is a classic example, it is by no means the only one; see for example the virulent opposition to Seymour expressed by Alma White, Sanders, *Seymour*, 75. Evangelical Fundamentalists (in particular) have

powerful signs of God's activity.

This raises an important issue; what criteria (if any) may be used to make judgements regarding the evidential value of the phenomena attendant to spiritual movements like Pentecostalism? Moreover, is it possible to judge the origin of such phenomena? Furthermore, do 'black and white' responses like *The Berlin Declaration* have any value?

Several points may be made in response to these questions. It is clear that 'charismatic' experiences (indeed any experiences) are equivocal[66] and are usually understood in line with the interpreter's presuppositions. Take, for example, the case of John Wesley and George Whitfield:

> Both had experience of people falling over in a dramatic way, but Wesley used this as justification of his Arminian theology, whilst Whitfield interpreted the events as a sign that he was correct in his Calvinism.[67]

As Middlemiss goes on to point out, there is a sizeable leap in the thinking of both Wesley and Whitfield here. The phenomenon is understood to be the gracious act of God and therefore a sign of His comprehensive endorsement of the preacher's theology. This step of logic would only be appropriate if one were to assume that God only acts where conditions are entirely to His liking; it is quite clear that neither Wesley nor Whitfield held such a view and it is therefore unsurprising that both of them changed their thinking later on.[68]

A mature view allows that spiritual experiences inhabit a murky world, and their interpretation is a tricky business. Middlemiss contends that the latter is only possible where different applied criteria produce judgements that converge (and hence build a 'cumulative case') in favour of a particular interpretation.[69] In any case, simplistic interpretations are usually suspect once they are confronted with a possible alternative interpretation of the same experience.[70]

How about the interpretation placed upon Pentecostal phenomena by the signatories to *The Berlin Declaration*? Firstly, we have an assertion that these originate 'from below'. This (probably deliberately) opaque statement is best understood in the light of a later statement: 'We do not want to assign or analyse how much of it is demonic, hysterical or psychological – such manifestations are certainly not from God.'[71] What is of interest to this study is

---

frequently viewed Pentecostal phenomena, particularly glossolalia as demonic. White, *When*, 40f. Cf. Wright, 'Revival', 134.

[66] Middlemiss, *Interpreting*, 49-52.

[67] Middlemiss, *Interpreting*, 177. Cf White, *When*, 126-128. See Wacker, *Heaven*, 78 for an account of a comparable, if somewhat more extreme, enthusiastic conflict between early Pentecostals, Charles Parham and William Durham.

[68] Middlemiss, *Interpreting*, 178.

[69] Middlemiss, *Interpreting*, 119-126, 155.

[70] Middlemiss, *Interpreting*, 156-193.

[71] Finis, *Quest*, Appendix 2.

not the validity of the Pentecostal phenomena as such, but the allegation that at least a proportion of them were of demonic origin. The reasoning given as justification of this rejection of Pentecostalism is weak and amounts in reality to a knee-jerk reaction against a new, unknown and potentially threatening movement.[72] It is a product of a manner of thinking that amounts to worshipping or damning that which cannot be immediately and comfortably incorporated into one's frame of reference.[73]

How does all this compare to Penn-Lewis' and Robert's reaction against similar phenomena occurring in the context of the Welsh Revival? Obviously *War on the Saints* represents a far more developed reaction than *The Berlin Declaration* and its analysis is more nuanced. Penn-Lewis' understanding of spiritual experiences is unusual in that she believed that an experience of the Holy Spirit may lead to negative effects because the recipient's understanding of, and reaction to the experience may be incorrect. Given this distinction her view of both passive 'sanctification by faith' and typical Pentecostal phenomenon was that they were inspired by, and open doorways to, demonic affliction. Penn-Lewis set out to outline exactly how the spiritual engages with the physical via the enthusiastic teaching and experiences she had witnessed in the Welsh Revival. In contrast, *The Berlin Declaration* was a straightforward condemnation of Pentecostalism that deliberately avoided analysis of this kind.

Nevertheless, *The Berlin Declaration* and *War on the Saints* both demonstrate the same schismatic enthusiastic tendency to ascribe aspects of enthusiastic Christianity to the activity of demons. Both demonstrate a certain intellectual superiority, however, carefully analysed, neither demonstrate much intellectual rigour or (in the case of *War on the Saints*) clarity and consistency. This is unsurprising since both emerge from within the wider enthusiastic

---

[72] *The Berlin Declaration* contains little in the way of dispassionate analysis of these Pentecostal phenomena. They are described as 'ugly' and therefore 'certainly not from God.' This is a purely subjective interpretation. Wright perceptively observes in relation to similar revival phenomena associated with the Vineyard Church and the so-called 'Toronto blessing' that, 'the waves of spiritual frenzy that we see attaching themselves to these events was also in each case marked by an equal and opposite frenzy, the frenzy to denounce and oppose the phenomena as demonic or occultic. Both tendencies are unhelpful. McCarthyism is a paranoid frenzy of its own, which panders to feelings of spiritual elitism and pride in its own way. To downplay the demonic ... and stress the sheer humanity of religious experience of the divine ought surely to help us behave more mercifully towards our fellow humans and offer fruitful possibilities for the future.' Wright, 'Revival', 134.

[73] Presumably if they had found the phenomena attractive rather than 'ugly' then they would have attributed them to God! Subjective reaction is clearly an extremely unreliable gauge of the merit of spiritual phenomena. Middlemiss, *Interpreting*, 174-175.

Holiness stream of Christianity.[74] Hence they are strong on assertion, conviction and confidence but weak on careful reflection, moderate language and theological acumen.

Hollenweger concludes that,

> The reason for this indiscriminate condemnation on the part of many German theologians of the Evangelical movement is the fact that their links with the Pentecostal movement are too close, with the result that the only remaining difference is the labelling of the same phenomena as 'spiritual' in their own camp and 'satanic' among Pentecostals.[75]

This is most helpful. The enthusiastic, eschatologically charged spirituality of the German Evangelicals and Penn-Lewis (and many others like them) meant that when they were faced with Pentecostal phenomena that they found unacceptable they were forced to demonise them. Any other, more rationalistic attack on the Pentecostals would have undermined their own spirituality. In short the demonisation of early / proto-Pentecostalism amounts to an *enthusiastic reaction against enthusiasm*.[76] Later in the century this pattern is repeated in EF and Charismatic demonisation of the Occult, New Age and NRMs which could be described as non-Christian forms of enthusiasm.

Unfortunately *War on the Saints* and *The Berlin Declaration* have made an impact that is out of proportion to their merit. The latter split German Evangelicalism causing a schism that is still evident.[77]

---

[74] Middlemiss identifies 'enthusiasm' as 'a sub-paradigm of Christian belief.' It is essentially anti-rational in that it stresses experience 'over reason as the basis of truth.' Middlemiss, Interpreting, 154, 66. It seems clear that although both *War on the Saints* and *The Berlin Declaration* take a rather superior attitude towards those phenomena they oppose and appear to employ rational language against them, their writers are judging such phenomena by subjective standards. Penn-Lewis writes in the Foreword of *War on the Saints* that the book 'will... only be clearly understood as the truths therein are put into practice in the hour of need... To the natural man, who has *but a mental grasp* of spiritual things, the language used may be meaningless' (Italics added). This is classic enthusiastic rhetoric and is fairly typical of the book as a whole. It has already been pointed out *The Berlin Declaration* relies upon a purely subjective analysis of Pentecostal phenomena. That the Gnadau Union itself was polarised from academic theology hints at its enthusiastic nature.

[75] Hollenweger, *Pentecostals*, 228.

[76] Wright argues that attributing all unusual revivalistic phenomena to the agency of either God or Satan is to naively ignore the human and thus ambiguous dimension to all such religious experiences. Wright, 'Revival', 121-135. However, it is observable that sectarianism of this most basic kind is a ubiquitous characteristic of religious enthusiasm. Wright is effectively arguing against the nature of religious enthusiasm rather than an undesirable and dispensable aspect of it.

[77] Finis, *Quest*, 1.

To conclude, the early twentieth century saw a dramatic revival of enthusiastic Christianity. This was marked by a persistent interest in divine healing, increased expectation and incidence of 'spiritual' manifestations which in turn led to a great deal of internal conflict.

The revival of enthusiasm stimulated interest in the demonic and strategies for dealing with it via the intemperate and also innately enthusiastic response of those who opposed the direction that the revivals were taking. The expectation and occurrence of 'Pentecostal' phenomena was frequently condemned as demonic by those who objected to these phenomena whilst accepting their 'spiritual' nature. The result was both schism and a focus on a form of spiritual warfare that was set to re-emerge mid century, particularly in the ministries of EF deliverance pioneers, Kurt Koch and Merrill Unger.

The Emergence of Distinctively EF Deliverance Ministry

The first notable examples of EF deliverance ministries are those of Kurt Koch and Merril Unger. Unlike Penn-Lewis, their deliverance ministry was not motivated *primarily* by an enthusiastic reaction to enthusiasm; it came out of an EF mileu that inherited her antagonism to Charismatic praxis and yet, like Penn-Lewis, at many points (including the practice of deliverance) closely resembled the praxis of the movement it demonised.

Kurt Koch

Kurt Koch became well known among EFs for his deliverance ministry in the 1970s although he was actually practising deliverance for many years prior to this.[78] Koch was a unique figure who delineated an approach to deliverance ministry that latterly came to be influential upon many Charismatics despite his explicitly anti-Charismatic outlook.

Koch's writings reveal his experience in the area of what he calls 'occult bondage' and a serious attempt to interact with sympathetic members of the medical profession in dealing with it.[79] He stresses Christ's power to overcome the power of Satan: 'The only real method of defense against the supernatural is

---

[78] Koch's books were published in the late sixties and early seventies and it was these that brought his ministry to international attention. Cuneo, *American*, 246. Koch's influence upon EF practitioners of deliverance ministry should not be underestimated. Cuneo, *American*, 276, 279. Koch's books in the area of demonology and deliverance ministry are as follows: K. Koch, *Between Christ and Satan* (Berghausen, Evangelisation, 1972); K. Koch, *Occult Bondage and Deliverance* (Berghausen: Evangelization, 1970); K. Koch, *The Devil's Alphabet* (Grand Rapids: Kregel, 1971); K. Koch, *Demonology, Past and Present* (Grand Rapids: Kregel, 1973).

[79] Koch, *Occult*, 71-81. The second half of this book is actually written by Alfred Lechler, a Christian psychiatrist who supported Koch's approach to demonology and deliverance ministry.

Christ... Christ leads us in triumph with all the defeated powers of the Evil One following in His train'[80]

Koch strongly asserts the reality of Satanic influence. He is keen to find members of the medical profession to support this and, for example, quotes an unnamed neurologist to the effect that sixty percent of his patients were actually suffering the symptoms of such influence rather than purely mental disorders.[81] His theological argument runs as follows:

> One can be sure that as the Son of God, Jesus had an accurate understanding of human nature and the human situation. We are therefore more than justified in accepting his actions at their face value, even when he was dealing with the demonically oppressed.[82]

Koch is anxious to establish the link between the occult and demonic influence. Sorcery ('a contract with the powers of darkness') can be the cause of compulsion neuroses, even across generations.[83] Satan accepts sorcery 'as his right to take people captive.'[84] Healing achieved from spiritist sources delivers 'a deathlike blow to [the patient's] faith.'[85] Occult paraphernalia 'carry with them a hidden ban.'[86] Living in a house where the occult is practised opens one to possibility of possession.[87]

At the root of Koch's approach to dealing with the demonic is his understanding of how demons exert influence over the individual which is taken from the experience of Alfred Lechler. Lechler divides demonic influence into four broad categories ranging from 'occult subjection' through 'demonization' and 'obsession' to full blown 'possession', although he realises that 'these four stages form a unity. These are merely different intensities of the same phenomenon.'[88] He often tends to collapse this framework into two categories of 'subjection' and 'possession'.

Of great concern to Koch is how the counsellor may discern between demonic influence and mental illness. Indeed, he asserts that distinguishing the two is 'one of the most difficult questions facing people engaged in counselling

---

[80] Koch, *Devil's*, 132.

[81] Koch, *Occult*, 12f.

[82] Koch, *Occult*, 135. Wheeling in Jesus' divinity as a foundation for disallowing recontextualisation is a powerful but ultimately inconclusive argument since, followed to its logical conclusion, it undermines Jesus' humanity.

[83] Koch, *Occult*, 80.

[84] Koch, *Occult*, 35, cf. 139.

[85] Koch, *Occult*, 47.

[86] Koch, *Occult*, 90.

[87] Koch, *Occult*, 70.

[88] Koch, *Occult*, 32. It is important to notice that, for all his theological conservatism, Koch has accepted as the basis for his understanding a model drawn from experience rather than the Bible.

work.'[89] This problem is compounded by what Lechler calls 'pseudo-possession.' That is, subjects believing themselves to be possessed and often behaving somewhat consistently with that belief which 'can be very contagious amongst a group of suggestible people.'[90] Lechler also points out that 'with Christians schizophrenia almost always appears in a religious guise.'[91] Koch identifies depression as possibly one form of demonic subjection.[92] One clear piece of advice is offered: a person who claims to be possessed is almost always mentally ill rather than suffering demonic subjection.[93]

Frequently implicit, and occasionally explicit, in Koch's writings is the assumption that mental illness and demonic activity are two separate and discrete categories; the medical profession should be allowed to deal with the former and the Christian counsellor the latter.[94] Nevertheless Koch does encourage these professions to work together particularly where the cause of disturbance is unclear,[95] and, furthermore, Lechler points out that 'demonic subjection and mental illness often occur simultaneously.'[96]

On the thorny issue of to what extent a Christian can be influenced by Satanic forces Koch is somewhat unclear. At one stage he seems to have an extremely positive view of the Christian's immunity: 'Jesus Christ has defeated all the powers of darkness. The true believer is therefore for ever guarded by him from all the devices of the devil.'[97] However, in practice both he and Lechler seem to suggest that believers may be subjected to demonic attack though not to full blown demon possession and even within these categories there may be some degree of greyness.[98]

With regard to the act of exorcism itself Koch is keen to point out that there are no fixed rules. Despite listing sixteen steps in 'counselling procedure' including confession, renunciation, prayer and fasting, Koch asserts that 'What we have been saying is not a recipe. The Lord in his sovereignty can at any time bypass each and every one of these steps.'[99] Perhaps most significantly, Koch allows that deliverance may take a lot of time and there is no guarantee of success. His description of the manifestations that accompany deliverance from demonic subjection bears resemblance to that of other, even the Charismatic,

---

[89] Koch, *Occult*, 61.
[90] Koch, *Occult*, 182.
[91] Koch, *Occult*, 158.
[92] Koch, *Occult*, 37.
[93] Koch, *Occult*, 155.
[94] Koch, *Occult*, 12-15, for example.
[95] Koch, *Occult*, 13.
[96] Koch, *Occult*, 160.
[97] Koch, *Occult*, 22.
[98] Koch, *Occult*, 70f., 190.
[99] Koch *Occult*, 127.

practitioners.[100]

Koch's attitude to alternative streams within the Christian traditions is both idiosyncratic and uncompromising. His work is obviously at odds with liberal approaches to Christian theology. He is, at points, quite amenable to Roman Catholic openness to the reality of the demonic and the need for exorcism,[101] although he goes on to dismiss liturgical formulae as 'obviously... of no use in the spiritual realm.'[102] His approach to the Pentecostal and Charismatic movements is condemnatory despite the previously noted similarity of his approach to Charismatic forms of deliverance ministry. Having adopted a mild cessationist position,[103] he warns against involvement in tongues speaking: 'It has nothing to do with the Holy Spirit!'[104] At another point he states: 'Many genuine Christians have had their Christian lives ruined through falling into this mediumistic stream.'[105] His polemic against Charismatic enthusiasm continues when he identifies the prominent healing evangelists William Branham and Oral Roberts as mediumistic healers. He erroneously asserts that Roberts may have 'received these mediumistic powers from an old Indian who once healed him in his younger days.'[106] Koch prefers a quieter and gentler emotional expression of spirituality.[107]

An important aspect of Koch's understanding is that Satan attempts to mimic the activity of God.[108] This is a fundamental assumption regarding the purpose of the occult and, significantly, he does not justify it by reference to Scripture. Koch does not develop this line of thinking as far as some but it is interesting that it surfaces in his writings.[109]

There can be no doubt that Koch's demonology was in symbiosis with his

---

[100] For example, he records the case of a woman who 'suddenly jerked and acted as if she was being sick.' Koch, *Occult,* 80.

[101] Koch, *Occult,* 10.

[102] Koch, *Occult,* 100. The fact that he feels no need to support this assertion is instructive of the manner in which evangelicals of Koch's enthusiastic stripe viewed spirituality. They tended to assume that liturgy was the hiding place for those with no lively personal faith.

[103] Koch, *Devil's,* 109. Like most mid century EFs Koch is not entirely opposed to the *charismata per se,* in fact he claims to believe in them. Koch, *Devil's,* 109, cf. Koch, *Day,* 127. This is an illustration of little there is to chose between EF and Charismatic enthusiasm. Mid century EFs tend to believe in the *charismata* in every way except practice.

[104] Koch, *Devil's,* 111.

[105] Koch, *Occult,* 95.

[106] Koch, *Occult,* 48-57.

[107] Koch, *Day,* 8.

[108] Koch, *Occult,* 22, 42. Cf. Koch, *World,* 55.

[109] Some practitioners have used this reasoning as the basis for analyses of demonic strategy that go well beyond the biblical material. For example see Horrobin, *Volume 1,* 50-53.

typically pessimistic premillenial eschatology. Koch viewed renewed interest in the occult among the developed world as one clear evidence of the nearness of the parousia with the attendant decline of the human race.[110] Hence, Koch's eschatology led him to expect increasing need for deliverance ministry and his perception of the increasing need for deliverance ministry supported his imminent, premillenial eschatology.

Koch's interest in deliverance appears to have been stimulated by his experience in overseas missions although he also quotes some European case studies. His influence was very significant; almost all of the American EFs examined below quote him as a source.

Moody Bible Institute and Dallas Theological Seminary[111]

Moody Bible Institute (MBI) and Dallas Theological Seminary (DTS) served as centres for EF deliverance ministry.[112] Interestingly (but probably coincidentally), Jessie Penn-Lewis had some links with MBI, teaching there in 1900.[113] The most significant American advocate of a characteristically EF deliverance ministry was Merrill Unger of Dallas Theological Seminary. Other key figures include Martin Bubeck and Fred Dickason (both of MBI). All three are examined in turn below. Finally, attention is given to Hal Lindsey whose name is synonomous with premillennial dispensationalism and who also advocated EF deliverance.

MERRILL UNGER

Merill Unger, a well-respected theologian within American evangelicalism, Unger was well known as a prolific writer prior to the publication of two books espousing deliverance ministry. Several of his books dealt with demonology and exorcism. He was concerned to outline a Christian approach to dealing with the demonic and to highlight the dangers of extreme Charismatic experientialism that he clearly deplored. Hence his work should be seen as a response not only to the problem of the demonic itself, but also to his frustration with his perception of confusion and spiritual naivete within the Pentecostal/Charismatic movement.

Unger adhered to a typically premillenial dispensationalist theology. At first he held tightly to the view that a Christian believer is immune from demonization.[114] His later position (based on a tri-partite anthropology) was that demons might wreak havoc in a believer's body and soul but may not affect the

---

[110] Koch, *World*, 31-33. Cf. K. Koch, *The Coming One* (Grand Rapids: Kregel, 1972).
[111] For first hand insight into DTS see Balmer, *Mine*, 31-47. Both DTS and MBI are marked by a strong historical adherence to premillenial dispensationalism.
[112] Powlison, *Power*, 32. Koch, *World*, 95.
[113] Jones, *Trials*, 97f., 103-105.
[114] Unger, *Biblical*, 100.

spirit, which is eternally secure.[115] This systematic argument is the foundation of his concept of the danger of progressive demonisation of Christians if they capitulate to demonic influence via sin. In the worst cases God may even allow demons to kill a Christian but never to divest him or her of salvation.[116]

Unger's latter work in the area of demonology and exorcism was initially published around the early and mid 1970s, although these books have gone through numerous reprints. He attempted to outline a 'middle of the road' approach, explicitly criticising the extremes of demythologisation of, or preoccupation with, the demonic. However, one wonders whether he is not guilty of the latter after all. He suggests that demons always lurk where there are patterns of persistent sin in the life of a Christian.[117]

His approach to exorcism, like that of Kurt Koch, appears simpler at face value than in reality, largely because the evidence of the case studies he uses is somewhat inconsistent. Having recorded that demonisation is characterised by personality shifts, use of unknown languages (vs Charismatics!), superhuman strength, antagonism to the 'things of God', and clairvoyance (among other things),[118] Unger goes on to take a very optimistic view. He notes that Jesus 'as Lord of the spirit world' could effect instantaneous deliverance from demons and although 'it may take more time with His finite, infirm servants... victory is *always* certain in His name.'[119] Some victories are only won by persistence over a long period of time however, this is more beneficial than an instant cure since it teaches deeper spirituality.[120] In order to remain free of demonic incursion the believer must fulfil certain conditions including complete dissociation from both the occult and heretical religion (apparently including

---

[115] Unger, *Saints*, 76f. This development was apparently due to the overwhelming evidence of 'numbers of letters and reports of cases of demon invasion of believers.' Unger, *Saints*, 69. Dickason claims that Unger's change of heart was largely driven by the experience of overseas missionaries C. F. Dickason, *Angels: Elect and Evil* (Chicago: Moody, 1975) 205. Moody actually published a compendium of such experiences from overseas in 1960; Various Authors, *Demon Experiences in Many Lands* (Chicago: Moody Press, 1960). Unger's U-turn made a considerable impact upon the Evangelical world. Cuneo, *American*, 246; cf. C. Arnold, *Spiritual Warfare* (London: Marshall Pickering, 1997) 77f.

[116] Unger, *Saints*, 86-98. Unger's emphasis upon God's sovereignty in the 'perseverance of the saints' surfaces here as it becomes apparent that demons are only operating in those areas that God allows them to and, despite their malevolent intentions, their actions ultimately serve to further God's ends.

[117] Unger, *Saints*, 57f.

[118] Unger, *Saints*, 129-140.

[119] Unger, *Saints*, 148. This commonplace argument attempts to disarm the criticism that the form of deliverance ministry looks very different from the form found in the NT.

[120] Unger, *Saints*, 164f.

Charismatic enthusiasm) and whole hearted surrender to God.[121]

Given his view of the apparent ease with which demons may begin to influence and take hold of a believer, and the complications involved in getting free of this, and (more demanding still) staying free, one wonders how Unger can assert that 'victory is always certain.' It seems that he has collapsed human experience into an overdeveloped dualism; all sin is always directly attributable to the nefarious influence of evil spirits and results in degrees of bondage to them.[122] Given the teaching both explicit and implicit in Unger's writings, one must draw the conclusion that his view is that *all* believers are plagued by demons to a greater or lesser extent (in so far as they capitulate to them through sinning) and that the only 'certain victory' is final, post-mortem salvation.[123]

An important aspect of Unger's work is the peculiar (though not uncommon) assertion that demons have names that describe the vice that they promote; English names apparently.[124] This is a rather difficult camel to swallow. Presumably, if demons have names at all (and there is little reason to assume that they do) it is surely improbable that they should be English.[125] If it is argued that demons present their name and characteristics according to the culture in which they are operating then this will readily be accepted as a possibility. However, this militates against Unger's legal (magical) approach to deliverance ministry in which the use of a demon's name grants authority over it.[126] His biblical basis for such an idea is extremely flimsy.

Perhaps Unger's most perceptive and original line of thought lies in his analysis of the character of demons. Typically, Christians present demons as

---

[121] Unger, *Saints*, 172-196. Unger was extremely critical of the Charismatic movement which he describes as 'a clever halo-crowned stratagem of Satan to divide God's people and to bring them under a subtle, yet real, type of occult bondage.' Unger, *Saints*, 203.

[122] Unger's understanding of the cause and effect of sin is therefore somewhat poorly thought out. He makes little allowance for, or analysis of, the fallen nature. Marrying this to Unger's tri-partite anthropology suggests that the work of regeneration has little practical benefit for the believer except in the sphere of the spirit where it becomes irreversible. This seems rather simplistic and takes a low view of the effects of salvation upon what Unger would call the soul. Most Christian theologians even EF theologians would prefer to take a more holistic view of human personality. Cf C. F. Dickason, *Demon Possession and the Christian* (Westchester: Crossway, 1987) 135f.

[123] This is demonstrably true in so far as all believers continue to struggle with sin. Nevertheless, Unger clearly believes that demonization goes far beyond this struggle; he holds that falling to sin leads (to a greater or lesser extent) to demonic control.

[124] Unger, *Saints*, 142, 163. Unger also briefly mentions that where demonization is achieved by several, or even numerous demons, there may be one demon who acts as a 'spokesperson'. Unger, *Saints*, 142. Again, most advocates of deliverance ministry hold this belief.

[125] Absurdly, one of Unger's case studies asserts the existence of demons of different nationalities. Unger, *Saints*, 152. One cannot help thinking that Unger is uncritical in his presentation of anecdotal evidence.

[126] Unger, *Saints*, 142.

utterly degraded and inveterate liars. Unger, however, avers that 'many demons are nice, refined, religious and "good" in a self-righteous sense.'[127] Demons are marked, not by their depravity (although some are certainly depraved) but by their opposition to 'the Word and the will of God.'[128] Sadly, Unger does not follow through on the implications of this, which would undoubtedly lead to some very interesting results. It would certainly stand in tension with his tendency to emphasise the occult when looking for causes of demonization.

Merrill Unger was along with Kurt Koch a pioneer of EF deliverance ministry. A respected Evangelical figure, his significance is great firstly, because he changed from a typically Evangelical position assuming that born again Christians are secure from demonic invasion to pioneering EF deliverance ministry; he seems to have played a major part in embedding deliverance in EF culture for years to come. Secondly, although opposed to Charismatic enthusiasm there is little doubt that his own espousal of deliverance was based upon a classically enthusiastic, eschatologically charged, capitulation to a spiritually immanent interpretation of events and experiences.

MARK BUBECK

Mark Bubeck has written a number of popular books dealing with the demonic. The first of these, *The Adversary*[129] was published in 1975 and has sold hundreds of thousands of copies. In 1991 he published *The Rise of Fallen Angels*.[130] Both of these were published by Moody Press.

Like Penn-Lewis, Bubeck's primary interest is not so much deliverance ministry as revival. Accordingly, he urgently calls every Christian to participate in aggressive spiritual warfare against the demonic forces that have infiltrated and dominated society. This warfare will include deliverance ministry but such ministry is actually only a small part of Bubeck's overall approach.

Bubeck's Sources

Bubeck acknowledges that he has been heavily influenced by Jessie Penn-Lewis's *War on the Saints*.[131] His approach is to deny Satan 'ground' and to take back such ground where it has been conceded;[132] this is the exact same concept that dominates Penn-Lewis's thought.[133] Similarly the concept of 'aggressive warfare prayer' and overriding interest in revival are in common with the latter's methodology.

The bibliography of *The Adversary* includes books by most of the prominent

---

[127] Unger, *Saints*, 116.

[128] Unger, *Saints*, 116.

[129] M. I. Bubeck, *The Adversary* (Chicago: Moody Press, 1975).

[130] M. I. Bubeck, *The Rise of Fallen Angels* (Chicago: Moody Press, 1991).

[131] Bubeck, *Adversary*, 129.

[132] Bubeck, *Adversary*, 34, 66, 89, 100, etc.

[133] See chapter 5, above.

evangelical advocates of deliverance ministry including John Nevius, Kurt Koch, Merrill Unger, Fred Dickason, but also, interestingly, one or two Charismatics. Donald Basham and Michael Harper make an appearance. His controlling premillenial eschatology is indicated by his inclusion of Hal Lindsey's *The Late Great Planet Earth.*[134]

Defeating the Adversary
Bubeck perceives the Christian life to be a struggle against the demonic forces of Satan. The Christian must fight against these as they seek to exploit the weakness of the 'flesh' and exert pressure through the 'world'.[135] This contest sometimes requires direct and authoritative confrontation;[136] however, this is not Bubeck's primary method. Taking Jesus' encounter with Satan as his example he urges Christians to confront the Devil by committing Scripture to memory, repeating it in what he calls 'doctrinal prayer' and 'applying it in my daily walk'.[137] This latter concept looks very much like the basis for the later approach of Neil Anderson,[138] who, tellingly, wrote the foreword in *The Rise of the Fallen Angels.*[139]

Other Issues in Bubeck's Work
In his later book *The Rise of the Fallen Angels*, Bubeck makes much of the prevalence of Satanic Ritual Abuse (SRA),[140] the rise of the New Age movement and other evidences that a 'Satanic revival' is under way. Despite obvious premillenialist leanings he does not draw the immediate conclusion that this heralds the imminent return of Christ, instead he urges Christians to engage in spiritual warfare to 'turn things around... Together, we can defeat the powers of evil.'[141]

Bubeck's attitude towards the Pentecostal and Charismatic Movements

---

[134] Bubeck, *Adversary*, 159f.

[135] Bubeck, *Adversary*, 25-44 and 45-54.

[136] Bubeck, *Adversary*, 115-125. Bubeck relates the story of the demonic oppression, and subsequent deliverance, of his youngest daughter. Bubeck's approach to, and interest in, deliverance ministry is far more moderate than most of his contemporaries. His approach to deliverance, and his understanding of demonisation, runs along the same lines as Unger.

[137] Bubeck, *Adversary*, 94f.

[138] Anderson is examined below, chapter 6.

[139] Bubeck, *Angels*, 11f.

[140] Bubeck, *Angels*, 23-25. On SRA, see below chapter 8. Bubeck accepts the thesis of Friesen that SRA lies behind around 25% of cases of Multiple Personality Disorder. Bubeck, *Angels*, 25. Cf. J. G. Friesen, *Uncovering the Mystery of MPD* (Nashville: Nelson, 1991) and the analysis of Cuneo, *American*, 248-255.

[141] It seems that Bubeck's eschatology was a good deal more 'imminent' in the 1970s. By the 1990s it seems to have cooled off a little. Bubeck, *Adversary*, 131, 156-158. Cf. Bubeck, *Angels*, 36.

shows the same ambivalence that one can detect in the earlier writings of Penn-Lewis. On the one hand he acknowledges that God is at work among Charismatics; on the other, he, like Penn-Lewis, has deep concerns regarding the dangers of uncritically seeking charismatic experiences.[142] With regard to deliverance ministry itself, Bubeck is very critical of what he calls the 'excesses and extremism of so-called faith healers'.[143]

To conclude, Bubeck (who is heavily reliant on Penn-Lewis) represents a moderate approach to deliverance ministry within an overall schema of spiritual warfare; his dominant recommendation is 'doctrinal prayer', a concept that Neil Anderson was to take further. Just as his attitude to deliverance ministry is moderate, so too are his eschatology and his attitude towards Charismatics.

FRED DICKASON

In the late 1980s Fred Dickason, who was at the time 'chairman of the theology department' at MBI, wrote a significant volume entitled *Demon Possession and the Christian.*[144] It is subtitled *A New Perspective*, which is somewhat misleading since it depends heavily on, and reiterates much of, the teaching of Kurt Koch, Merrill Unger and Mark Bubeck. Nevertheless there are new angles on their work and, on occasion, explicit criticism of it.

Dickason demonstrates genuine integrity in his attempt to outline and defend his approach to demonisation and deliverance ministry. He deals with the biblical data conscientiously and acknowledges that there is uncertainty regarding the precise manner of interaction between the believer and the demonic.[145] Nevertheless, with a great deal of qualification, like Unger before him, he asserts that *experience* indicates that a Christian may be demonised. As he outlines his approach to deliverance one becomes increasingly aware that this precept is driving much of his interpretation of scripture.

The main point of divergence with his forerunners is in the area of anthropology. He recognises the over-simplification of Unger's analysis and argues instead that 'man is two parts – body and spirit, and that his whole being is termed soul.'[146] Dickason believes that demonisation is usually achieved by demonic control of the mind.[147] He outlines an explanation of the psychological repercussions of this.[148] Thus he replaces the weakness of Unger's anthropology

---

[142] Bubeck, *Adversary*, 40-42.

[143] Bubeck, *Adversary*, 116.

[144] Dickason had already published a book entitled *Angels: Elect and Evil* in 1975. This earlier publication was fairly brief in regards to demonisation and deliverance (and very similar in content to the work of Koch and Unger); it examined the angelic as a whole rather than purely the demonic. This earlier work is typical of his contemporaries in its antipathy towards Charismatic Christianity, Dickason, *Angels*, 221f, 223, 236.

[145] Dickason, *Demon*, 127.

[146] Dickason, *Demon*, 136.

[147] Dickason, *Demon*, 225.

[148] Dickason, *Demon*, 222-229.

with speculations at least partially justified by purported exchanges with the demons themselves.[149] His approach to deliverance is to locate the highest ranking demon (the 'throne' demon) and to negotiate this spirit into an acceptance that he has no legal right to demonise the subject.[150]

Dickason's teaching, largely founded on his experience grows steadily less convincing and internally inconsistent. At the same time his tone becomes less temperate and he expresses less tolerance of those who disagree with him.[151] In common with all the work from this school of evangelical theology, his analysis of the case evidence is often outlandish and is certainly open to alternative interpretation.

HAL LINDSEY

Hal Lindsey is one of the best known EF names largely as a result of his bestselling book *The Late Great Planet Earth*,[152] first published in 1970, outlining Lindsey's imminent premillenial eschatology. Two years later Lindsey followed up with *Satan is Alive and Well on Planet Earth*[153] which was also enormously popular.

The book opens with the story of Lindsay's encounter with a young woman demonised as a result of occult involvement.[154] As is so often the case, Lindsay uses this story as the thin end of the wedge to establish the need for much greater awareness of the demonic:

> I knew what the Bible had to say about such manifestations, but I had never been called upon to deal with someone who was under the influence of an evil spirit...

> What happened during the following hours was an amazing experience... At this point it is sufficient to say I witnessed a miracle! This woman was freed from an evil spirit. Not in Africa, not in the remote regions of the Amazon, but in the sunshine of an American college campus.

> This incident awakened me to the widespread phenomenon of the occult.

---

[149] Dickason, *Demon*, 238-240.

[150] Dickason, *Demon*, 187-213. This is a common technique – other practitioners sometimes refer to a 'strongman'. As with Bubeck there is a clear parallel with Penn-Lewis's concept of 'ground'.

[151] For example, 'Antagonism to the casting out of demons is irrational and morally perverted religion.' Dickason, *Demon*, 277.

[152] H. Lindsey, *The Late Great Planet Earth* (London: Lakeland, 1973).

[153] H. Lindsey, *Satan is Alive and Well on Planet Earth* (London: Lakeland, 1973).

[154] Lindsey, *Satan*, 15-17.

It alarmed me that the increase in astrology, extrasensory perception, witchcraft, black magic, fortunetelling and Satan worship, which you might expect among the youth of the West Coast, was evident in other places. The occult influence went deeper into American life than I had imagined.[155]

Fundamental to all streams of enthusiastic understanding of demonisation and implicit here is the assumption that the primary way to reach such a condition is via conscious commitment to Satan or idolatry (which amounts to much the same thing) and Lindsay treads a familiar path in expressing his amazement that such religious practices have permeated Western culture. He spends the next two chapters establishing the extent of this permeation identifying the emergence and startling popularity of various occult activities including Satanist cults involved in appalling abuse.[156] Included alongside these, Lindsey identifies two NRMs – Nichiren Shoshu and Scientology.[157] His analysis is typically exaggerated and alarmist.

After outlining a reasonably orthodox Biblical demonology,[158] Lindsey analysed various academic and cultural trends which he believed were inspired by Satan.[159] After an extended refutation of the famous psychic, Jeane Dixon,[160] the reader is warned against following her example of occult involvement; it is in this immediate context that Lindsey discusses Charismatic enthusiasm and particularly glossolalia.[161] Whilst he attempts to be irenic and counters the cessationist position,[162] Lindsey has grave concerns about the Charismatic Movement and initiates his critique by summarising Penn-Lewis to the effect that the 'great revival in Wales was completely neutralised by an invasion of demonic power. The demons began to get into this movement through people who sincerely wanted to know God in a deeper way and began to open themselves up for all kinds of spiritual contact and leading.'[163] A demon can

---

[155] Lindsey, *Satan*, 17.

[156] Lindsey, *Satan*, 17-40.

[157] Lindsey, *Satan*, 34, 36. The EF and Charismatic tendency to lump NRMs and the occult together is not usually based upon a socio-cultural analysis of these groups. It is an instinctive parochial reaction to the effect that they all represent the increasingly transparent activity of Satan. The underlying assumption is that this represents an active allegiance to Satan heretofore unknown in the 'Christian West' which means that one might expect to see demonisation close to home and not just on the 'mission field'.

[158] Lindsey, *Satan*, 41-83.

[159] Lindsey, *Satan*, 84-113.

[160] Lindsey, *Satan*, 114-128.

[161] Lindsey, *Satan*, 133-149.

[162] Lindsey, *Satan*, 136-149.

[163] Lindsey, *Satan*, 134. Elsewhere he describes *War on the Saints* as 'an old and priceless book which has some deep perceptions into the subject. The authors were scholars and Christians of great understanding and depth.' Lindsey, *Satan*, 163.

'get into a person's life' through seeking a spiritual encounter that will supposedly lead to 'instant maturity' and this forms the basis for his critique of glossolalia. However, having made a brief and rather negative analysis of Charismatic practice of glossolalia Lindsey contents himself with an assertion that Charismatics may become deceived and they may cause controversy which will please Satan. He does not follow through to spell out the possibility of demonisation through glossolalia although that was the clear implication at the start of his discussion.[164]

Lindsey goes on to discuss typical symptoms of demon possession[165] including most of the usual candidates: significantly enhanced intelligence or physical strength, mental illness, facial expression, uncontrolled swearing, and personality shift (the demon's personality displacing that of the host).[166] Lindsey argues that it is observing combinations of these characteristics that one may make a correct diagnosis regarding possible demon possession but this seems in some tension with the case study he outlines where he diagnosed the possession of a Muslim man largely on the basis of his facial expression observed in a photograph.[167] Lindsey believes 'that a non-Christian can be totally controlled and manipulated by demonic power, but a Christian *rarely* has the same degree of complete subjection.'[168] Note the use of the word 'rarely'. Lindsey accepts that there are exceptions, particularly in 'countries where there is open worship of idols, such as China.'[169] Of course, the underlying theme of his book is that this susceptibility to possession is now a reality in the post-Christian West and the eschatological significance of this.

Lindsey makes a brief but intriguing assessment of the interest in exorcism generated by the film *The Exorcist*.[170] In effect he claims that the style of exorcism demonstrated in the film is equivalent to pagan rites: 'When we read and hear of the methods of casting out demons used by unbelievers, we understand that it is even possible under the power of Satan to cast out demons,

---

[164] Lindsey, *Satan*, 133f, cf. 147f.

[165] In this section of the book Lindsey quotes Unger on an incidental point describing him as 'one of the finest Bible scholars in the world.' Lindsey, *Satan*, 154.

[166] Lindsey, *Satan*, 156-159.

[167] Lindsey, *Satan*, 150f.

[168] Lindsey, *Satan*, 159f. Italics added for emphasis.

[169] Lindsey, *Satan*, 160. There is a fair tradition emanating from missions work (particularly that of the China Inland Mission) in China on EF deliverance in this context. See Taylor, *Pastor*. Hsi, a Chinese national Christian leader, became known as 'Conqueror of Demons'. The book features a foreword from the redoubtable Martyn Lloyd-Jones. See also Kinnear, *Watchman*, 92. Nee was much influenced by Penn-Lewis 'on the questions of soul and spirit and of triumph over Satanic power.' Kinnear, *Nee*, 65. Cf. Murphy, *Handbook*, 412-415. Of course, Nevius' *Demon Possession and Allied Themes* emerged as a result of his ministry in China.

[170] Lindsey, *Satan*, 162.

if it furthers his teaching and purposes.'[171] A clearer demonstration of EF anti-Catholicism is harder to imagine!

Lindsey does not give much in the way of case studies to illustrate his approach to deliverance; however he does give one example where he issued a command to evict the demon and procured a simple confession of faith from the subject.[172] He does not, however, seem to think that every occasion will be that simple: 'If a believer encounters ... demon possession, I believe he should, in most cases, call upon a trusted, mature believer and the two should pray for guidance together as to how to proceed.'[173]

Satan is Alive and Well on Planet Earth is perhaps the most straightforward example of how deliverance functions within a premillenial eschatologically charged EF enthusiasm.[174] The metanarrative runs something like this: *The Lord's return is nearing and this is evidenced by the growing idolatry and occult activity of the post-Christian West. As a result of this 'satanic takeover' demonic possession is now afflicting increasing numbers of Westerners and there is a consequent need for deliverance.* Hence deliverance functions as a secondary support to the overall premillenial eschatological framework.[175]

Enthusiastic Fascination with Demonology and the Occult[176]

Fascination with demonology and the occult has emerged as a common theme amongst the Charismatic and EF practitioners of deliverance ministry examined thus far. This fascination coheres well with the basic thesis that enthusiastic spirituality is formed in part by an impulse toward an immanent spirituality. Furthermore, the perceived revival of the occult in Western society lends ballast to the other great symptom of enthusiasm, namely imminent eschatology. Attention is now focused on this fascination in order to establish its function within the outlook of the enthusiastic practitioners of deliverance ministry and, specifically, how it exists in collaboration with a perceived need

---

[171] Lindsey, *Satan*, 162.

[172] Lindsey, *Satan*, 164-166.

[173] Lindsey, *Satan*, 164. Lindsey goes on to admit that his experience of deliverance is not extensive.

[174] Of course Lindsey's *The Late Great Planet Earth* had already done a great deal to popularise EF eschatology.

[175] Imminent premillenial eschatology is also a frequent characteristic of Charismatic enthusiasm however, the consequent pessimism is somewhat mitigated by their dynamic Christian optimism. See Wacker, *Heaven*, 251-265 for an examination of the function of premillenial eschatology within the environment of early Pentecostalism.

[176] Such fascination is very frequently used by practitioners to serve as justification for the growing need for deliverance ministry. I have chosen to include it as this point since it surfaces most often and most obviously in the EF literature. This obsession is foundational for the later excitement generated by celebrated conversions (see 4.3.1) from occult entanglement.

for the widespread practice of such a ministry.

Orthodox Christians have always held to a belief in a personal devil; among evangelicals, in the face of liberal scepticism, such a belief is almost a theological shibboleth. John Wesley himself believed in the power of witchcraft, demon possession and frequently practised exorcism himself; moreover, he used this belief to refute 'sceptics denying supernatural intervention in the world.'[177] In other words, in the light of growing Enlightenment scepticism, Wesley realised that the 'same intellectual developments which made the Devil and the witch redundant ate away at belief in God himself... If Satan and his covens were no longer needed to explain events, neither was God.'[178]

During the 1970s and 1980s enthusiastic interest all things demonic sky-rocketed. Countless studies of the occult were made - usually at a popular and decidedly unscientific level. Most books advocating deliverance ministry made at least some study of this subject[179] whilst other books were written addressing the subject directly which then made some reference to deliverance ministry.[180] Most of the analysis was popular and polemical, usually adopting a scattergun methodology stacking up alarming examples of how the occult had penetrated secular culture, particularly the media. When specific quantitative assessments were made they tended to be much higher than those suggested by more scholarly studies.[181] The situation is identical with regard to NRMs. Their

---

[177] H. D. Rack, *Reasonable Enthusiast: John Wesley and the Rise of Methodism* (London: Epworth Press, 1989) 187, 195-197 and 387.

[178] R. Cavendish, *The Powers of Evil in Western Religion, Magic and Folk Belief* (London: Routledge & Keegan Paul Ltd, 1975) 226. Actually Wesley was by no means the first to make such a connection. J. Redwood, *Reason, Ridicule and Religion* (London: Thames and Hudson, 1976) 46; P. C. Almond, *Heaven and Hell in Enlightenment England* (Cambridge: Cambridge University Press, 1994) 33-37; M. Heyd, *Be Sober and* Reasonable (Leiden: E J Brill, 1995) 80. In the face of the widespread decline of their religion, Christian writers both asserted the veracity of medieval demonologies and utilised their apologetic (even evangelistic) value. Almond, *Heaven*, 41, 85-90.

[179] See, for example, Richards, *Deliver*, 19-90; M. Perry, *Deliverance* (London: SPCK, 1987) 53-70; Prince, *Expel*, 113-141.

[180] P. Anderson, *Talk About the Devil* (London: Word, 1973) 99; M. F. Unger, *Demons in the World Today* (Wheaton: Tyndale, 1971) 177; Cruz, *Satan*, 125-139.

[181] See, for example, Anderson's contention (made in 1973) that the number of practising witches in Great Britain was 40,000 'and growing daily'. Anderson, *Talk*, 14. This figure was taken from a report in the Daily Mirror. The occult is of course an extremely attractive subject for sensational media reporting. The various motivations of Christian enthusiasts, practitioners of deliverance ministry, the media and those involved in the occult all converge to encourage inflation of the numbers of people involved in the occult revival. Anderson goes on to quote Kurt Koch to the effect that half the population of Great Britain is involved in the occult in some way. Anderson, *Talk*, 16. Cf. Cruz, *Satan*, 92-117. These sort of analyses are highly dubious; more sober analysis

significance is inflated and they are viewed as secretive, manipulative and damaging organisations, at best; at worst, they are perceived as demonically inspired.[182] Enthusiastic Christians were at the forefront of the Anti-Cult movement, which opposed and, in some cases, forcibly removed people from, NRMs.[183]

It must be borne in mind that it suited enthusiasts to exaggerate the impact of the Occult Revival and NRMs for several reasons.[184] Firstly, and probably most importantly, widespread Occult activity and deviant religion is often interpreted as an indication of the imminent eschaton.[185] Since imminent premillenial eschatology is almost an article of faith amongst EF, and to a somewhat lesser extent Charismatic, enthusiasts this all sits together very neatly. Secondly, since occult activity is usually understood to be the primary way in which to become demonised it suits practitioners of deliverance ministry to present occultism as an extremely widespread activity. Thirdly, among more extreme enthusiasts there is a tendency towards conspiracy theories. The Occult Revival and the emergence of NRMs may be construed as one symptom of a widespread demonic conspiracy.[186] Fourthly, some Christians have built extremely lucrative

---

indicates that the numbers are actually far lower. See, for example, T. M. Luhrman, *Persuasion of the Witch's Craft* (Oxford: Blackwell, 1989) 5; D. Burnett, *Dawning of the Pagan Moon* (Eastbourne: MARC, 1991) 197-201.

[182] See J. McDowell and D. Stewart, *Understanding the Cults* (San Bernadino: Here's Life, 1986); D. Hunt, *The Cult Explosion* (Eugene: Harvest House, 1980); W. Martin, *The Kingdom of the Cults* (Minneapolis: Bethany House, 1985); D. Breese, *Know the Marks of Cults* (Wheaton: Victor, 1975). Cf. L. L. Dawson, *Comprehending Cults* (Ontario: Oxford University Press, 1998) 7. Much could be said about the anti-cult movement, which was energised to a great extent by enthusiastic Christians. Also, Cf. J. G. Melton, *Encyclopedic Handbook of Cults in America* (New York: Garland, 1986).

[183] J. G. Melton, 'Anti-Cultists in the United States' in B. Wilson and J. Cresswell (eds.), *New Religious Movements: Challenges and Response* (London: Routledge, 1999) 217-232.

[184] In relation to the heretics of the Middle Ages, Knox observed in like fashion that 'both friends and foes tend to exaggerate in such matters.' Knox, *Enthusiasm*, 74.

[185] The idea that renewed interest in occult spiritualities is a sign of the approaching eschaton, is commonly asserted by enthusiastic Christians. See, for example, Lindsey, *Late*, 107, 114-134. With reference to the Occult Revival note that Warnke's organisation was initially named 'The Alpha Omega Outreach' because 'we are beginning a new ministry for the Lord for the end times.' M. Warnke, *The Satan Seller* (Plainfield: Logos International, 1972), 202. In regard to the emergence of NRMs see Hunt, *Cult*, 199-201. This assertion ignores the fact that the occult/NRMs are still 'minority sports' and that the far more dominant secularism of Western culture is no more conducive to Christianity and, some argue, is less so. Appeals to Bible passages such as 1 Timothy 4:1 should be balanced by reference to 2 Peter 3:3-9.

[186] 'Sign watching' for the eschaton and conspiracy theories are 'integral to fundamentalist dualist constructs.' S. Hunt 'The Devil's Advocates: The Function of

ministries through peddling their testimonies of occult involvement; this provided them with a strong motivation to keep the occult to the forefront. [187] Lastly, despite their strong opposition to the Occult and NRMs, twentieth century enthusiasts, like Wesley before them, often make apologetic capital from them, arguing (perhaps with some justification) that their popularity represents evidence for the indefatigable human instinct for noumenal experience.[188]

Hunt observes that within a fundamentalist, dualist worldview 'evidence for the powers of evil bring as much confirmation of a world view as does that of the powers of good.'[189] Along with the reasons given above, this sheds a great deal of light on the motivations behind Christian demonology, alarmism over the occult revival and (to a lesser extent) the emergence of NRMs, and interest in deliverance ministry. In a secular, agnostic wider culture, enthusiastic Christians seized upon the Occult Revival as evidence of evil supernatural activity. Never mind the need for sober assessment, just feel the apologetic value. In this way the Occult Revival and enthusiastic Christianity enjoyed a perverse symbiotic enmity.[190]

Celebrated Conversions

In the light of all this it is unsurprising that those who convert from a

---

Demonology in the World View of Fundamentalist Christianity' in M. Percy and I. Jones (eds.), *Fundamentalism: Church and Society* (London:SPCK, 2002) 81.

[187] As in the case of Mike Warnke (see below). With reference to the way in which Enthusiastic Christians fanned the flames of hysteria surrounding Satanic Ritual Abuse (again, see below) Ross points out: 'In the cosmic battle against Satan, it is essential that Satan actually present himself on earth for combat; otherwise, the danger will not be tangible, and donations of faith, support, money and allegiance will not be so readily forthcoming.' C. Ross, *Satanic Ritual Abuse* (Toronto: University of Toronto Press, 1995) 96.

[188] Expressed sensibly, this oft-used argument has some validity. At its worst, it leads enthusiastic Christians to exaggerate claims about the scope of Occult/New Age/ Cult activity. It can also lead to an over emphasis on the Satanic/demonic within Christian theology and even a neurotic desire to witness manifestations of the demonic. Cf J. S. Victor, *Satanic Panic: the creation of a contemporary legend* (Peru, Illinois: Open Court, 1996) 99, cf. 282. Cf. also, Warnke, *Satan*, 126.

[189] Hunt, 'Devil's', 74.

[190] The Occult fits the category of what Wacker describes as a 'symbolic foe': 'the... folk that saints encountered indirectly, either on paper or by word of mouth'. Wacker, *Heaven*, 179. In the midst of all the enthusiastic furore one wonders how many enthusiasts actually had any personal contact with an Occultist. In actuality, the Neo-Paganism, New Age and the emergence of the NRMs is partially a result of the same reaction to secularisation and depersonalisation. M. York, 'New Age Millenarianism and its Christian Influences' in S. Hunt (ed.), *Christian Millenarianism* (London: Hurst, 2001) 227-238.

background of occult activity especially excite enthusiastic Christians.[191] Two prominent examples are Doreen Irvine and Mike Warnke.[192] They have both written autobiographical accounts of their conversion from occultism to Christianity entitled *From Witchcraft to Christ*[193] and *The Satan Seller*[194] respectively.

Doreen Irvine was converted to Christian faith in June 1964 as a result of attending a revivalist campaign held by Eric Hutchings.[195] She had previously held the position of 'queen of the black witches', having graduated to occultism from a dissolute life as a prostitute, stripper and drug addict.[196] Her involvement in the occult began with Satanism before leading on to black witchcraft;[197] Irvine relates lurid details of the ceremonies and evil supernatural manifestations she experienced. On one occasion she claims to have made an entire gathering of witches invisible in order to avoid detection by a local preacher and two reporters.[198] During the ceremony at which the queen of the black witches was to be chosen Irvine asserts that Lucifer himself materialised and guided her unharmed through a large bonfire as evidence that she was his choice.[199]

Following her conversion Irvine experienced an awful spiritual struggle during which she encountered a great deal of demonic oppression including another appearance of Satan and many problems typically associated with demonic activity.[200] It is at this point in the story that Arthur Neil, an experienced exorcist gets involved.[201] After 5 months of distilled Christian

---

[191] A point not lost on Anton LaVey according to Hertenstein and Trott. Hertenstein, *Selling*, 428.

[192] Wacker observes that early Pentecostals employed an 'apostate narrative' to celebrate the conversion to Pentecostalism of Roman Catholics. In the case of Irvine and Warnke (among others) we have a dynamic equivalent. Wacker, *Heaven*, 182. Others include the story of Elaine in Brown, *Captives* and G. Trinkle, *Delivered to Declare* (London: Hodder, 1986). The latter is more of a Charismatic version of this narrative (featuring Frank Hammond and John Wimber). Trinkle and Irvine are far more moderate than Warnke and Brown; this probably reflects the respective European and American authorship.

[193] D. Irvine, *From Witchcraft to Christ* (Cambridge: Concordia, 1973).

[194] Warnke, *Satan*. Warnke's co-author Dave Balsiger was a former associate of Morris Cerullo – an interesting link with healing revivalism.

[195] Irvine, *Witchcraft*, 111-117.

[196] Irvine, *Witchcraft*, 64-80, 88-110.

[197] Irvine, *Witchcraft*, 88-95.

[198] Irvine, *Witchcraft*, 99f.

[199] Irvine, *Witchcraft*, 101f. Irvine claims that Lucifer appeared on more than one occasion during Satanist rituals. Irvine, *Witchcraft*, 95.

[200] Irvine, *Witchcraft*, 118-127.

[201] Irvine, *Witchcraft*, 126-144. Neil wrote a couple of books focusing on the broader subject of spiritual warfare with occasional relevance to deliverance ministry. A. Neil,

enthusiasm including numerous sessions with Neil during which forty eight demons were evicted Irvine was finally delivered.[202] At this time she had been mistakenly admitted to a psychiatric unit having been diagnosed with 'religious mania.'[203] It was the spiritual aid she was receiving that proved decisive in her final deliverance rather than the medical and psychiatric help.[204] She was finally discharged from hospital dumbfounding the medical staff with her miraculous recovery. Still feeling troubled Irvine went to the countryside to convalesce. Here she was delivered from further depression and demonic affliction by another vision of Jesus. At the conclusion of the book Irvine tells us of her own deliverance ministry but warns the reader not to be obsessed with the demonic.

The problem with Irvine's warning at the end of the book is that it is completely out of synch with the story she tells. Having shared hair raising tales of the reality and power of the demonic from which she was only delivered by an extremely arduous process of deliverance she then attempts to relativise the significance of the demonic. Once the demonic hordes are exposed to the reader's sight in this way it seems unlikely that they can be marginalised thereafter. The implication of Irvine's experience is that there is an increasing and imperative need for deliverance ministry and (whilst wishing not to appear irresponsible) that appears to be the conclusion Irvine wants us to draw.

Irvine sees the occult revival as clear evidence of the imminent return of Jesus:

> The Word of God plainly states that unseen forces of evil are at work, and that wickedness will wax worse and worse as the coming of the Lord draweth nigh. We do not have to look very far to see that wickedness is far worse today than ever it was, with more and more people in the trap of the occult, with more and more people in the evil web of witchcraft.[205]

Irvine's testimony is extremely powerful within the framework of enthusiastic Christianity. She is able to call upon her own experience to assert the reality and power of both demons and Christ. She then interprets her own experience

---

Aid Us in Our Strife (No location given: Heath, 1989) and A. Neil, *Aid Us in Our Strife: Volume 2* (Newton Abbot: Nova, 1990).

[202] Irvine, *Witchcraft*, 143. D. Irvine, *Set Free to Serve Christ* (Cambridge: Concordia, 1979) 33.

[203] Irvine, *Witchcraft*, 140-143, particularly 142.

[204] Irvine points out that the cure for her psychiatric condition came when she was delivered from a demon called dementia. In the light of her persistent negative comments about the medical help that she received, one cannot but think that she is making a somewhat wider point about the relative merits of psychiatry and deliverance ministry.

[205] Irvine, *Witchcraft*, 179. Cf. D. Irvine, *Spiritual Warfare* (Newton Abbot: Nova, 1992) 29, 89, 102-117.

in line with the imminent eschatology of the worldview of the group within which she operates. What sets Irvine apart from the average practitioner of deliverance ministry is that she not only has expertise and experience in deliverance ministry but she has experienced demonic power first hand. She is a fine example of the aforementioned symbiotic enmity between the occult and enthusiastic Christianity.[206]

Mike Warnke's story follows essentially the same lines as that of Irvine although it is somewhat more extreme in every sense. Warnke was brought up in a Roman Catholic home but quickly fell away from any Christian faith. A college dropout, he was drawn into Satanism via drug addiction and sex orgies.[207] The satanic cult he was involved with were heavily involved in drug smuggling and pushing; Warnke raises the curtain on some unspeakable ritual activities over which he presided, including dismemberment and gang rape.[208] His first contact with Christianity was when the victim of the latter offered him forgiveness.[209] During his involvement with this Satanic cult Warnke visited Salem (where he learnt that some of the witch hunters were actually witches themselves)[210] and later met Anton La Vey (Warnke detected 'a certain phoniness about him') whose Church of Satan was gaining ground.[211]

Having been thrown out of the Satanic cult Warnke decided to join the Navy where he converted to Christianity partially as a result of the influence of two Christian colleagues.[212] His experiences in Satanism led him to conclude that since he knew that Satan was real, 'it stood to reason that his arch-adversary was equally real.'[213] Warnke then details how, as a result of his Christianity, the cult became frightened of him and attacked both him and his fiancé, Sue. Warnke relates that Sue and her flatmate decided to move in order to evade the attentions of the cult members and their supernatural allies:

> The girls found a place to move and decided it would be best to move at night so they would not be seen and no one would know where they had

---

[206] On 'symbiotic enmity' see Hertenstein, *Selling*, 420f.

[207] According to Warnke the orgies were used as bait to attract new recruits to the Satanist cult.

[208] Warnke, *Satan*, 101, 110-112. Whilst Irvine is reasonably restrained in her accounts of Satanic rituals, Warnke is more explicit. Having said that it seems odd that Warnke never appeared to be involved in or even to have heard about SRA if the latter was as rife within Satanism as many would later claim. Indeed the present author cannot find any convert to Christianity who admits to perpetrating SRA which is odd considering the many thousands who claim to have been victims of it.

[209] Warnke, *Satan*, 121f.

[210] Warnke, *Satan*, 96.

[211] Warnke, *Satan*, 102. But see below for the claim that Warnke never actually met La Vey at all.

[212] Warnke, *Satan*, 123-132.

[213] Warnke, *Satan*, 126.

gone. They might as well have moved in the daylight, though, because they were followed by two bats, everywhere they went.

After they were moved in and settled, I noticed there was a big black cat that kept hanging around outside the front gate. It gave me the creeps every time I went by, and I did not tell the girls I thought it was a demon too. They already know about the bats.[214]

Warnke went to become acquainted with Tim LaHaye who informed Warnke of the identity of the *Illuminati*, a clandestine Satanic organisation attempting to secretly control the world. Intriguingly, there is no definitive deliverance episode in Warnke's testimony, however, two experiences are worth noting. Firstly, in his battle against the demonic forces he was taught of the 'power of the blood.' When under Satanic attack a prayer claiming the 'protection of Jesus' name' proved an effective response.[215] Secondly, Warnke received the baptism in the Holy Spirit in 1970 after a tour of duty in Vietnam.[216] This experience not only gave him a release from guilt but also seems to have been the catalyst for a new ministry:

This wonderful elixir or (sic) life made us look around at the loose ends we had left scattered in our lives. We also had a new spiritual burden for young people trapped by occult practices.

By the time Sue and I received the Baptism, I had already given my testimony of how Christ delivered me from occult bondage at Jesus People coffee houses in Coronado, La Mesa, and San Diego in addition to giving it at two Baptist churches and an Assembly of God church.

But now we had a new burden to really dig into the occult scene and learn how to counsel young people who had been caught in occult bondage.[217]

Warnke was allowed to leave the Navy in order to embark upon this new, full time, Christian ministry. The work was given the name 'The Alpha Omega Outreach' partially due to conviction that 'we [Warnke and his wife] are *beginning* a new ministry for the Lord for the *end times*, the anti-occult

---

[214] Warnke, *Satan*, 142.

[215] Warnke, *Satan*, 154f.

[216] Warnke, *Satan*, 172-181.

[217] Warnke, *Satan*, 183.

ministry.'[218] It is clear that an imminent, premillenial eschatology stood at the cradle of this new work.

Like his British counterpart Irvine, Warnke's story was very influential. His first hand experience of supernatural evil was extremely attractive to enthusiastic Christians. It included all the elements listed above including a cosmic conspiracy theory, imminent eschatology, Christian apologetics based upon spiritually immanent experience of evil and, of course, taken at face value it is suggestive of the widespread need for deliverance ministry. *The Satan Seller* was the foundation of Warnke's prominent and lucrative ministry.[219]

Warnke's credibility has been brought into considerable doubt by the publication in 1993 of Hertenstein and Trott's book *Selling Satan*. Having undertaken considerable investigation of Warnke's personal history and his ministry activities they convincingly assert that Warnke fabricated much of the material in *The Satan Seller*.[220] Furthermore, Warnke's lifestyle has been persistently inconsistent with the traditional Christian values he appeared to stand for.[221] At its peak 'Warnke Ministries' generated millions of dollars each year ostensibly to minister to victims of occult abuse.[222] One of the more damaging claims against Warnke is that no such ministry ever took place.[223] Instead Warnke enjoyed a lavish lifestyle; Warnke and his third wife Rose drew salaries of over $230,000 in 1990 alone.[224]

Enthusiastic Christianity's obsession with the occult (and Satanism in particular) and consequent gullibility and vulnerability to fraud was by no means confined to the USA. The UK enjoyed a scandal of its own, though on a much smaller scale, when Derry Knight managed to defraud a group of Christians of £200,000 on the grounds that he would use the money to purchase Satanic cultic items which he would subsequently destroy. He was convicted of 'obtaining' the money 'on false pretences' at Maidstone Crown Court in 1986.[225]

---

[218] Warnke, *Satan*, 202. Second italics added for emphasis.

[219] It is important to understand that Warnke is examined here as prominent example of a wider trend. In America during the early 1970s there were many ex-occultists peddling their testimony within Charismatic/Evangelical circles. Hertenstein and Trott identify several of them and give evidence of the sense of competition between them. Hertenstein, *Selling*, 163-165. Conversely, Irvine's story, although significant within the UK Evangelical scene, is unique.

[220] Hertenstein, *Selling*, 47-83.

[221] Hertenstein, *Selling*, 218-249 In 1993, Warnke made public admission of 'previous ungodliness.' 389. He has been through three divorces and according to Hertentstein and Trott's findings has repeatedly embarked on extra-marital affairs. 337-340.

[222] Hertenstein, *Selling*, 305f.

[223] Hertenstein, *Selling*, 301-307, cf. 342.

[224] Hertenstein, *Selling*, 305.

[225] Wright, *Theology*, 14. Cf. M. Barling, 'Satan, the church and a con-man' in *Renewal* (No 124, August/September 1986) 4-7.

The same enthusiastic impulses lie behind the emergence of a major scare surrounding the extent to which Satanism and witchcraft were penetrating society.[226] Briefly, the eighties and nineties played host to wholesale Satanic panic as police, lawyers, psychologists and social workers became convinced of the existence of widespread Satanic Ritual Abuse (SRA). Although this was largely an American phenomenon there were numerous cases of Satanic panic in Europe.

The evidence for SRA was usually unearthed by psychologists practising a form of hypnosis to discover 'repressed memories'[227]. The normal scenario played out as follows.[228] A subject would seek help for fairly serious psychological disturbance and be diagnosed as suffering from Multiple Personality Disorder (MPD). Some psychologists (almost exclusively American) were convinced that MPD (itself a controversial diagnosis) was triggered as the subject developed new personalities under extreme stress (commonly SRA) during childhood. Hence a methodology was developed for the uncovering and acceptance of these experiences as a key to reintegrating the personality. Often, where a Christian psychologist adopted this methodology (and many of them were enthusiastic Christians) some of the 'personalities' would be identified as demons and exorcised.

The 'memories' that were recovered in this process were of such a gruesome and criminal nature that they inevitably caught the attention of both the media and law enforcement agencies. Legal cases were won and lost, children were removed from the care of certain individuals and organisations and, once again, many enthusiastic Christians seized upon this new evidence of Satanic activity to further their own agendas. At its peak the SRA panic became a major issue in the USA and, to a lesser extent, Europe with many legal cases and much media interest.

The SRA scare began to unravel, as it became clear that there was little hard evidence for the widespread practice of SRA.[229] Victor, on the basis of his own extensive research into the SRA phenomenon, concludes that: 'The dark imaginings of Satanic Cult Crime against children has been constructed out of false testimonies, misinformation and distortions of real incidents.'[230]

---

[226] Early Pentecostals tended to indulge in similar conspiracy theories but at this time their *bête noir* was Roman Catholicism. See Wacker, *Heaven*, 242.

[227] Given that most psychiatric patients likely to be diagnosed as MPD are extremely vulnerable and suggestible, it is not difficult to see how such 'memories' might be 'recovered'.

[228] See Friesen, *Uncovering*, for what follows. Friesen is a typical example of a professional Christian psychologist advocating the diagnosis and treatment of MPD as caused by widespread SRA. Christian practitioners of deliverance ministry sometimes quote him, particularly those with a psychotherapeutic bent. See for example Sandford, *Deliverance*, 166, cf. 199f.

[229] For what follows see Victor, *Satanic* and Arnold, *Spiritual*, 133-137.

[230] Victor, *Satanic*, 130.

There is now general agreement that the SRA panics of the eighties and early nineties were largely unfounded. Whilst there may be some evidence for isolated cases of SRA their incidence is nothing like the wild speculations commonplace at that time. It is clear that enthusiastic Christians were often those most anxious to propagate the myth of widespread SRA for the reasons identified above.[231]

This is one of the most shameful episodes in the history of twentieth century enthusiasm. The refusal to approach the issue of Occultism critically and empathetically led to embarrassing gullibility and the development of widespread yet completely unnecessary 'Satanic Panic' with tragic consequences. For the many children who were removed from their parents as a result of unfounded fears of SRA the effects have been most serious.

Most of the advocates of deliverance ministry in the early 1970s asserted the growth of occultism making it serve their theological agendas. From around 1975 onwards SRA usually featured in their analysis. What is perhaps most alarming is that many deliverance advocates are still asserting the existence of widespread SRA and claim to be treating the victims of it. Much could be said about the failure of many enthusiastic Christians to engage critically with these religious trends. However, it will suffice for this study to observe that enthusiastic Christians have used the 'Easternisation' of the West to further their own objectives, largely by engendering an uncritical reactionary movement. This movement created an environment, which was of course extremely hospitable to the practice of deliverance ministry.

Conclusion: The Significance of EF Deliverance Ministry

EF is an anomalous movement finding its identity in opposition to Charismatic enthusiasm. It so closely resembles the Movement it opposes that it is unlikely to be able to sustain itself in the longer term. The Third Wave Movement represents the first major collapse of EF and it seems likely that the latter will eventually fall away completely.[232]

EF deliverance ministry is a strange beast. It first surfaced among those who rejected the Pentecostal movement and was motivated by their understanding that the Pentecostals were themselves in need of deliverance from the Satanic

---

[231] Ironically the early Pentecostals were themselves unfairly accused of child abuse. Wacker, *Heaven*, 186. Cohn observes that accusation of cannibalistic infanticide are not unusual when new religious groups emerge. N. Cohn, *Europe's Inner Demons* (London: Pimlico, 1993) see index under 'Cannibalistic infanticide, accusations of' (pg 264) for an extensive list of examples

[232] Another good example of this in the UK this time is that of the Keswick Convention. For many years this was self-consciously anti-Charismatic, however, over recent years this antagonism has eroded. Fervent opposition to the Pentecostal / Charismatic Movement, the lifeblood of EF is ebbing away. C. Price and I. Randall, *Transforming Keswick* (Carlisle: OM, 2000) 245-258.

deception which lay behind the Pentecostal teaching and experience. Later, an enthusiastic EF form of deliverance emerged in parallel to Charismatic deliverance, which was in many ways identical to Charismatic deliverance and yet remained in settled opposition to the Charismatic Movement.

Laying aside the irony of its existence, it is important to recognise the evidential value of EF deliverance for the thesis that exorcism is a persistent secondary characteristic of Christian enthusiasm. One might have expected EFs to avoid deliverance ministry on the basis that they would reject all things Charismatic. Actually, despite this rather obvious hurdle, deliverance did surface among EFs therefore lending support to the thesis advanced.

CHAPTER 5

Enthusiastic Sacramental Exorcism

As has already been noted in the consideration of Catholic Charismatic deliverance ministry there was already a long history of Sacramental exorcism within the Catholic tradition at the start of the period in question. What is beyond doubt is that this rite (with the usual exceptions) had largely fallen into disuse at the beginning of the twentieth century under the pressure of Modern rationalism. Equally, it is certain that this was to some extent reversed during the latter half of the twentieth century.

Of course the title of this chapter immediately begs the question as to whether an historic rite of the Church practised by priests in good standing within an institutional ecclesiastical setting could be appropriately understood as 'enthusiastic'. There can be no doubt that a sense of vocation to ministry within an institutionalised church militates against enthusiasm. Nevertheless, one should not conclude that the enthusiastic impulse is therefore excluded from such settings; Knox himself observed that there is a mystical strand of enthusiasm which often finds its home in a Roman Catholic environment.[1] Furthermore, it should not escape the reader's attention that the Charismatic Movement, which Middlemiss has convincingly demonstrated to be typically enthusiastic, penetrated deep into the sacramental churches.

It should immediately be confessed that the figures studied in this chapter conform less readily to the principal driving assumptions of enthusiasm identified in the introduction, in that imminent eschatology is not usually a feature of their writings. This is largely due to the institutional, routinised ecclesiastical setting in which they operate. However, they do (sometimes with a good degree of drama) hold to an assumption of spiritual immanency. In the environment of 'high' sacramentalism, this often leads to the expectation and description of the most outlandish of demonic manifestations and spiritual confrontations. In the 'broader' sacramentalism of the Anglican Church it leads to eccentric rather than dramatic approaches.

In this brief survey of Sacramental Exorcism it will become clear that the historic rite was to enjoy something of a revival during the second half of the twentieth century and that its practice is often surrounded and supported by beliefs and practices typical of enthusiasm and, in many cases, parallel to those

---

[1] Knox, *Enthusiasm*, 581.

already encountered in Charismatic and EF circles.[2] The re-emergence of sacramental exorcism is explored via an examination of practitioners of sacramental exorcism under two broad categories: Roman Catholic sacramental exorcism (Malachi Martin, Ed and Lorraine Warren, Scott Peck and Gabriele Amorth); and sacramental exorcism within the Anglican Church (Dom Robert Petitpierre, Christopher Neil-Smith, Michael Perry and Martin Israel). Malachi Martin and The Warren's significance lie in their extreme enthusiasm which pushed them to the margins of the institutional Church. Scott Peck, heavily influenced by Martin was America's best known psychologist so his books advocating exorcism are of great importance. Gabriele Amorth's ministry of exorcism sat squarely (though in a degree of tension) within the Roman Catholic establishment; he was the appointed exorcist for the diocese of Rome. Petitpierre was recognised as the most authoritative figure in Anglican exorcism / deliverance during the seventies and eighties. In many respects Perry inherited this mantle. Christopher Neil-Smith enjoyed a degree of media profile as an 'expert' exorcist whilst Israel represents the extreme of eccentric Anglican exorcism. Preceding the study of these figures and their approach to sacramental exorcism attention is directed toward early twentieth century exorcism and the significance, for this study, of the film *The Exorcist*.

Sacramental Exorcism Prior to 1970

As is the case within the Charismatic and EF milieus, examples of enthusiastic sacramental exorcism emerge far more frequently in the last three decades of the twentieth century. In this necessarily brief study, the emphasis is placed upon these examples in order to demonstrate that late century enthusiastic sacramental exorcism emerged to a modest degree of prominence in a parallel manner to the emergence of enthusiastic Charismatic and EF deliverance ministry.

Nevertheless, a few words about sacramental exorcism prior to 1970 are in order. It is important to note that within sacramental circles there was an existing liturgy of exorcism which, in theory at least, all sacramentalists accepted.[3] Therefore, there was an existing authority to which practitioners of exorcism might appeal. Conversely, one must acknowledge that exorcism was largely marginalised by the established sacramental denominations and the rite of exorcism certainly was not generally practised.[4]

---

[2] Writing in 1999, A Findlay reflects that both the Roman Catholic and Anglican Churches 'have experienced a recrudescence of belief in recent times in possession and the efficacy of exorcism.' Findlay, *Demons*, 199.

[3] On the development of the Roman Catholic ritual of exorcism see Findlay, *Demons*, 121f.

[4] Cuneo notes that even in the mid-nineties there was only one accredited priest-exorcist in the United States. Cuneo, *American*, 309.

The situation prior to the 1970s was generally, therefore one of theoretical acceptance and practical rejection of exorcism within most sacramental circles. Of course there were exceptions, particularly within Anglican sacramentalism, but the general picture is one of stifling institutionalisation which was of course not conducive to the innately enthusiastic rite of exorcism.

Sacramental Exorcism and *The Exorcist*

When one thinks of the historic, sacramental rite of exorcism one cannot but think of the 1974 film *The Exorcist* which was undoubtedly one of the twentieth century's most powerful pieces of cinema. Whilst Charismatics and EFs are keen to distance themselves from the type of exorcism portrayed in this film, sacramental exorcists often affirm it as a fair representation of what they encounter in an exorcism. *The Exorcist* was based on a novel by William Peter Blatty purportedly based on real events. This film genre has proved surprisingly popular and one might be forgiven for speaking of an enduring cultural obsession with gothic forms of exorcism and associated demonology.

The Exorcist depicts the exorcism of a young girl called Regan which develops into a life or death struggle for the priests concerned; in fact, both of the exorcists lose their lives in their struggle to free Regan. Blatty deliberately spiced up the demonic manifestations reported from the exorcism on which he based the book and it is certainly these that proved the major attraction at the box office. For the purposes of this study they are the first indication of a profound difference between sacramental exorcism and the various forms of deliverance ministry considered above.

Most enthusiasts are restorationists,[5] that is to say that they look back to a golden age of the church and desire to restore the perceived glory of that time to present day church. For Charismatics and EFs alike that golden age is perceived to be the earliest church presented in the Acts of the Apostles. Consequently, their over-riding aim (in deliverance as in everything else) is to mimic the early church. For enthusiastic sacramentalists the hankered after halcyon era is more likely the middle ages when the Catholic Church reigned supreme in matters spiritual and (via the Emporer) temporal or perhaps more simply the pristine pre-Modern theology and ecclesial practice of pre-Vatican II Catholicism.[6] Consequently, while Charismatic and EF deliverance ministry is generally presented in terms of a decisive pneumatic (neo apostolic) power encounter with no real doubt as to the outcome and no significant danger to the exorcist who is in proper relationship to Christ, enthusiastic sacramental

---

[5] The enthusiast 'has before his eyes a picture of the early Church, visibly penetrated with supernatural influences; and nothing less will serve him as a model'. Knox, *Enthusiasm*, 2.

[6] 'Fundamentalist' Roman Catholism is marked by a suspicion of Vatican II. Malachi Martin viewed it as a fundamental betrayal of traditional Catholicism.

exorcism is at the extreme presented in terms of a supernatural life or death struggle amidst eerie phenomena that would not be out of place in a gothic horror film such as *The Exorcist*.

Cuneo, the only scholar to make a serious attempt to analyse exorcism and deliverance in socio-historic terms, attributes the rise of sacramental exorcism (and to a lesser extent deliverance as well) primarily to the creation of a conducive climate by the popular media,[7] pre-eminently via *The Exorcist*. It seems more likely that it was the general revival of interest in the occult that actually lay behind both the rise of interest in exorcism and the popularity of films like *The Exorcist* however, the film certainly made a massive impact, not least because of the sensational depictions of lurid demonic manifestations.[8] Perhaps the censorious reaction of various Christian groups to the film helped create an aura of credibility around the film.

Practitioners of Enthusiastic Sacramental Exorcism

Malachi Martin (1921-1999)

Malachi Martin is undoubtedly the most colourful character in the revival of enthusiastic sacramental exorcism; an intriguing and mysterious figure, he exhibits classic hallmarks of enthusiasm including an emphasis upon imminent spirituality, conspiracy theories[9] and eschatological speculation. He has published several books a number of which vilify the post-Vatican II Roman Catholic Church; a brief biography will help to put his advocacy of exorcism in proper context.

BIOGRAPHY

Born in Ireland, Martin became a Jesuit at age 18 and then underwent a rigorous education. From 1960 he taught in Rome at the Pontifical Institute and in time became close to Pope John XXIII. Only four years later he felt compelled to leave his teaching post and shortly afterwards made a break with the Society of Jesus. He was also released from his ordination vows (with the exception of a commitment to celibacy), and moved to Paris before settling down in New York. This much is universally accepted though the reasons why he left Rome and his ecclesial status thereafter are hotly contested. The arguments cannot be rehearsed here except to note that even an ardent admirer

---

[7] Cuneo, *American*, 325-337.

[8] Precisely what that impact was is almost impossible to assess. At first glance one might assume that only a fool could take the film seriously, however, no less a figure than Scott Peck cites it as formative in his interest in exorcism (see below).

[9] Cuneo describes him as 'American Catholicism's foremost connoisseur of conspiracy' Cuneo, *American*, 35.

like Peck accepts that Martin's behaviour was far from exemplary.[10] Martin became an influential critic of the Catholic hierarchy, a purveyor of grand conspiracy theories involving the Free Masons, the Vatican, the Mafia, global financial institutions and widespread (Satanic) priestly sexual abuse. Cuneo takes a fairly dim view of Martin's reliability, describing his books as 'religious potboilers' and suggesting that Martin's motives were mainly financial, which has evinced a predictably furious response from Martin's supporters.

HOSTAGE TO THE DEVIL[11]

In 1976 Martin published *Hostage to the Devil* purporting to be a faithful account of 'the possession and exorcism of five contemporary Americans'; Martin assures the reader that each of the five were known to him personally.[12] This book undoubtedly had a major effect on the credibility of sacramental exorcism; no less a figure than Scott Peck, America's premier psychologist at the time, was greatly influenced by it and came to a belief in demons and the efficacy of exorcism himself (see below). In 2005 he retrospectively described the by now dead Martin as the 'greatest expert on the subject of possession and exorcism in the English-speaking world.'[13] Martin's status as an authority on the subject was confirmed when he appeared alongside Erwin Prange on the Oprah Winfrey show on April 30 1987 as an expert in the field of Satanism and exorcism.[14]

Firstly, it should be noted that *Hostage to the Devil* is a truly riveting read; Martin is a gifted writer and the narrative style he adopts is a very powerful medium for conveying his approach to exorcism. Martin believed that possession, although rare was a present reality and that the cost of freeing a victim of such was very great:

> The exorcist is the centrepiece of every exorcism. On him depends everything. He has nothing personal to gain. But in exorcism he risks literally everything that he values… every exorcist must engage in a one-to-one confrontation, personal and bitter, with pure evil. Once engaged, the exorcism cannot be called off. There will and must always be a victor and a vanquished. And no matter what the outcome, the contact is in part fatal for the exorcist. He must consent to a dreadful and irreparable pillage of his deepest self. Something dies in him. Some part of his

---

[10] M. S. Peck, *Glimpses of the Devil* (New York: Free Press, 2005) 251.

[11] M. Martin, *Hostage to the Devil* (New York: Reader's Digest, 1976). Note that subsequent references are to the 1992 edition.

[12] Martin later informed Cuneo that he had been present as assistant exorcist at each of the case studies. It seems strange that he did not say this at the time. Cuneo, *American*, 43.

[13] Peck, *Glimpses*, 11.

[14] Cuneo, *American*, 80f.

humanness will wither from such close contact with the opposite of all humanness – the essence of evil; and it is rarely if ever revitalised. No return will be made to him for his loss.[15]

Before leading the reader through his five case studies, Martin composes 'a brief handbook of exorcism'. He first addresses the thorny issue of diagnosing possession which he candidly admits is not straightforward. Martin asserts that the candidate for exorcism should be thoroughly scrutinized by medical professionals prior to any diagnosis of possession. Since 'there is usually no one physical or psychical aberration or abnormality in the possessed person that we cannot explain by a known or possible physical cause'[16] the Church must evaluate medical assessments and other factors from a faith perspective.[17] The other factors include pre-eminently the presence or otherwise of 'a peculiar revulsion to symbols and truths of religion [which] is always and without exception a mark of the possessed person'[18] and various phenomena such as:

> the inexplicable stench; freezing temperature; telepathic powers…; a peculiarly unlined or completely smooth or stretched skin, or unusual distortion of the face…; "possessed gravity"…; levitation…; violent smashing of furniture constant opening and slamming of doors, tearing of fabric in the vicinity of the possessed, without a hand laid on them and so on.[19]

Where a case with no obvious medical explanation converges with some or all of these characteristic factors then 'the decision will usually be to proceed and try Exorcism.'[20] Demonic possession should be viewed as a process rather than a static, instantaneously incurred condition;[21] taken to its conclusion it will result in 'perfect possession' which is Martin considers to be, in all likelihood, irreversible.[22]

The exorcist who should normally be a priest outstanding for 'his qualities

---

[15] Martin, *Hostage*, 10. MacNutt unsurprisingly considered this an overly pessimistic view and told Martin so. Cuneo, *American*, 197. MacNutt believed that the problem was that Martin was ministering deliverance without the fullness of the Holy Spirit, a predictable Charismatic critique MacNutt, *Deliverance*, 274-277.

[16] Martin, *Hostage*, 12.

[17] Martin, *Hostage*, 13. In a later section of the book Martin specifies the path by which a person becomes possessed. Martin, *Hostage*, 435-443. A key stage of this process involves the victim of possession to some extent acquiescing to control 'by a force or presence he clearly feels is alien to himself'. Martin, *Hostage*, 436.

[18] Martin, *Hostage*, 13.

[19] Martin, *Hostage*, 13.

[20] Martin, *Hostage*, 13.

[21] Martin, *Hostage*, xx.

[22] Martin, *Hostage*, xxiiif., 441.

of moral judgement, personal behaviour and religious beliefs'[23] should only proceed having procured 'official Church sanction for he is acting in an official capacity, and any power he has over Evil Spirit can only come from those officials who belong to the substance of Jesus' Church... Sometimes a diocesan priest will take on an exorcism himself without asking the bishop, but all such cases known to me have failed.'[24]

The exorcism is 'usually [performed in] the home of the possessed person, for generally it is only relatives or closest friends who will give care and love in the dreadful circumstances associated with possession.'[25] Due to the dramatic and dangerous supernatural manifestations that occur during an exorcism Martin offers advice on making the location as safe as possible for those involved.[26] Any unnecessary items should be removed and a few sacred items should be placed upon a small table.[27] The possessed person will often be physically restrained, possibly via the use of a straightjacket.[28]

The exorcist should be joined by a younger priest in order to train the latter in exorcism; the assistant's role is to provide support and to act as substitute for the exorcist 'if he dies, collapses, flees, is physically or emotionally battered beyond endurance – and all have happened during exorcisms.'[29] The priests should be accompanied by a doctor and a team of (usually four) lay assistants. The team needs to be comprised of people who are fairly unshockable:

> The exorcist must be as certain as possible beforehand that his assistants will not be weakened or overcome by obscene behaviour or by language foul beyond their imagining; they cannot blanch at blood, excrement, urine; they must be able to take awful personal insults and be prepared to have their darkest secrets screeched in public in front of their

---

[23] Martin, *Hostage*, 14. Cuneo quotes Scott Peck to the effect that Martin was to have played role of assistant exorcist to the latter in two exorcisms despite the fact that Peck was not ordained or even a practising Catholic. Cuneo, *American*, 71.

[24] Martin, *Hostage*, 12. Cuneo reports that Martin came to believe that this Episcopal permission was 'beside the point'. Cuneo, *American*, 44. It is unthinkable that Martin was unaware of deliverance forms of exorcism. It is surprising that he does not pass any comment on them although one can imagine that he would (at this early stage at least) consider them 'beyond the pale'. Peck quotes 'one of his mentors' (probably Martin) to the effect 'The charismatics generally are not dealing with true demons, but occasionally they catch one.' Peck, *Lie*, 192.

[25] Martin, *Hostage*, 14.

[26] Martin, *Hostage*, 14f. The manifestations he describes are certainly more violent than anything described by Charismatics and EFs.

[27] Martin, *Hostage*, 15.

[28] Martin, *Hostage*, 16.

[29] Martin, *Hostage*, 15.

companions. These are routine happenings during exorcism.[30]

The team should be prepared for the exorcism to last at least a few hours and possibly a lot longer.

The official liturgy of the Church should only be regarded as a 'framework'; 'in fact, the conduct of an exorcism is left very much up to the exorcist.'[31] In spite of this, Martin finds general agreement among exorcists that every exorcism will usually proceed along a common course. He quotes a colleague who identified the stages as 'Presence (a clear yet inexplicable awareness of possession that transcends the symptoms discussed previously), Pretense (the evil spirit will seek to disguise its presence and its name; the exorcist must endeavour to uncover the demon and get it to reveal its name), Breakpoint (when the evil spirit begins to manifest openly), Voice (the evil spirit speaks in an alien and confusing, disturbing 'babel' – the exorcist must still the 'Voice' by means of a challenge 'with his own will, but always in the name and by the authority of Jesus and his Church.'), Clash (the exorcist locks wills with the spirit and as much as possible force the spirit to reveal itself) and Expulsion.'[32] Martin employs the full range of his not inconsiderable literary skills to graphically picture the final stages of an exorcism:

> All sense may suddenly seem nonsense. Hopelessness is confirmed as the only hope. Death and cruelty and contempt are normal. Anything comely or beautiful is an illusion. Nothing, it seems, was ever right in the world of man. He is in an atmosphere more bizarre than Bedlam.

> If, in spite of his emotions and his imagination and his body – all trapped at once in pain and anguish – if, in spite of all this, the will of the exorcist holds in the *Clash*, what he does is to approach the final function in this situation as an authorized human witness for Jesus. By no power of his, on account of no privilege of his own, he calls finally on the evil spirit to desist, to be dispossessed, to depart and to leave the possessed person.

And if the exorcism is successful, this is what happens.[33]

The exorcist will pay a heavy personal price for their ministry; the trauma they carry can only be shared with God.[34]

---

[30] Martin, *Hostage*, 16.

[31] Martin, *Hostage*, 17.

[32] Martin, *Hostage*, 17-24.

[33] Martin, *Hostage*, 23.

[34] Martin, *Hostage*, 23f.

There follows the five sensational accounts of possession and exorcism selected from the many available to Martin 'because... they are dramatic illustrations of the way in which personal and intelligent evil moves cunningly along the lines of contemporary fads and interests.'[35] The factors causative of possession in the five accounts are respectively nihilism, rationalism, gender confusion, individualism and an attempt to demythologise spirituality.[36]

Narratives of possession and exorcism present a golden opportunity to justify theological perspectives. Martin's case studies certainly add ballast to his pre-Vatican II outlook. One demoniac reacted with 'extreme violence when a rosary or crucifix was put to her lips';[37] a priest became possessed when he adopts religious practices consistent with Vatican II and Teilhardian theology;[38] a newly exorcised demoniac chants the Ave Maria in the traditional Greek;[39] and an evil spirit reacts negatively to an icon of the Virgin.[40]

SIXTEEN YEARS LATER

The passing of time certainly did not dampen Martin's enthusiasm. In his preface to the 1992 edition of *Hostage to the Devil*, he asserts that American cultural conditions are most propitious for the work of evil spirits:

> To a far greater degree than most of us could have imagined fifteen years ago, a favourable climate for the occurrence of demonic Possession has developed as the normal condition of our lives...

> Now in America of the 1990s, there is little question of demonic Possession as entertainment. Among families everywhere and at every level of society, there is instead a justifiable fear. Most of all this fear is for children. And in point of fact, there are few families not already affected in some way by Satanism.[41]

Martin goes on to affirm that SRA is a present and widespread phenomenon in America: 'Ritualistic Satanism and its inevitable consequence, demonic Possession, are now part and parcel of the atmosphere of American life.'[42] Conversely, diminishing belief in Satan, even amongst the Catholic faithful, is

---

[35] Martin, *Hostage*, 24.

[36] Martin, *Hostage*, 24f. Note that Martin effectively demonises certain philosophical and theological emphases that he is opposed to.

[37] Martin, *Hostage*, 59.

[38] Martin, *Hostage*, 83-171.

[39] Martin, *Hostage*, 166.

[40] Martin, *Hostage*, 278.

[41] Martin, *Hostage*, xif.

[42] Martin, *Hostage*, xiii..

opening the door to Possession since 'the belief that he does not exist at all is an enormous advantage that he has never enjoyed to such a degree. It is the ultimate camouflage. Not to believe in evil is not to be armed against it.'[43]

Martin observes that the many Catholic bishops are antipathetic to the practice of exorcism. Consequently an 'Exorcism underground' has emerged and this underground is hard at work. Martin states that a 750 percent increase in exorcisms took place between the early 1960s and the mid-1970s; apparently '800 to 1,300 major Exorcisms, and some thousands of minor Exorcisms are performed.'[44]

Malachi Martin stands alongside Derek Prince and Jessie Penn-Lewis as the dominant figures of the revival of the three streams of enthusiastic deliverance / exorcism identified in this study. Whether Martin is a reliable witness is open to serious question and he certainly had his share of critics but his influence was undoubtedly significant.

Ed and Lorraine Warren

Like others in the field, Ed and Lorraine Warren's ministry of exorcism came to wider attention in the 1970s although by that time they had been working in the field for thirty years.[45] In collaboration with them Gerald Brittle wrote a book about their ministry entitled *The Demonologist*[46] which was first published in 1980. They came to a degree of public awareness as a result of their involvement in a case upon which the macabre film *The Amityville Horror* was based.[47]

The Warrens were practising Roman Catholics and their understanding of exorcism is certainly sacramental, however, they accept that this is only one form of exorcism, and others, including those practised by adherents of non-Christian religions, may be equally successful. Their experience and understanding of demonic activity is the most fantastic and medieval considered in this study.

Brittle is certainly not reticent in asserting the significance of the Warrens'

---

[43] Martin, *Hostage*, xv.

[44] Martin, *Hostage*, xviii. He gives no source for these figures.

[45] After Ed's discharge from the Navy at the end of World War II, the Warrens decided on a career that combined their interest in painting and the paranormal; they decided to paint haunted houses. G. D. Brittle, *The Demonologist* (Lincoln: BackinPrint, 2002) 19. They became aware of the demonic when they came across sinister cases of paranormal activity which could not be accounted for by the presence of deceased human spirits.

[46] Brittle, *Demonologist*. The Demonologist in question is presumably Ed Warren.

[47] The house was owned at the time by George and Kathy Lutz who were later to receive 'a blessing of deliverance' from Christopher Neil-Smith. Their experience of the house have 'yielded a best-selling book and no fewer than nine films.' *The Daily Telegraph* (May 12, 2006) B17.

work: They are 'called in because in professional circles, they are considered to be perhaps this country's [USA] leading authorities on the subject of spirits and supernatural phenomena.'[48] They claim to have 'investigated over three thousand cases of supernatural disturbances.'[49] Ed functions as the 'demonologist', diagnosing the problem in each case and calling in an exorcist where the problem is demonic in origin; Lorraine's contribution is to assist Ed by virtue of her being 'a penetrating clairvoyant and light-trance medium' which is understood as the spiritual gift of discernment of spirits.[50]

Claiming that over half the cases of spiritual disturbance they encounter are demonic in origin,[51] the Warrens have constructed a clear and unique three stage understanding of the demonic's strategy in proceeding towards the possession of their victim(s). At first they *infest* the home of the intended victim(s), then they *oppress* those living there through a variety of outlandish and fearful manifestations of their presence, breaking the will of the victim(s) until they are ripe for *possession*.[52] This process is not uncommon and presents a terrifying prospect for those subjected to it; like Malachi Martin, the Warrens paint a dramatic picture of the activity of demons.

Infestation will only occur when one of two conditions occur; the victim(s) must either *invite* the demons to infest their home, perhaps unconsciously or they must *attract* the demons through unnatural behaviour.[53] Demonic activity at this stage will be disturbing but comparatively harmless aimed at producing 'fear – through incidents of inexplicable phenomena.'[54] Initially the demon(s) may cause unexplained noises such as knocking or footsteps and temperature changes in certain areas of the house which will generate a sense of an unearthly presence. As this stage advances the activity becomes more dramatic; the sounds will be louder, objects may be moved around in a deliberately mischievous manner, electrical and mechanical devices may behave erratically. Children and animals, more sensitive to demonic presence, may become inexplicably terrified.[55] The sense of evil presence may become palpable even at this early stage.[56]

'Although the terror experienced during infestation is bad enough, it's really

---

[48] Brittle, *Demonologist*, 2.

[49] Brittle, *Demonologist*, 2.

[50] Brittle, *Demonologist*, 7. This equation of psychic sensitivity with the so called 'gift of discernment' is not unusual in sacramental schemas.

[51] Brittle, *Demonologist*, 57.

[52] Brittle, *Demonologist*, 99.

[53] Brittle, *Demonologist*, 99f.

[54] Brittle, *Demonologist*, 104.

[55] Brittle, *Demonologist*, 106f. Apparently, these manifestations may equally indicate the presence of a disembodied human spirit. The difference is that in the latter cases activity is likely to be arbitrary and chaotic; where demons are involved there is evidence of a strategy behind the activity. Brittle, *Demonologist*, 107.

[56] Brittle, *Demonologist*, 107.

only a warm-up to the pandemonium that's liable to happen with the next stage.'[57] Once the demon has become 'entrenched' the activity will develop into a campaign of *oppression*, either 'a bombardment of incredible phenomena, or... a surreptitious psychological attack, dedicated to the complete domination of the victim's will.'[58] Specifically, the demon seeks to 'dehumanize' its victim to the point where they become ripe for the final stage - *possession*. The specific activity will include manifestations that may make the house inhabitable although it seems that in some cases these will follow the victim even if he or she leaves the home in question. The manifestations[59] themselves will be utterly terrifying and on occasion fatal for the victim without even proceeding to possession.[60] It is vital for the subject(s) of this attack to retain 'personal control' otherwise possession becomes a real possibility.[61]

Where the victim's will is broken by this oppression the 'individual is then invaded by one, or even a multitude, of possessing entities.'[62] The Warrens distinguish between demons who may be involved in the external aspects of the first two phases of infestation and oppression and devils ('a higher order of angel before the Fall') which tend to get involved in the internal oppression of the victim's personality and ultimately their possession. [63] Once the victim is possessed 'the spirit will... either seek to mutilate the body it inhabits – as was portrayed in *The Exorcist* – or take off on a spree of wild physical mayhem. The demonic spirit isn't content simply to possess the body; its mind is fixed on death.'[64] More seriously still, the ultimate purpose of a possessing devil is to dominate a person's soul.[65]

---

[57] Brittle, *Demonologist*, 107.

[58] Brittle, *Demonologist*, 108.

[59] These include 'disgusting smells, ghoulish moans, bloodcurdling screams, knockings, rappings, poundings, heavy breathing and magical whisperings, disembodied footsteps, rapid changes in room temperature, ghastly visions, and so on. When a disturbance really gets going, say into what we call a diabolical siege, then you get phenomena like materializations, de-materializations, teleportations, levitations – of both people and objects, strangling sensations about the neck, arms being grabbed from behind, cuts, burns, gouges, wounds, sudden critical illnesses, blinding headaches, vulgarities and blasphemies written on the wall by unseen hands, spontaneous outbreaks of fire, inhuman voices calling on the phone, demon faces showing up on the television screen... Sometimes the victims are held prisoner inside their own home... even killed, by these forces of inhumanity and evil.' Brittle, *Demonologist*, 109.

[60] Brittle, *Demonologist*, 109.

[61] Brittle, *Demonologist*, 108.

[62] Brittle, *Demonologist*, 164.

[63] Brittle, *Demonologist*, 121f. The Warrens are extremely unclear about this. Other passages in the book appear to contradict this point. See, for example, Brittle, *Demonologist*, 164.

[64] Brittle, *Demonologist*, 167.

[65] Brittle, *Demonologist*, 195f. The Warrens quote Christopher Neil-Smith to support this assertion although he is actually making a point that runs counter to their

Given the above, how do the Warrens respond when asked to intervene in a suspected case of demonic presence? Firstly, there is the matter of diagnosis. Usually Ed interviews those subject to the attack whilst Lorraine uses her psychic awareness; between these two different approaches they are able to ascertain whether the problem is demonic.[66] Once a demonic presence has been diagnosed in this way it must be flushed out. Apparently the demon may not be keen to reveal its presence and this may mean that Ed has to engage in what he terms 'religious provocation.'[67] This will involve the use of religious items such as a crucifix or holy water to cause the spirit sufficient discomfort that it will manifest itself in order to intimidate Ed into leaving or perhaps to cause him physical harm.[68] The Warrens do not claim to be exorcists; Ed might be able to 'take care of the matter' where he catches the demonic infestation at an early stage, otherwise the 'religious provocation' is mainly designed to throw up enough evidence to justify a Catholic exorcism.[69] If he does manage to evict a demon, Ed still recommends a blessing from a 'clergyman' and an attempt to 'keep up an emotional atmosphere that does not attract such entities.'[70]

Where a devil has successfully possessed a person, the only answer is a full-blown solemn exorcism.[71] Specifically, these are performed where 'an inhuman spirit has possessed a person's body and soul, and that soul has *got* to be saved.'[72] In these cases there is invariably a particular spirit at work:

It is a black day indeed when this ritual must be performed. Because if it has been determined necessary to perform a major exorcism, church authorities will have so judged after long and diligent deliberation that a human being has been possessed by that which calls itself Legion. And this is no frivolous decision...[73]

Being Roman Catholics themselves, the Warrens usually work with Catholic

---

understanding of the process of demonic activity. Brittle, *Demonologist*, 195. The general tenor of the Warrens' ministry is certainly at serious odds with Neil-Smith's understanding.

[66] Brittle, *Demonologist*, 69. According to Ed, Lorraine's gift of discernment has proved accurate on every occasion: 'Lorraine's an excellent clairvoyant and she's never been wrong about the nature of a spirit that's present.' Brittle, *Demonologist*, 50.

[67] Brittle, *Demonologist*, 77.

[68] Brittle, *Demonologist*, 78-80.

[69] Brittle, *Demonologist*, 77. Ed is not averse to commanding demons to leave the homes of those they are oppressing using the threat of an imminent exorcism to encourage an early departure. Brittle, *Demonologist*, 77-80.

[70] Brittle, *Demonologist*, 81.

[71] Brittle, *Demonologist*, 195-206. The Warrens do not state this explicitly but it appears to be the only legitimate interpretation of these pages.

[72] Brittle, *Demonologist*, 196.

[73] Brittle, *Demonologist*, 196. The logic of this statement may suggest that the Warrens could envisage a situation where a possession could be terminated by means of a minor exorcism. This would, however, run counter to their statements on the previous page.

priests however they are open to exorcism being successfully practiced by any 'ordained Christian clergyman'.[74] Despite their chilling and idiosyncratic depiction of diabolic possession, the Warrens place a great deal of faith in the Roman Ritual's rite of exorcism which, they claim, evicts around six in ten possessing devils on first reading.[75] A substantial minority of exorcisms prove difficult; the victim will display varying degrees of abnormal and disturbing behaviour and in some cases supernatural phenomena not unlike those portrayed in *The Exorcist* will occur:

> In at least six cases, I have seen the possessed levitate off the bed. I have seen the victim's hair yanked out of the scalp by invisible hands. I have seen the possessed individual throw up *gallons* of putrid, disgusting substances, usually smelling of excrement. I have seen psychic burns and slashes show up all over the body of the possessed, causing frantic, painful screaming when the individual is not unconscious during the ritual.

> In the case of a thirteen-year-old girl who was possessed by an Incubus, we saw teeth marks appear on the girl's arm... I have also seen the demonic bloat up the body of the possessed individual to twice its normal size. The head, the torso, the arms, the fingers, the legs, the whole body was so bloated and disfigured that the skin began to split open and ooze blood; we actually thought the individual was going to explode![76]

Despite the horrific nature of these manifestations, they are only short term. Once the exorcism has successfully evicted the devil any physical effects simply fade away leaving behind an atmosphere of 'peace and tranquillity'.[77] After such a successful exorcism (and Brittle does not record any that were unsuccessful) the devil(s)/demon(s) may seek to deal out reprisals to those involved.[78] Hence Ed Warren believes that the exorcist has the most dangerous job in the world, his own role (that of demonologist) following in second place.[79]

Ed Warren is confident that he could prove the existence of ghosts and evil spirits in a court of law.[80] Furthermore he asserts that the various phenomena he has encountered are so dramatic and self-verifying that they 'could not have

---

[74] Brittle, *Demonologist*, 200.

[75] Brittle, *Demonologist*, 203.

[76] Brittle, *Demonologist*, 204f.

[77] Brittle, *Demonologist*, 205.

[78] Brittle, *Demonologist*, 154.

[79] Brittle, *Demonologist*, 220.

[80] Brittle, *Demonologist*, 14.

been influenced by what we believe.'[81] Moreover they dismiss those who 'philosophize about the demonic as being a purely psychological event, or say it's not even there at all': 'these people have never witnessed the phenomena themselves, or they wouldn't make such empty statements. Just *once*, they need the experience of walking into a home where these inhuman spirits have manifested.'[82] This by now familiar appeal to imminent spirituality establishes the Warrens' enthusiasm. The extremity and indeed arrogant naivety of their claim to pure objectivity is consistent with, though more obvious than, the usual appeal to spiritually immanent interpretations of experience and events made by religious enthusiasts. The Warrens are at least straightforward and honest and one must concede that the demonic manifestations recorded by the Warrens would, if witnessed exactly as they are recorded, be paradigm shattering for the sceptical observer. Middlemiss is of course right to assert that experience is usually equivocal and therefore an unreliable foundation for belief in isolation from other factors. Nevertheless, the Warrens make the typical and instinctive enthusiastic play in presenting their experiences in such a way that the reader is forced to either surrender to the force of their experience or assert dishonesty. In the final analysis the reader must conclude that the Warrens like the other more extreme examples considered in this study have presented their experiences so as to batter the reader into credulity. They even go so far as to suggest that the evidence for demonic activity is deliberately covered up and so one can only find out about it through first hand experience.[83] Like most conspiracy theories this unprovable contention is of course a crude apologetic manoeuvre designed to explain why their experiences are so out of step with the everyday experience of the reader.

Unusually, the Warrens do not use their experiences as apologetic value for Christianity; surprisingly they appear to advocate religious pluralism. They have collaborated on exorcisms performed by adherents of other faiths[84] and it appears that their preference for the Roman Catholic ritual is merely the choice appropriate for them as Roman Catholics.[85] This begs a host of questions which are largely unanswered. One implication that is clear is that the factors that cause demonic activity are vague ('negative or patently unnatural things'[86]) in order to span the varying faith traditions, rather than the specific terminology that would be used if the subject were to be studied through the lens of a particular faith.

---

[81] Brittle, *Demonologist*, 37.

[82] Brittle, *Demonologist*, 37

[83] Brittle, *Demonologist*, 138.

[84] Brittle, *Demonologist*, 201. Ed is sufficiently open to other religious perspectives to be receptive to the possibility of reincarnation. Brittle, *Demonologist*, 182.

[85] Nevertheless, they do assert that Jesus was the greatest exorcist and that it is only in his name that one can find protection from evil spirits. Brittle, *Demonologist*, 200, 87.

[86] Brittle, *Demonologist*, 99.

The Warrens present the demonic as a routine part of their daily experience, not least due to many cursed objects that they have in their house which seem to serve as a magnet for their activity.[87] Ed explains that they have to retain these macabre items since destroying them could cause further trouble and it is often not safe to leave them with the victims.[88] In one particularly disturbing case he experienced demonic activity through a black lace veil that had been used in a ceremony of marriage to Satan.[89] This macabre 'Occult Museum' also contains the records of the many cases in which the Warrens have been involved.[90]

Prior to visiting the Warrens, Cuneo understandably wondered whether he would find tell-tale signs of dissemblance.[91] He could uncover nothing of the sort: 'Not only was there no nudging and winking, the Warrens gave every indication of being completely sincere in their beliefs and mission.'[92] The Warrens' claimed experiences are among the most, if not the most, outlandish and improbable considered by this study. Assuming they are serious, they are either crooked, deluded or the world is a very much stranger place than most are inclined to believe.

M. Scott Peck

Psychologist Scott Peck became a household name after writing *The Road Less Travelled*[93] which was first published in 1978. Advocates of exorcism and, by implication, deliverance received an unexpected but considerable fillip when his next book *People of the Lie*,[94] published in 1983, espoused an orthodox Christian demonology, including belief in a personal devil and possession. Furthermore, the by now openly Christian, Peck claimed to have gained first hand experience by participating in two exorcisms himself.[95] His approach to possession and exorcism comprises only a part of this book, the whole being a wider study of evil. Recently, in 2005, Peck published *Glimpses of the Devil*. Dedicated to Malachi Martin, this book comprises thorough case histories of the two aforementioned exorcisms.

Whilst *People* received a muted response and was not successful in its stated aim of putting possession and exorcism on the agenda for serious consideration by the medical establishment, it did provide powerful cognitive underpinning

---

[87] Brittle, *Demonologist*, 168.

[88] Brittle, *Demonologist*, 168.

[89] Brittle, *Demonologist*, 169-174.

[90] Brittle, *Demonologist*, 168.

[91] Cuneo, *American*, 54.

[92] Cuneo, *American*, 54f.

[93] M. S. Peck, *The Road Less Travelled* (London: Arrow, 1990).

[94] M. S. Peck, *People of the Lie* (New York: Touchstone, 1985).

[95] Peck, *People*, 183.

for those already involved in exorcism / deliverance.[96] Peck clearly favours sacramental exorcism and explicitly criticises Charismatic deliverance;[97] one does not need to agree with his prescription to accept his diagnosis.

Peck's original interest in possession and exorcism was piqued after viewing *The Exorcist* and reading *Hostage to the Devil*.[98] He contacted Malachi Martin who started to pass cases to him. Peck recollects that the third person passed to him in this way was in his view possessed, not by just any demon, but by Satan 'itself'.[99] Peck described his newfound belief in Satan as a 'conversion' and in this context made some comments of significance for this study:

I don't hope to convince the reader of Satan's reality. Conversion to a belief in God generally requires some kind of actual encounter – a personal experience – with the living God. Conversion to a belief in Satan is no different. I had read Martin's book before witnessing my first exorcism, and while I was intrigued, I was hardly convinced of the devil's reality. It was another matter after I had personally met Satan face-to-face. There is no way I can translate my experience into your experience. It is my intent, however, that, as a result of my experience, closed-minded readers will become more open-minded in relation to the reality of evil spirit.[100]

This is of great interest since it indicates that Peck realised firstly, that the justification for exorcism was entirely experiential and secondly, he understood the epistemological limitations of second hand experiences. This bears out the central contention of this study (that exorcism / deliverance are secondary characteristics of enthusiastic 'experience driven' religion) and raises the important issue of how one can draw others into the circle of experience; in other words, how does enthusiasm spread? Peck, like MacNutt (but somewhat more emphatically), insightfully recognises the limitation of the written word in this process and sets his sights somewhat lower than an expectation that his experiences related in this way will lead to the 'conversion' of his readers.

To be credible, it is obviously important for the writer to speak with confidence regarding the experiences that lie behind their practise of exorcism /

---

[96] Cuneo, *American*, 69.

[97] Peck, *Lie*, 193. Peck resists the idea of 'oppression' instead he 'pays some heed to one of my mentors [surely Martin] who believes… that there is either possession or not and there is either an exorcism or not.' Peck, *Lie*, 193. Twenty years later Peck's reflections in *Glimpses* indicate greater openness towards Charismatic deliverance. Peck, *Glimpses*, 36, 53, 153, cf. 164, 248.

[98] Cuneo, *American*, 70. Later, Peck argues that The Exorcist 'was a very good read on those stormy nights, but it was in no way believable by the light of day.' Peck, *Glimpses*, 2.

[99] Peck, *People*, 183 and Cuneo, *American*, 70f.

[100] Peck, *People*, 184. Cf. Peck, *Glimpses*, 238f.

deliverance and in this regard Peck's commitment to objectivity, whilst commendable, somewhat emasculates his attempt to open closed minds:

> A confirmed atheist who witnessed the same exorcisms did not have that same experience [of God's presence] although there is much about them he cannot explain. For me, however, the power of God on these occasions was palpable.[101]

To confess to such subjectivity might be honest and perceptive but it exposes Peck to the accusation that he has simply misinterpreted an essentially equivocal experience. To a large extent then both Peck and his atheist colleague interpreted the same experience in different directions in line with the worldview they brought with them. Peck confesses that at the end of both the exorcisms nothing seemed to have changed: 'The patients had returned largely to their pre-exorcism condition. Nonetheless, within a few hours it was possible to discern a subtle but extraordinary change.'[102]

It is when Peck isolates the aspects of the exorcism that convinced him that something supernatural occurred he sounds most credible:

> As a hardheaded scientist – which I assume myself to be – I can explain 95 per cent of what went on... by traditional psychiatric dynamics... But I am left with a critical 5 percent I cannot explain in such ways. I am left with the supernatural – or better yet, subnatural. I am left with what Martin called the Presence.[103]

> When the demonic finally spoke clearly in one case, an expression appeared on the patient's face that could be described only as Satanic. It was an incredibly contemptuous grin of utter hostile malevolence... Yet when the demonic finally revealed itself in the exorcism of... [the] other patient, it was with a still more ghastly expression. The patient suddenly resembled a writhing snake of great strength, viciously attempting to bite the team members. More frightening than the writhing body, however, was the face. The eyes were hooded with lazy reptilian torpor – except when the reptile darted out in attack, at which moment the eyes would open wide with blazing hatred.[104]

Nevertheless, Peck acknowledges in *Glimpses* that the strange demonic expressions that made such an impact upon him were not picked up by the

---

[101] Peck, *People*, 186.

[102] Peck, *People*, 197.

[103] Peck, *People*, 195.

[104] Peck, *People*, 196.

video recordings of either case and, furthermore, that the patients never spoke in anything other than their own voices. In the first of his two cases, Peck's diagnosis of demon possession was based largely upon an unusual and unexpected comment from the patient.[105]

Years later Peck startlingly revealed to Cuneo that he had himself been the lead exorcist in the two cases reported in *People* and that Malachi Martin (with whom he had developed a good relationship) 'coached him in the role.'[106] This begs the question why didn't he make his own role clear in *People*? It certainly must have affected his objectivity in interpreting his experience. Was not the aforementioned atheist observer in a better place to make such an interpretation? Furthermore, why did Malachi Martin break with his view that the exorcist should be a priest only a short time after writing it? According to Peck, who was not even a Catholic, Martin did not raise this which seems surprising.[107] According to *Glimpses*, Martin accepted Peck as a member of the 'Church Invisible' despite Peck's liberal theological leanings and manipulated him into becoming an exorcist.[108]

In *People*, Peck accepts the reality of multiple personality disorder and draws a distinction between this and demon possession.[109] Later he came to the conclusion that a diagnosis could include both of these conditions.[110] Despite various comments on MPD Peck does not mention SRA which suggests that he had his doubts about it.

Peck in many respects apes 'his big mentor' Martin[111] in his approach to possession and exorcism but differs from him in one or two important respects. Firstly, he believes that Martin may have over emphasised the physical and spiritual danger to those involved in exorcism; nevertheless he believed the psychological dangers to be 'real and enormous.'[112] Peck is open to having non-Christian team members[113] whereas Martin implies that lay-assistants should be Christians 'not consciously guilty of personal sins at the time of the

---

[105] Peck, *Glimpses*, 19-22, cf. 246.

[106] Cuneo, *American*, 71. Apparently it had been Martin who had passed cases to Peck which resulted in Peck encountering possession for the first time.

[107] Cuneo, *American*, 71.

[108] Peck, *Glimpses*, 11, 253.

[109] Peck, *People*, 192f. Later still, in *Glimpses*, he seems somewhat less certain about the reality of MPD. Peck, *Glimpses*, 101f. He also comments that none of his patients have ever recovered a memory which they had *entirely* forgotten. Peck, *Glimpses*, 119.

[110] Cuneo, *American*, 72.

[111] Cuneo, *American*, 70. His great admiration for Martin is most evident in *Glimpses*. Peck, *Glimpses*, 1-11. Despite his high regard for Martin, he is well aware of the latter's capacity for dishonesty and manipulation. Peck, *Glimpses*, 5, 9.

[112] Peck, *People*, 189. Peck reports that in both cases the patient needed two hours of psychotherapy daily 'for some weeks' after their exorcism.

[113] Peck, *People*, 198-200.

exorcism.'[114]

People of the Lie is a quirky book. In one sense Peck's status lent respectability to exorcism and by derivation deliverance too, however, the attempt to open the secular mind to these things was doomed to failure. Peck's aspiration was that the institutional church should collaborate with secular healthcare to research and implement exorcism in a controlled and professional manner and he hoped his book might provoke some progress towards this.[115] It did not and indeed could not. Exorcism and deliverance live in the context of religious enthusiasm; deprived of this clement environment they cannot survive for long.

Gabriele Amorth (1925-)

On June 6, 1986 Gabriele Amorth was appointed assistant to the experienced exorcist for the diocese of Rome, Candido Amantini. In 1990, realising that Amanitini's health was declining and anxious that his expertise should not be lost, Amorth published *An Exorcist Tells His Story*[116] intended as a testimonial to Father Candido's experience as an exorcist, for the benefit of all those who are interested in the subject.'[117] The book proved to be a best-seller, greatly raising Amorth's profile in Catholic circles. Two years later he published *An Exorcist: More Stories*[118] which covers much of the same ground as his previous offering. In 1993 Amorth co-founded the *International Association of Exorcists* for Roman Catholic priest exorcists which boasted 200 members by the year 2,000.[119] By November 2000 Amorth claimed to have performed over 50,000 exorcisms.[120]

Amorth outlines and defends orthodox Catholic demonology justifying this from Scripture, various statements of Catholic authorities (including several popes) and experience.[121] He follows standard Catholic practice in dividing demonic activity into ordinary and extraordinary forms.[122] The former involves temptation which is the common experience of all humanity; the latter includes

---

[114] Martin, *Hostage*, 16.

[115] Peck, *People*, 200-202. *Glimpses* is another attempt to achieve this goal.

[116] G. Amorth, *Un Escorista Raconta* (Rome: Edizioni Dehoniane, 1990). I have used the English translation *An Exorcist tells His Story* published by Ignatius Press in San Francisco in 1999.

[117] Amorth, *Exorcist*, 17

[118] G. Amorth, *Nuovi Racconti di un Esorcista* (Rome: Edizioni Dehoniane, 1992). Again I have used the English translation *An Exorcist: More Stories* published by Ignatius Press in San Francisco in 2002.

[119] www.news.bbc.co.uk/1/hi/uk/728180.stm.

[120] G. Brandreth, *The Devil is Gaining Ground* (*Daily Telegraph*, 29 October, 2000) Review Section 1f.

[121] Amorth, *Exorcist*, 19-41 and *More*, 29-56.

[122] Amorth, *Exorcist*, 32.

'external physical pain', 'demonic possession' (the rarest and gravest form), 'diabolic oppression', 'diabolic obsession', 'diabolic infestation' and finally 'diabolic subjugation or dependence'.[123] The reasons for these various demonic attacks may be assembled under four headings:

- 'With God's permission'. Here God allows the demonic attack for some greater good usually the deeper sanctification of the victim.[124]
- 'When we are subjected to an evil spell'. In this instance an individual is subjected to demonic attack via a curse or spell placed by a third party.[125]
- 'A grave and hardened state of sin'.[126]
- 'Association with evil people and places'. This largely refers to occult involvement of one kind or another.[127]

Amorth takes a positive view of the priest's authority over demons. He claims (unlike Martin) to be unintimidated by any of his experiences and claims that the would be exorcist has nothing to fear from getting involved in such a ministry,[128] but this claim is somewhat undermined by a story he relates of his mentor, Father Candido, suffering long term health problems following an attempt to destroy a cursed item without following the correct procedure.[129]

Amorth argues that an unnecessary exorcism will not cause any harm[130] since it is in effect a specialised form of blessing; indeed, he performs his exorcisms in Latin, so it seems that initially the subject may not even be aware that an exorcism is taking place.[131] Wishing to appear responsible in the light of much criticism practitioners of exorcism / deliverance are usually keen to stress their hesitancy to indulge in this ministry so this confidence is unexpected. Furthermore, it enables Amorth to assign a diagnostic function to the rite.

Amorth in common with other comparatively thoughtful advocates of deliverance / exorcism recognises the impossibility of diagnosing demonic involvement in any given case, particularly since demons usually try to disguise their presence.[132] While he makes room for the usual diagnostic routines

---

[123] Amorth, *Exorcist*, 33-35. He admits that these categories are not watertight: 'there is a lot of mingling and compounding of symptoms.' Amorth, *More*, 60.

[124] Amorth, *Exorcist*, 56f.

[125] Amorth, *Exorcist*, 57f.

[126] Amorth, *Exorcist*, 58f.

[127] Amorth, *Exorcist*, 59f.

[128] Amorth, *Exorcist*, 194 and *More*, 184f.

[129] Amorth, *Exorcist*, 139.

[130] Amorth, *Exorcist*, 45.

[131] Amorth, *Exorcist*, 77.

[132] 'Every phenomenon that we encounter, no matter how strange or inexplicable, may have a natural explanation.' Amorth, *Exorcist*, 44, cf. 78.

(charismatic discernment,[133] aversion to the sacred,[134] the use of reason based upon long experience[135]) and a few that are less common (examination of the eyes during exorcism,[136] the judgement of 'sensitives' namely people who are sensitive to spiritual disturbance[137]), Amorth argues that finally the only test is to examine the reaction of the subject to the rite of exorcism. Indeed, he goes as far as to suggest that the *primary* function of exorcism is diagnostic.[138] This places Amorth in a diametrically contrary position to almost every other practitioner of exorcism / deliverance. The usual argument runs that exorcism / deliverance is reluctantly adopted and initially despite theological misgivings as a result of unambiguous personal experience of the demonic. Amorth moves in precisely the opposite direction; he has a fundamental commitment to the efficacy of exorcism, however, evidence of demonic possession is so ambivalent that exorcism must be practiced in order to establish its need. Nevertheless, Amorth does detail numerous cases where startling supernatural manifestations have taken place and he is not afraid to use his experience as a club with which to beat those who criticise his practise of exorcism.[139]

With regard to the rite itself Amorth does not accept the Charismatic distinction between simple and formal exorcism, instead arguing that Charismatic 'deliverance prayers' as he calls them do not fit into the category of exorcism at all, the latter being restricted to priests.[140] Even so, he welcomes deliverance prayers[141] as part of a normal, sacramental Christian lifestyle - the most powerful means of achieving freedom from demonic attack. Indeed, for all his focus upon exorcism. Amorth readily admits that within the wider context of a healthy spiritual discipleship exorcism plays an important but marginal role.[142]

Assuming that the presence of what Amorth refers to as 'negativity' is confirmed, liberation may be achieved in various ways. Sometimes a simple exorcism may relieve the victim; conversely, years of exorcism may, in extreme cases appear to have little effect.[143] Amorth presents the process of exorcism as one of causing the demon sufficient discomfort that they finally decide to leave:[144] 'The secret is to find your demon's weak spot. Some demons cannot bear to have the Sign of the Cross traced with a stole on an aching part

---

[133] Amorth, *More*, 160-162.
[134] Amorth, *More*, 78.
[135] Amorth, *Exorcist*, 68-70.
[136] Amorth, *Exorcist*, 78f.
[137] Amorth, *More*, 160-162.
[138] Amorth, *Exorcist*, 45.
[139] Amorth, *Exorcist*, 68, 167, and *More*, 155.
[140] Amorth, *Exorcist*, 43, *More*, 91-99.
[141] Amorth, *Exorcist*, 95.
[142] Amorth, *Exorcist*, 112.
[143] Amorth, *Exorcist*, 48-50, cf. 169.
[144] Amorth, *Exorcist*, 115f.

of the body; some cannot stand a puff of breath on the face; others resist with all their strength against blessing with holy water.'[145]

The most extreme cases of demonic attack are often those involving a curse.[146] In these there is, according to Amorth, often a cursed item that must be destroyed before the victim may be liberated; alternatively, and bizarrely, the victim may have unconsciously eaten or drank something that was cursed; in this case the victim will need to vomit out whatever has been consumed.[147] This can often be effected by the consumption of blessed water or oil.[148]

Amorth notes that the ancient *Roman Ritual* allows any priest to exorcise water, oil and salt and that these are of great benefit to the process of liberating and thereafter protecting the victim of demonic attack.[149] Blessed incense and clothing may also assist.[150] He chides the Church for its apparent lack of interest in exorcism noting that following Vatican 2 the only sacramental without a revised liturgy is that of exorcism.[151]

Demons do not restrict their oppressive activities to people; Amorth has experienced demonic infestations of houses and even animals and includes guidance on exorcising these.[152] Some of the most sensational material is found with reference to this kind of demonic activity including houses where blood runs from the taps[153] and disappearing cats.[154]

Amorth's credibility is somewhat questionable in the light of occasional inconsistencies in his claims. The most serious of these concerns the number of exorcisms he has undertaken. In his first book he claims to have performed 'over thirty thousand' with a mere ninety three involving patients who were possessed over nine years of ministry.[155] Two years later in his second book this has been down-sized to 'more than twenty thousand' over eight years of ministry.[156]

Amorth swims in the stream of traditional sacramental exorcism and he is certainly enthusiastic in his application of this ancient rite; but is he a religious

---

[145] Brandreth, *Devil*, 1.

[146] When Amorth refers to a curse he is thinking of the 'deliberate harming [of] others through demonic intervention.' Amorth, *Exorcist*, 129. This explicitly occult activity does not include some of the more trivial 'curses' identified by many Charismatic / EF deliverance ministers.

[147] Amorth, *Exorcist*, 132-135.

[148] Amorth, *Exorcist*, 118.

[149] Amorth, *Exorcist*, 117.

[150] Amorth, *Exorcist*, 119f.

[151] Amorth, *Exorcist*, 165.

[152] Amorth, *Exorcist*, 123-127.

[153] Amorth claims that this was verified by two academics who had the 'blood' tested in their laboratory. Amorth, *More*, 156

[154] Amorth, *More*, 163.

[155] Amorth, *Exorcist*, 169.

[156] Amorth, *More*, 197.

enthusiast? In his own view he is simply continuing an ancient practice which continues to have sizeable pastoral benefits; moreover, he is an establishment figure, appointed by the bishop of Rome to an official position within the diocese. Nevertheless, tell-tale signs of enthusiasm emerge which indicate that a muted religious enthusiasm is certainly present:

1. An emphasis upon foundational religious experience is present even if in a somewhat different form to that of other deliverance / practitioners. In Amorth's approach the key test of whether an exorcism is required is to perform one and see what happens – this is a neat solution to the problem raised by the multivalent nature of the ecstatic manifestations / symptoms which other practitioners use as their own justification, however, it is open to the rather obvious accusation that his exorcism itself provokes the reaction that he identifies as demonic. Furthermore, in responding to the scepticism of theologians Amorth resorts to the typical enthusiastic defence – don't criticise what you haven't experienced and therefore do not understand. Of course underlying Amorth's whole approach is an impulse towards an immanent spirituality.

2. There are indications of a bent towards conspiracy theories. For example, Amorth includes a quote from a magazine article which alleges that an American group of practicing Satanists under the name WICCA have powerful interests in the music industry which they are using as a vehicle to promote records that have been 'consecrated to Satan.'[157]

3. There is some evidence of restorationist thinking which in sacramental circles tends to hanker after pre-Vatican 2 (possibly medieval) Catholicism.[158] To some extent the mere practice of sacramental exorcism tends in this direction and Amorth's stress on the traditional forms of liturgy underline this commitment. Amorth desire to portray himself as theologically reliable means that he is cautious in what he writes, but occasionally mistrust of contemporary theology becomes explicit.

4. Amorth's affirmation of Charismatic forms of worship and their 'deliverance prayers' in particular is instructive. Whilst he does not favour the laity practising exorcism, which on the surface appears to be a damning judgement on Charismatic deliverance, his scruples are more to do with the maintenance of proper Catholic norms of worship and ministry rather than a rejection of any aspect of Charismatic practice. It is fair to describe Amorth's reaction to Catholic Renewal as love/hate; the enthusiasm appeals to him but the consequent 'liberation of the laity'

---

[157] Amorth, *More*, 72-74.
[158] Amorth, *More*, 24.

concerns him.

5. Within a Catholic context Mary is often the focus of enthusiastic forms of worship.[159] Amorth has a lively devotion to the Virgin and has written four books on the subject.[160] Based on the scriptural injunction of enmity between her and the Devil, Mary features prominently in most Catholic approaches to spiritual warfare in general and exorcism in particular.

Gabriele Amorth occupies an official role in the heartland of institutional Catholicism. His ministry of exorcism is nevertheless enthusiastic although it is a form of enthusiasm mitigated somewhat by his involvement with the hierarchy of the Church. Tellingly, and despite his best and not unsuccessful efforts to embed the ministry of exorcism within the normal ministry of the Church, Amorth's approach was rejected by the Church authorities when the revised ritual of exorcism was approved.[161]

Anglican Sacramental Exorcism

A closer look at several key twentieth century Anglican sacramental exorcists will be instructive to see how enthusiastic sacramental exorcism functioned within, and was affected by, a broad church setting. Eccentric yet nevertheless enthusiastic, sacramental versions of the ritual of exorcism emerge within this context.

---

[159] Whilst Knox does not make this point it seems reasonable that the orthodox Roman Catholic enthusiast will be drawn towards veneration of Mary who symbolises divine warmth, acceptance and above all immanence.

[160] Amorth, *Exorcist*, 197.

[161] The Catholic Church appeared reluctant to reform the ritual of exorcism following Vatican II but came under pressure to do so following the emergence of Charismatic deliverance ministry within its ranks. Its initial lack of enthusiasm was wholly understandable; perhaps no other historic rite of the church held the power to divide theologically liberal progressives and conservative traditionalists. The former might smile indulgently while the Church held to its historic theological commitment to belief in a personal Devil (as can be illustrated from a string of papal statements in the second half of the twentieth century); allowing this article of theological dogma to grow legs in the form of a renewed official affirmation of exorcism might stir up serious controversy. Those responsible for the revised ritual would need to steer through some choppy water.

The revised ritual was finally published in 1999. It appears to be a fairly typical compromise between traditionalists and progressives whilst delivering a firm slap-down to enthusiastic practitioners. Firstly, demon possession is accepted as a reality and therefore the need for the rite of exorcism is affirmed. However, exorcism is only to take place where the presence of the demonic has been established with certainty. *Roman Ritual, Rite of Exorcisms 22nd November 1998* (Vatican City, 1999). Unsurprisingly, Amorth did not approve of the new ritual. Brandreth, *Devil*, 2.

Dom Robert Petitpierre

Robert Petitpierre was the editor of the Church of England's 1972 report on exorcism,[162] long-time chair of the Study Group on Exorcism and a recognised authority on sacramental exorcism throughout the Anglican Church.[163] He had an awareness of things psychic from a young age before he was introduced to the practice of sacramental exorcism by one Gilbert Shaw while studying chemistry at Merton College, Oxford in the early 1920s.[164] His own contribution to exorcism was entitled *Exorcising Devils* and was published in 1976[165] by which time he had been practising exorcism for around fifty years.

Petitpierre's book is best understood as a response to (and an attempt to steer a course between) two threatening and contrasting challenges to his gentle sacramental approach. In 1975, an open letter was sent from a group of Anglican theologians to the episcopacy of the Church asserting that exorcism is irrelevant and indeed dangerous in the modern era. Their case rested upon a liberal demonology and was bolstered by the growing number of horror stories surrounding the explosion of exorcism.[166] Petitpierre mentions this and immediately and predictably refutes their argument; defence against this kind of rationalism runs throughout the book.[167] Conversely, he is clearly unhappy about the extreme demonology and practice of 'certain evangelical groups who, apparently, cannot conceive of ordinary human sin.'[168] In steering between the Scylla of rationalism and the Charabdis of what he terms 'angelism' Petitpierre presents a gently eccentric theology of exorcism largely focused on appropriate Christian responses to the paranormal.

It has already come to light that Sacramentalists are much more ambivalent regarding things psychic and occult than Evangelicals and Charismatics though it is fair to say that a degree of fascination is present among all the groups.

---

[162] R. Petitpierre (ed.), *Exorcism: The Findings of a Commission Convened by the Bishop of Exeter* (London: SPCK, 1972).

[163] Intriguingly Michael Harper relates how Petitpierre helpfully exorcised a house in which he was living prior to any experience that Harper was to have of Charismatic deliverance. Petitpierre gives further detail of the incident. Petitpierre, *Exorcising*, 85. This gives some indication of how close the various streams of exorcism flow within the Church of England.

[164] Petitpierre, *Exorcising*, 10f.

[165] R. Petitpierre, *Exorcising Devils* (London: Robert Hale, 1976).

[166] Petitpierre refers to the infamous 'Barnsley Case' and commendably, on the basis of his own research, defends those involved in ministering to Michael Taylor. Petitpierre, *Exorcising*, 135-137. He observes reaction to the tragic events 'almost amounting to hysteria.' Petitpierre, *Exorcising*, 163.

[167] Petitpierre, *Exorcising*, 32-37.

[168] Petitpierre, *Exorcising*, 53. For 'evangelical' one should read 'Charismatic'. Petitpierre also turns his guns upon extremist sacramental exorcism by describing *The Exorcist* as 'absurd'. Petitpierre, *Exorcising*, 134.

Charismatic and EF dualism tends to firmly demonise and anathematise any paranormal experience that does not have a specifically Christian significance yet are sufficiently fascinated by the occult to go into glorious and usually spurious analyses of it; the former are only a little less fascinated and certainly point out the dangers involved however, they often have a pseudo-scientific approach, interpreting much that the former would demonise as simply the little understood workings of (human) nature. Petitpierre is certainly typical of the former group. Very little of his attention is given to the alleviation of demonic oppression which he understands to be extremely rare in any case. Instead he focuses on the much more common episodes where unconscious natural psychic forces may cause unpleasant or unnerving events to occur. Petitpierre's methodology in such circumstances is to give an 'antiseptic' simple exorcism in case there is something inhuman involved before proceeding to celebrate a requiem mass if the problem appears to be one of 'unquiet dead'.[169] Indeed Petitpierre acknowledges that in these cases caused by psychic disturbance rather than 'little devils' (as he prefers to call demons[170]) exorcism is not the primary solution in any case.[171] Hence his title is really a misnomer since the book is not really focused on devils (demons) to any extent.

That said, Petitpierre genuinely believes in the 'little devils'[172] and accepts that there are cases that require exorcism proper. In fifty years he claims to have experienced 'genuine demonic control' only once and would prefer that use of the word 'possessed' be discontinued.[173] In the vast majority of cases (even those concerning occult involvement) a simple exorcism prayer suffices to expel the little devils.[174] Petitpierre does give some basic guidelines for formal exorcism (operate in a team, be careful to avoid the demon transferring from the afflicted person to others, bind then expel the demon and then follow up the session with ongoing healing[175]) which is certainly not the perilous, tortuous affair described by Malachi Martin or the Warrens. Nevertheless, his real concern is to advocate simple exorcism or, preferably 'deliverance',[176] which unlike formal exorcism holds no danger if the real problem is not demonic.[177]

Petitpierre's tone is both moderate and thoughtful; nevertheless the tell-tale signs of religious enthusiasm are not absent. These are most clearly evidenced

---

[169] Petitpierre, *Exorcising*, 46, 68f., 85.

[170] Petitpierre, *Exorcising*, 29.

[171] Petitpierre may perform a minor exorcism before 'finding out what the real trouble is'. Petitpierre, *Exorcising*, 42.

[172] He holds to the orthodox Christian view that they are fallen angels. Petitpierre, *Exorcising*, 26.

[173] Petitpierre, *Exorcising*, 26, 37.

[174] Petitpierre, *Exorcising*, 34.

[175] Petitpierre, *Exorcising*, 157-163.

[176] Petitpierre, *Exorcising*, 135.

[177] Petitpierre, *Exorcising*, 30-40.

in some of the downright bizarre interpretations of events that led Petitpierre to initiate an exorcism, and on the usual emphasis upon experience. Petitpierre's attempts along with Gilbert Shaw to 'exorcise the ancient mound in the middle [of Burgh-le-Marsh]' in order to alleviate 'occult pressures... directed at Britain from Russia during the General Strike of 1926' are a prime example of the former and furthermore demonstrate a quirky (rather than paranoid) form of conspiracy theorising.[178] The (quintessentially English) tale of an assistant to a bishop who humourously discovered the reality of the demonic whilst telling a vicar/exorcist that he was 'a "silly chump" – or words to that effect' for believing in such things provides an opportunity for Petitpierre to highlight the importance of first-hand experience.[179]

Whilst Petitpierre's underlying approach to exorcism is unquestionably sacramental, it shows the influence of the moderate Charismatics with whom he had shared lengthy discussions on the study group. Firstly, he warmly acknowledges John Richards' book *Deliver Us From Evil*[180] which outlines a moderate Charismatic approach. Secondly, he prefers the term 'deliverance' to 'exorcism' perhaps because he fears that there is a tendency to understand the latter term as describing a 'magical' rite.[181] Thirdly, his preferred, simple approach that is not entirely dissimilar to the deliverance prayers of more moderate Charismatics.[182] Nevertheless, he is suspicious of more extreme Charismatics who he accuses of overemphasising the demonic to the exclusion of a balanced understanding of human sinful nature.[183] Furthermore, he appears to accuse such groups of straying into the practice of magic themselves when they seek to 'tell God what to do... and establish their power and influence over other people.'[184]

Petitpierre's career as a moderate if quirky sacramental exorcist began when the practice was very much a marginal activity; he was therefore, well placed to take a leadership role within the Church of England's impressively proactive engagement with the issue. His book, published as exorcism began to emerge centre stage, advocates a gentle sacramental approach with substantial moderate Charismatic influence in evidence.

---

[178] Petitpierre, *Exorcising*, 17.

[179] Petitpierre, *Exorcising*, 107, cf. 13.

[180] Petitpierre, *Exorcising*, 7.

[181] He doesn't make this point explicitly, but his expression of his preference for the term 'deliverance' comes out of the blue following a discussion regarding magic in which he points out that 'Christian exorcism and Christian prayer in general are not forms of magic.' Petitpierre, *Exorcising*, 134, cf. 34.

[182] Petitpierre defines minor exorcism as 'nothing more than a simple prayer.' Petitpierre, *Exorcising*, 37.

[183] Petitpierre, *Exorcising*, 35, 53. Although he doesn't mention Charismatics by name it seems pretty clear that Petitpierre's criticisms are aimed in this direction.

[184] Petitpierre, *Exorcising*, 114.

Christopher Neil-Smith

Anglican priest, Christopher Neil-Smith's idiosyncratic practice of exorcism was outlined in *The Exorcist and the Possessed*,[185] published in 1974. By this time he had been performing exorcisms for twenty-five years including one that was filmed for television. Though standing within the High Church tradition of the Church of England, Neil-Smith (like Petitpierre) had considerable sympathy with the Charismatic Renewal and his exorcisms are best understood as a hybrid of Sacramental exorcism and Charismatic deliverance with more than a nod in the direction of liberal theology and the popular culture of his day.[186]

The first chapter deals with the reality of evil which Neil-Smith understands as an objective though impersonal reality.[187] The presence of evil 'vibrations' may be discerned via a mystical approach ('based on the ancient mystics particularly the writings of St John of the Cross') that he learnt from a mentor:

> I had to learn spiritual detachment. I had to be quite clear that if I was to be of any value as an exorcist, that my sense of perception must be completely dulled, and what I discerned or diagnosed in people whom I interviewed was the evil force picked up from them and not my own imagination.[188]

Neil Smith argues contra Harper and quoting John Robinson as an authority that *daimonieozai* should be translated as possessed rather than 'having a spirit' although his understanding of such a 'possession' is rather opaque and appears to include addictions and various other forms of 'slavery to Satan'.[189] Once the presence of an evil influence on a person is discerned in this way, Neil-Smith would, without further ado, proceed to exorcism.[190] He argues that this liberation is attractive and appropriate within a contemporary culture that has lost a sense of sin but not of evil.[191] In contrast to Sacramentalist practitioners, Neil-Smith does not favour ritual in the administration of exorcism and considers the formula used unimportant; he believes that the essential

---

[185] C. Neil-Smith, *The Exorcist and the Possessed* (Andover: James Pike, 1974).

[186] Indeed, Neil-Smith's eclecticism is a wonder to behold. He blithely quotes Muggeridge, Lennon, Graham, McLuhan and John Robinson in the first two pages!

[187] Neil-Smith, *Exorcist*, 20f.

[188] Neil-Smith, *Exorcist*, 16. He claims that his initiation into exorcism came about as a result of his healing ministry. Laying hands upon an 'unfrocked priest, who had been practising Black Magic... [he] felt the impact of an evil force come upon me.' Gilbert Shaw then exorcised this influence. Neil-Smith, *Exorcist*, 15f.

[189] Neil-Smith, *Exorcist*, 44f.

[190] He disagreed with the Exeter Report's requirement that candidates be prepared for exorcism in advance. Neil-Smith, *Exorcist*, 61. Tellingly he is quite happy to accept the term 'deliverance' but sticks with exorcism himself. Neil-Smith, *Exorcist*, 31.

[191] Neil-Smith, *Exorcist*, 32.

components are 'a word of command combined with a... touch' by which the power of the Holy Spirit is mediated.[192] In common with other Sacramentalists he makes a distinction between major and minor exorcisms, uses holy water[193] and allows that multiple exorcisms may be required to achieve liberation.[194]

Throughout *Exorcist* the author's enthusiasm is clearly evidenced in his mystical approach to discerning 'possession' but there is a marked lack of any emphasis upon demonic manifestations. Neil-Smith's enthusiasm is best understood as a gentle, eclectic and vague mysticism and irregular theorising. The impression he leaves behind is of an unconventional yet genuinely caring individual seeking to meet fairly extreme pastoral needs by developing an idiosyncratic hybrid approach to exorcism.

Considerable attention is given to the paranormal and occult. Here Neil-Smith adopts the same ambivalence that is characteristic of sacramental exorcists in contra-distinction to Charismatic and EF approaches. The usual distinction is made between witchcraft and black magic which are certainly sinful, harmful and dangerous and 'psi-phenomena'[195] which are, of themselves, natural and morally neutral, but may become dangerous if they lead on to occult activities.[196]

In a final chapter which further reveals his allegiance to Anglo-Catholicism, Neil-Smith makes extensive reference to the Charismatic Movement. His commitment to the former is revealed by his sacramentalism (which even extended to scourging as long as it is done 'under spiritual direction to avoid the pitfalls of spiritual pride.'[197]), reference to the Pope[198] and familiarity with the Roman Ritual.[199] Recognising that exorcism is 'a part of the Charismatic Movement'[200] Neil-Smith criticises the Exeter Report for making no mention of the latter or indeed the spiritual gift of discerning spirits[201] and like many Charismatic practitioners believes that exorcism may often profitably be used in tandem with healing of the memories.

One can only admire Neil-Smith's endeavour to wed sacramental exorcism with a somewhat less than conservative understanding of the demonic and an innovative methodology geared towards the contemporary culture. It is best

---

[192] Neil-Smith, *Exorcist*, 36-39.

[193] Neil-Smith, *Exorcist*, 43.

[194] Neil-Smith, *Exorcist*, 31.

[195] Including communication with the dead – it is not for nothing that the book is published by James Pike Ltd. James Pike was an Anglican Priest who came to accept the validity of spiritism.

[196] Neil-Smith, *Exorcist*, 26f., 63-91.

[197] Neil-Smith, *Exorcist*, 120.

[198] Neil-Smith, *Exorcist*, 120.

[199] Neil-Smith, *Exorcist*, 118.

[200] Neil-Smith, *Exorcist*, 97.

[201] Neil-Smith, *Exorcist*, 97. Actually, as John Richards points out, the Report was written prior to the eruption of Charismatic Renewal. Richards, *Deliver*, 117, 183.

understood as his attempt to develop a loosely sacramental approach that would be acceptable within the broad Anglican Church.

Michael Perry – Deliverance

Michael Perry's book, entitled *Deliverance*, was published in 1986.[202] Although his name appears on the book, it is in fact his compilation of the work of the Church of England's 'Christian Exorcism Study Group'. Perry, like John Richards, is an Anglican and develops an approach to exorcism with a broad Church in mind. Unlike Richards, however, his foundations are in Anglo-Catholicism and his approach is mainly liturgical.

Whilst his approach is similar at many points to that of Petitpierre, Perry has a somewhat different understanding of the demonic. He describes demons themselves as 'spiritual bacilli which attack the soul and personality',[203] apparently downplaying any element of demonic personality. The first area to come under examination is poltergeist activity. Perry views this as paranormal but nevertheless natural activity caused by an individual under 'a combination of stress, worry, fear and strained relationships'.[204] Therefore counselling and prayer are more appropriate than exorcism.

This understanding of the paranormal (common in sacramental circles) continues throughout. Perry distinguishes between the occult and the psychic; the latter includes telekinesis, telepathy, 'inner seeing', dowsing, various 'intuitive abilities' and even magic.[205]

> What they have in common is that, despite appearances to the contrary, they are all part of the realm of nature and created by God. Like all created powers, the psychic needs to be 'hallowed and directed aright', but in itself it is as morally neutral as any other human ability – artistic or musical ability, scientific or financial expertise.[206]

Perry warns against involvement in divination and mediumship, not because of the commonly feared inevitable demonic deception and or infestation they entail, but because they *may* lead to deception either from evil spirits or from

---

[202] M. Perry *Deliverance* (London: SPCK, 1986). In 1997 Dominic Walker, who was, at the time, co-chairman of the Christian Deliverance Study Group, published a smaller book along very similar lines. D. Walker *The Ministry of Deliverance* (London: DLT, 1997).

[203] Perry, *Deliverance*, 7.

[204] Perry, *Deliverance*, 25.

[205] Perry, *Deliverance*, 44.

[206] Perry, *Deliverance*, 44. One can almost hear the shocked responses or Pentecostal / Charismatic practitioners of exorcism. Unsurprisingly Michael Perry is the editor of *The Christian Parapsychologist*. He goes on to disarm the biblical injunctions against sorcery and attacks Kurt Koch's suspicion of psychic gifts. Perry, *Deliverance*, 47f.

the person's own subconscious.[207]

Perry defines the occult as 'fringe' or 'alternative science.'[208] Again, there is no clear mention of any danger of demonic oppression; instead, he seems to see the occultist as someone practising natural but as yet unexplained arts which may entail unforeseen and possibly dangerous repercussions. He describes various groups and the type of occult practices they engage in before looking at religious and quasi-Christian 'cults', since they 'share some of the same methods of recruitment... and since the process of deliverance from them has aspects in common.'[209]

Possession syndrome, namely the mistaken belief that one is possessed by evil spirits, is examined at some length.[210] Perry's familiarity with modern psychology emerges here and he helpfully exposes and explains the human tendency towards such a delusion.[211] People may consider themselves possessed as a result of mental illness, 'neurotic and personality disorders', poltergiest activity, occult involvement[212] and, controversially, involvement with Charismatic Christianity.[213]

Perry then turns his attention to genuine possession which he accepts alongside less severe cases of demonic oppression. In genuine possession 'the person's will is taken over by an intruding alien entity'[214] a diagnosis which seems a little vague and open to alternative interpretation. However, his description of the consequences and cure for this possession are relatively typical.[215]

Perry is a respected representative of a stream of Christian thought that believes the paranormal is ontologically neutral. The danger involved stems from our lack of understanding of it. Reckless and uninformed involvement in the paranormal will usually result in personality disturbance, which requires deliverance rather than full blown exorcism. This approach is anathema to the much more dualistic world view of many of the Charismatic practitioners /

---

[207] Perry, *Deliverance*, 49. Perry does not rule out the positive use of the paranormal and only warns that 'some people cannot retain their balance in respect of psychic forces and have to forgo the use of them.' Perry, *Deliverance*, 48.

[208] Perry, *Deliverance*, 51.

[209] Perry, *Deliverance*, 55.

[210] Perry, *Deliverance*, 71.

[211] Perry, *Deliverance*, 71-81.

[212] 'Various degrees of mental disturbance can result from involvement in occult practices... exorcism as such will rarely, if ever, be the right form of treatment.' Perry, *Deliverance*, 76f.

[213] He asserts that many of those drawn to Charismatic Christian sects are psychologically or spiritually distressed and that 'the more zealous groups [in particular] may become enmeshed in psychological and spiritual manipulation, with the most tragic consequences.' Perry, *Deliverance*, 77.

[214] Perry, *Deliverance*, 82.

[215] Perry, *Deliverance*, 82-89.

writers examined above. Indeed, Perry is extremely suspicious of Charismatic Christianity as a whole not least due to the latter's approach to deliverance ministry.

Perry's enthusiasm is not as obvious as that of the Charismatic ministers of deliverance he so disdains. Indeed he is probably the least enthusiastic minister of exorcism / deliverance carefully distancing himself from the dangerous and eccentric practices of his contemporaries. Nevertheless, there are strains of enthusiasm to be found in his case studies which often bear a close resemblance to those of the groups which he criticises.[216]

Martin Israel

Ordained priest, Martin Israel is another significant figure within the Anglican Sacramentalist stream under consideration. His approach is broadly similar to that of Perry who warmly endorses Israel's book on the subject *Exorcism: The Removal of Evil Influences*,[217] however, his approach is idiosyncratic in the extreme.[218]

Israel is 'sympathetic to the concept of' reincarnation[219] and holds to a form of universalism[220] and these inform his approach to exorcism. He believes that people or locations may need deliverance from psychic memories, psychic disturbance (eg poltergeists) ghosts (the souls of the departed) and evil spirits. In every case Martin believes that these will benefit from being sent to the presence of God who aims to reconcile all things to himself.[221] In any case, Israel understands deliverance to mean liberation from external domination which leads him to utterly reject some 'fanatical [Charismatic] groups... because they are controlled by a master figure or figures that interfere with the lives of lesser members of the group to the extent that their own will is impugned.'[222] Israel reveals that he is more drawn towards spiritualism than a Charismatic approach.[223]

Israel freely speaks of his psychic gifts which enable him to discern where deliverance may be required,[224] but in cases where he cannot be sure he has

---

[216] For example see Perry, *Deliverance*, 64-66, 88f.

[217] M. Israel, *Exorcism: The Removal of Evil Influences* (London: SPCK, 1997).

[218] It should be noted that *Exorcism* is a difficult book to read, Israel is not a clear writer and the book generally lacks focus, meandering around its subject. Nevertheless, the reader is struck by the evident eccentricity of Israel's approach.

[219] Israel, *Exorcism*, 39f.

[220] Israel, *Exorcism*, 1, 95.

[221] Israel, *Exorcism*, 34, 42, 100, 102.

[222] Israel, *Exorcism*, 77.

[223] Israel, *Exorcism*, 78.

[224] Israel, *Exorcism*, 29. Israel subsequently asserts 'that no one devoid of a special psychic gift or sensitivity should get involved.' Israel, *Exorcism*, 134.

developed an interesting and unusual methodology: he adopts a system of coin flicking mixed with intervening prayers in order to detect the presence of an evil or negative influence, and subsequently to ensure that it has been removed.[225]

For many years Israel teamed up daily with an older lady by the name of Geraldine.[226] After her death, Israel's pseudo-spiritualism enabled him to continue to work with her despite the fact she was no longer bodily present:

> In this work [of deliverance from demonic spirits] my helper, Geral, whom I have mentioned already (and died four years ago) and I work in close collaboration. The work is far too dangerous to be conducted alone, but unfortunately there are few who can contribute their share to it. That I continue my deliverance work with my beloved helper Geral who died four years ago can hardly avoid disturbing some readers, but the fact remains that her living soul works in close contact with my own.[227]

There are elements of liberal theology in Israel's understanding of the demonic in addition to his universalism. He understands Satan as a metaphor for 'demonic agencies'.[228] Similarly he allows that successful exorcism may be achieved by exorcists from religions other than Christianity.[229]

Israel represents the end of the line in terms of the pseudo-spiritualist, Anglican sacramental exorcism. His theological liberalism, sacramentalism and personal idiosyncrasies fuse into an altogether aberrant approach to exorcism which defy categorisation. Undoubtedly, his approach evidences a large degree of enthusiasm, but it is fairer to describe him as merely eccentric.

Conclusion: Enthusiastic Sacramental Exorcism Overcomes Institutional Hurdles

The renewed popularity of sacramental exorcism during the latter decades of the twentieth century is an established fact. In the UK the main developments took place during the 1970s following the publication in 1972 of an ecumenical report commissioned by the Bishop of Exeter.[230] This report seems to have galvanised and lent profile to a gentle Anglican form of sacramental exorcism

---

[225] Israel, *Exorcism*, 98-101.

[226] Israel, *Exorcism*, 34.

[227] Israel, *Exorcism*, 100.

[228] Israel, *Exorcism*, 44.

[229] Israel, *Exorcism*, 33.

[230] This was a remarkably proactive venture. Most of the other established churches took little interest in deliverance / exorcism until the infamous Barnsley case and others like it meant that some kind of official response was required. In contrast, the Bishop of Exeter convened an ecumenical, sacramentalist commission 'to consider the theology, techniques, and place in the life of the Church of exorcism'. Petitpierre, *Exorcism*, 9.

roughly in parallel to the much more significant growth of Charismatic deliverance.

The picture among Roman Catholics is somewhat different. Prior to the 1990s it seems that exorcism was largely confined to clandestine, unauthorised rituals hidden away from the church hierarchy, or to anti-establishment figures who had long since stopped caring about the official legitimacy of their actions. It was only during the 1990s that Roman Catholic enthusiastic sacramental exorcism became confident to emerge from the shadows. Books were published and priest-exorcists were appointed. Even the Pope performed an exorcism during this time.[231]

Why did Roman Catholic enthusiastic sacramental exorcism lag behind exorcism / deliverance which elsewhere seemed to come to prominence in the 1970s? The reason is simple and lends powerful credence to the thesis explored in this study. The Roman Catholic Church is institutionalised to a greater degree than any of its Protestant counterparts and sacramental exorcism (in contrast to Charismatic deliverance) may only be practised by an ordained priest with the permission of his bishop. Furthermore, sacramentalists will tend to respect the Church's hierarchy in direct proportion to their level of enthusiasm. Hence a truly enthusiastic Roman Catholic sacramentalist is likely to feel compelled to respect the divine authority of the Roman Catholic hierarchy *even though he may disdain the lack of vital charismatic authority exerted via that same hierarchy*. What all this adds up to is that enthusiastic sacramental exorcism had some fairly powerful institutional hurdles to clear in the Roman Catholic setting. Hence the time lag of twenty years or so. The same forces that led, during the 1970s, to the flowering of Charismatic and EF deliverance ministry and the gentle Anglican version of sacramental exorcism, produced a harvest in the Roman Catholic Church too; it took twenty or so years longer in the latter because the soil was not so easy to work with.

---

[231] Brandreth, 'Devil', 2.

CHAPTER 6

Enthusiastic Convergence: Late Century Trends in Exorcism and Deliverance Ministry

As has been shown, enthusiastic practice of exorcism reached its zenith in the 1970s particularly within the shepherding stream of the Charismatic Renewal and the 1980s as an integral part of John Wimber's theology and practice of the 'power encounter'.[1] However, the progress of exorcism is not a simple story of decline thereafter; instead the three major streams of exorcism / deliverance have tended to converge towards the dominant Charismatic centre ground. This can be seen in the generally positive relationship between sacramentalists and the Charismatics and, more significantly, improving relationships between Charismatics and former EFs as is perhaps most clearly and prominently demonstrated in the 'Third Wave' movement.

This convergence should be understood as clear indication of a trend towards a post-Modern undermining of denominational and theological ties by the apparently irresistible march of Christian enthusiasm in the Pentecostal/Charismatic Movement; nevertheless, this triumph of enthusiasm, often contains within it the pragmatic seeds, if not the saplings of the routinisation of the very enthusiasm around which the various strands are converging.

Exorcism / Deliverance in Late Century Popular Culture

If exorcism and demonology were an increasingly popular theme within popular culture from the 1960s onwards it is fair to say that this trend continued throughout the 1990s. Popular fascination with all things diabolic may have intensified but, conversely, research into society's religious convictions indicates that belief in Satan has decreased in the latter half of the twentieth century.[2] Popular interest in the demonic is, therefore, largely for the purposes of entertainment and titillation and appears to have little impact on the secular

---

[1] Wimber was himself influenced by several Roman Catholic Charismatics notably Francis MacNutt.

[2] S. Bruce, *Religion in Modern Britain* (Oxford: OUP, 1995) 51.

beliefs of the majority of those so interested.[3]

Sacramental Exorcism Converges with Charismatic Deliverance

Every attempt to identify and explain historical trends are fraught with the potential for over-simplification and this is most certainly the case when examining the tendency of sacramental exorcism to veer towards Charismatic deliverance ministry. Unlike EFs, Sacramentalists were not necessarily negatively predisposed to Charismatics and largely ignored them until the latter began to penetrate their ranks in the 1960s. Thereafter the Charismatics tended to be viewed with cautious approval by the more lively Sacramentalists on the basis of a shared religious enthusiasm although the individualistic impulse of the former and the 'High Church' principles of the latter were the cause of much friction. As has been clearly explicated above, Sacramentalist practitioners of exorcism have, whilst retaining a definite and distinctively sacramental thrust to the ancient rite of exorcism, managed to incorporate a Charismatic dimension consistent with their overall sympathy towards the Charismatic Movement.

Anglican Charismatic Deliverance Ministry

Within the broad Anglican church two distinct approaches to exorcism /

---

[3] Contra Cuneo, whose thesis is the outlandish suggestion that the explosion of interest in Christian exorcism / deliverance was largely fuelled by the popular media, particularly the film *The Exorcist*. This grants far too much credence to the power of the media to effect religious change and would need (in order to be proven) to establish far more than a coincidence of the appearance of such media attention with renewed interest in Christian quarters in order to avoid a chicken and egg dilemma. His thesis would be more credible if he provided other examples of the media motivating internal religious change (which he does not). Cuneo himself highlights that *The Exorcist* is obviously fictionalised (if not fictitious) and that he, as a young man, interpreted its function purely in terms of entertainment. But, he argues, subsequent proponents of exorcism often took it seriously, motivating a renewed emphasis on exorcism. One example he quotes is Scott Peck, who according to Cuneo viewed *The Exorcist* and 'decided that I must take this stuff more seriously.' Cuneo, *American*, 70. Peck, later stated that he had 'devoured the book during two consecutive stormy nights in a house on a New England hilltop... Intellectually I did not take the book seriously.' Peck, *Glimpses*, 1. Peck's interest in exorcism was *coincident with* rather than *caused by* media attention to this most sensational aspect of religious practice. This leads to the far more plausible thesis that wider sociological factors motivated coincident developments throughout late twentieth century culture. In this case the wider factors included the disenchantment with a demythologised world and hence the superficial respiritualising of the Western world evidenced outside the church by the media's interest in more spiritual themes, the New Age Movement and the gradual Easternisation of the West, and within the Church by a revival of Christian enthusiasm.

deliverance have been observed, the exorcism of the sacramentalists and the deliverance of the Charismatics.[4] There were usually good relationships between the leading exponents of both groups due to their mutual service on the Exorcism Study Group. It has also been noted that sacramentalists were often happy to include charismatic deliverance in their schema as a form of minor exorcism. Furthermore, later non-sacramental Charismatics began to include sacramental aspects into their practice such as the use of blessed water.

This convergence is exemplified by two inclusive Charismatic Anglicans who made written contributions during the 1990s. Graham Dow, later to become the bishop of Carlisle, authored a Grove Booklet in 1990 entitled *Those Troublesome Intruders*.[5] John Woolmer's book *Healing and Deliverance*[6] emerged nine years later in 1999. Both represent a desire to take a sensible approach to the ministry avoiding the pitfalls of more extreme practitioners.

As their book titles indicate both Dow and Woolmer favour a form of Charismatic deliverance ministry, however, both accept the use of holy water (Dow even includes information on how to acquire the correct prayers for 'consecrating holy water) and Woolmer also accepts the use of blessed oil. It seems that use of these sacramentals has undoubtedly made inroads into moderate Charismatic practise of deliverance. Even a more extreme Charismatic such as Horrobin has included the use of blessed water and oil in his approach.

Sacramental Exorcists Soften Their Approach to Charismatic Deliverance

When Charismatic deliverance arrived on the denominational scene in the early seventies; contemporary mainstream sacramental exorcists tended to be suspicious, if not hostile, to the former practice. Malachi Martin and even the far more moderate Robert Petitpierre believed that Charismatics were far too inclined to diagnose the need for deliverance,[7] largely thinking in terms of possession which of course most Charismatics rejected (following Prince who was by no means the first person to argue this). Even a champion of the Charismatic Renewal such as Suenens rejected the attempt to equate Charismatic deliverance with minor exorcism thus undermining the latter's

---

[4] EF deliverance does not seem to have penetrated the Church in the UK. In fact the enthusiastic reaction against Pentecostalism does not appear to have left much of an *enthusiastic* legacy in the UK to compare with that of the States. This may be down to the natural reticence of the British which easily settled for a more scholastic evangelicalism.

[5] G. Dow, *Those Troublesome Intruders* (Nottingham: Grove, 1990). This booklet was republished in slightly expanded form in 2003: G. Dow, *Deliverance* (Tonbridge: Sovereign, 2003).

[6] J. Woolmer, *Healing and Deliverance* (Crowborough: Monarch, 1999).

[7] The early Peck certainly had his concerns over the Charismatic approach to deliverance even if he seemed to retrospectively take a more positive view later.

status within the sacramental tradition. The battle lines at this early stage were clear.

In contrast, by the 1990s, sacramental exorcists tended to express a much more positive outlook on Charismatic deliverance, usually broadening the category of minor exorcism sufficiently to include it within that aegis. Writing in the early 1990s, Gabriel Amorth values Charismatic 'deliverance prayers' acknowledging their efficacy whilst retaining a special place for priestly exorcism.

By the end of the twentieth century sacramental exorcists generally accepted, even welcomed the presence of Charismatic deliverance, whilst the latter began to include aspects of the former's practice in their own approach.

EF Deliverance Converges with Charismatic Deliverance

Deliverance ministry was not only practiced by Charismatics. A parallel development took place among a Christian faction that might be termed Evangelical Fundamentalists. These latter were to some extent bedevilled by two conflicting impulses at the heart of their identity. On the one hand they were undoubtedly religious enthusiasts, on the other, their very existence was founded on the rejection of Charismatic spirituality. Hence they have been characterised as an enthusiastic rejection of enthusiasm; a classic expression of the visceral conflict that is a mark of enthusiasm as defined by Knox.

With regard to the practice of deliverance, it is therefore no surprise that EFs practiced this essentially enthusiastic ministry in a manner practically identical to that of their Charismatic *bêtes noir*. Neither should it be any surprise that they demonised the Charismatics in the process by asserting that Charismatic spirituality to a greater or lesser extent was empowered by demons and may result in the need for deliverance. Nevertheless, taking a wider perspective this position is simply a particularly clear example of the anomalous relationship between Charismatics and EFs. Ultimately the boundary between these two parties is hard to sustain, at least as far as the practice of deliverance was concerned, as the historical motivations for their separation became ever more distant. The partition between EFs and Charismatics in the important area of enthusiastic deliverance ministry has been significantly eroded.

The 'Third Wave'[8]

The emergence of a 'Third Wave' of Charismatic renewal, among evangelicals, and in many cases among those who might have been designated EF in the 1980s, is easily demonstrated: Whilst his own background was evangelical Quaker, John Wimber's conversion to Charismatic forms of ministry led to great controversy within Fuller Theological Seminary where he was teaching at

---

[8] See above, chapter 3.

the time;[9] Peter Wagner, Timothy Warner, Neil Anderson and Ed Murphy all had EF roots. An immediate consequence of this breaching of the boundary between Charismatics and evangelicals (and EFs in particular) was that EF practitioners of deliverance could not so easily demonise the almost identical and far more significant practice of deliverance among Charismatics. Since EF practitioners were a minority group within Evangelicalism as a whole the attraction of seeking allies among Charismatic practitioners was great.[10]

The equation of Charismatic deliverance with minor exorcism was the theological bridge over which mutual acceptance of sacramental exorcism and Charismatic deliverance could pass. In reference to Charismatic and EF practitioners of deliverance a less predictable development took place which allowed a similar rapprochement to occur. The hybrid 'Third Wave' movement pursued and interpreted Charismatic experience in the context of their over-riding commitment to effective evangelism. The deployment of Charismatic experience and particularly Charismatic deliverance in a context of optimistic and ambitious evangelism led to Wimber's concept of the 'power encounter' and ultimately to the popularity of 'strategic level spiritual warfare' (SLSW).

Subordinating deliverance ministry to the practical goal of world evangelisation and the spiritual warfare necessary to achieve it proved to be a banner around which EF practitioners of deliverance could join Charismatics, particularly since the boundaries between the two groups had already substantially eroded in any case.

Late century openness of EF practitioners of deliverance to their Charismatic

---

[9] Cuneo, *America*, 247.

[10] Conversely, Charismatics had been doing the opposite for a long time. Kurt Koch in particular would from time to time turn up in the bibliographies of the more highbrow Charismatic practitioners (namely those who had read around the subject) who were inclined to acknowledge the desirability of any source in addition to direct religious experience. With regard to EFs, the opposite was the case. The more highbrow types such as Unger and Dickason purposefully exclude Charismatic practitioners from their acknowledged sources, only quoting them in order to criticise. Koch who goes so far as to quote a Roman Catholic priest's openness to exorcism with approval *never* does the same with regards to a Charismatic. All this may be explained by recognition of the fact that the enthusiastic Charismatics were so focused on religious experience that they were free to claim even EF religious experience if it looked similar to their own. EF practitioners of deliverance had less room to manoeuvre; they had to ensure that an enthusiastic commitment to the experience of deliverance would not lead to an uncritical acceptance of Charismatic enthusiasm. In hindsight it seems inevitable that these EFs would reach a rapprochement with their Charismatic counterparts – their approach was basically identical, separated only by a historic and increasingly irrelevant dispute over the origins of Pentecostalism. None of this should be understood as suggestive that there is no longer any division between Evangelical and Charismatic. The boundary eroded is between EF practitioners of deliverance and Charismatic practitioners of the same. Any suggestion of a larger rapprochement is outside the boundaries of this study.

counterparts is clearly visible in the revival centred approach of Mark Bubeck, Ed Murphy's inclusive Third Wave approach, Neil Anderson's post-EF / Charismatic slant and Lozano's attempt to bridge the gap between Catholic Charismatic deliverance and a less sensational approach that he picked up from 'third-waver' Pablo Bottari. Ed Murphy's exhaustive *Handbook for Spiritual Warfare* represents the zenith of this trend. A self-confessed 'Third Waver', Murphy's roots are in EFism but his approach is a comprehensive fusion of EF deliverance to a Third Wave (Charismatic) Spiritual warfare agenda. In contrast, Neil Anderson has delineated an approach to personal spiritual warfare that resembles a traditional cessationist approach and yet is couched in terms attractive to jaded post-EF/Charismatics. Anderson exemplifies the routinsation of enthusiastic deliverance.

Ed Murphy

The Handbook for Spiritual Warfare represents the zenith of the late century EF / Charismatic convergence around the theme of spiritual warfare. Murphy's EFism is demonstrated by his exhaustive survey of the Scriptures built upon similar though somewhat less extensive (and fanciful) treatments by the likes of Merrill Unger. Murphy's hermeneutic is informed by a typical Third Wave claim, namely that the assumptions of animist cultures encountered are more comparable to the Worldview of the writers of the Scriptures than that of the post-Enlightenment West. Consequently, experience of an animist Worldview, particularly the belief that a parallel spiritual sphere teaming with competing spirits is the underlying reality behind the physical world of everyday experience, enables an approach to scripture that discerns implied spiritual warfare motifs at every turn. The amount of material that Murphy finds relevant to his subject is a wonder to behold and at points demonstrates considerable ingenuity.

The rest of the book is largely taken up with pastoral / ministerial application of this militant anti-Enlightenment spirituality read into the Scriptures in the way outlined above. Murphy adopts an eclectic approach to this application integrating the outlook and practice of a wide range of EF and Charismatic sources. All the expected EF sources are present (Penn-Lewis,[11] Koch, [12] Unger,[13] Bubeck,[14] Dickason[15]) alongside fellow 'Third Wavers' (Wimber,[16] Wagner,[17] Kraft,[18] Arnold,[19] Silvoso[20]) and traditional Charismatics

---

[11] Murphy, *Spiritual*, 554.
[12] Murphy, *Spiritual*, 580.
[13] Murphy, *Spiritual*, 20, 49-51, 277.
[14] Murphy, *Spiritual*, 64, 67f., 76, 545f.
[15] Murphy, *Spiritual*, 51, 103, 223, 278, 556.
[16] Murphy, *Spiritual*, 282, 342, 543.
[17] Murphy, *Spiritual*, 554.

(Michael Green[21]) and a wide variety of others including (Friesen,[22] Anderson,[23] Peck[24] and Peretti[25]). He even notes the growing demand for exorcism among Roman Catholics in Italy even mentioning Gabriel Amorth in the process.[26]

What conclusions if any may be drawn from Murphy's eclecticism? It seems that Murphy represents the triumph and simultaneous decline of enthusiastic exorcism / deliverance. The triumph in that commitment to deliverance is now so developed that it may dissolve traditionally strong boundaries, even those between EFs, Charismatics and even Sacramentalists. The decline, in that the exhaustive and analytical manner in which Murphy approaches his subject, and the way in which so much very traditional evangelical doctrine is incorporated in his understanding of deliverance, smacks of routinisation.

Neil Anderson's 'Truth Encounter' Approach

Neil Anderson's best selling book *The Bondage Breaker* [27] was first published in 1990. In some respects his approach to deliverance is an extension of that of the EFs considered above in chapter seven. However, like Bubeck, Anderson generally refrains from attacking the Charismatic Movement and makes explicit what is implicit in the former's approach, namely that demonisation requires a 'truth encounter' rather than a power encounter.[28] *The Bondage Breaker* makes positive reference to both Unger and Penn-Lewis frequently making use of the latter's concept of 'ground'.[29]

It is instructive to compare the Hammonds' memorable metaphor for deliverance as a crisis power encounter (evicting 'Pigs' from the 'Parlour') with that of Anderson:

People's lives are like houses. Suppose a family hasn't taken the garbage out of their house for months, and they have spilled food and beverages

---

[18] Murphy, *Spiritual*, 539.

[19] Murphy, *Spiritual*, 262, 344-345, 393, 395-396, 401-407, 406f., 410, 564, 571, 572.

[20] Murphy, *Spiritual*, 548, 577f.

[21] Murphy, *Spiritual*, 7, 48, 332, 418, 579.

[22] Murphy, *Spiritual*, 469, 584.

[23] Murphy, *Spiritual*, 48f., 104, 110, 434.

[24] Murphy, *Spiritual*, 541.

[25] Murphy, *Spiritual*, 540.

[26] Murphy, *Spiritual*, 568.

[27] N. T. Anderson, *The Bondage Breaker* (London: Monarch, 2002).

[28] Anderson, *Bondage*, 261. Anderson's basic thesis is that instilling biblical concepts in the subject is the best way to lead an individual from demonic bondage to Christian maturity. Arguably this could be understood as a Christianised form of Cognitive Behavioural Therapy. This approach is most explicit in N. T. Anderson, *Living Free in Christ* (Harpenden: Monarch, 1993).

[29] Anderson, *Bondage*, 96, 195, 195f., 231, 233, 243, 250.

without cleaning up. That will attract a lot of flies. To resolve this problem, I don't think it is necessary to study the flight patterns of flies and determine their names and rank structure in the insect hierarchy. There may be some value in doing this which I am not aware of, but I don't think the answer is primarily found in gaining knowledge about and getting rid of the flies. Similarly, to "focus on the flies" in our lives is to allow the devil to set the agenda for us and distract us from the real issue – which is to get rid of the garbage. Repentance and faith in God have been and will continue to be the answer in this present church age.[30]

Here, Anderson makes a key move in switching cause and effect. Where most Charismatic (and some non-Charismatic) practitioners would argue that demons are the root cause of people's problems and hence deliverance is required before one can achieve any progress (indeed that is Prince's primary contention), Anderson identifies sin as the root problem and, therefore, his seven step solution entitled *Freedom in Christ* is largely focused on repentance rather than deliverance.[31] Indeed, Anderson rejects terms such as 'exorcist' or 'exorcism' and by implication, 'deliverance ministry'.[32]

The relevance of Anderson's approach for this study should not however be underestimated. He shares with practitioners of deliverance the general pessimism over the spread of the occult including a belief in widespread SRA and consequent MPD, the ubiquitous presence of demons seeking to oppress the Christian and that progress in sanctification is coterminous with success in the spiritual war against Satan and his hosts.[33] However, Anderson has moved away from the enthusiastic drive for a power encounter towards a traditional repentance led approach. Powlison notes that Anderson is 'weaving features of EMM [deliverance ministry] into a more traditional evangelical perspective.' [34]

---

[30] Anderson, *Bondage*, 257.

[31] The question of whether human bondage to sin is caused by, or the cause of demonisation is a central theological issue for this study and runs parallel to a similar discussion regarding the role of the Holy Spirit in sanctification. Among popular treatments debate is polarised consequently no synthesis is attempted. The fact that no recent, serious scholarly attempt has been made to resolve the former issue in the way of a pastoral theology of sanctification is indicative of the current neglect of underlying pastoral theology in favour of techniques and strategies. Stackhouse, *Gospel*, 224-229. It probably also reflects how deeply reluctant even evangelical scholarship is to treat things demonic seriously.

[32] Anderson, *Bondage*, 256.

[33] Hence Anderson maintains the key features of what Walker calls the 'paranoid universe'. Anderson, *Bondage*, 18-29, 44, and 125-136.

[34] Powlison, *Power*, 33. Whilst Anderson holds appeal for Charismatics, EFs and mainline evangelicals alike, Walter Wink has attempted an altogether more ambitious synthesis, namely the attempt to wed a Jungian liberal demonology to third wave SLSW language. The result is a series of books that might, at first glance, appear extremely

In so doing he has designed a methodology that holds appeal across the Charismatic / non-Charismatic divide.

Neal Lozano

Neal Lozano, a committed Roman Catholic Charismatic, published his own approach to deliverance, entitled *Unbound*, in 2003.[35] Whilst this places his published work outside of the period under scrutiny, his practice of deliverance ministry developed subsequent to the Charismatic Renewal. Like his cousin, Michael Scanlan, Lozano is committed to a Christian community which accounts for his impressive pastoral emphasis.

Like many other Charismatic practitioners, Lozano asserts that deliverance is an essential component of Christian discipleship. Futhermore he subsumes large areas of Christian spirituality under the category of deliverance. The effect of this, however, is not as in the case of Horrobin to elevate the practice of deliverance ministry, so much as to revert to marginalise the deliverance component within a fairly traditional model of Christian discipleship.

a godly man, through the power of God, delivered me from an evil spirit. It was real spiritual bondage rooted in a deep human wound. Over the years I have been able to assist hundreds of others to do the same. That event was significant, and yet I believe that 98 percent of deliverance from evil spirits is learning the truth - of who God is, what He has said and whom He has made us - resisting temptation, repenting of sin, renouncing the works of the devil an forgiving those who harmed us. Perhaps two percent or less is commanding the enemy to leave. This book is not so much about evil spirits as it is about acknowledging the doors we have opened to their influence and how to close them. We are set free from the devil's influence when we pray, read the Bible, participate in church services or receive the sacraments. *Deliverance is not a one-time event but an ongoing and normal part of the Christian life.*[36]

The final sentence could equally read: *Deliverance is a relatively insignificant component of the normal Christian discipleship.* It is also important to observe the 'truth-encounter' nature of this model. Lozano prescribes a method of deliverance that emphasises repentance and renunciation by which the right of a

---

conducive to the practice of SLSW.[34] See, for example, W. Wink, *Engaging the Powers* (Minneapolis: Fortress, 1992). Upon closer inspection they deny most of doctrine underlying the Third Wave and instead rest upon Jungian psychology and classic liberal demythologisation.

[35] N. Lozano, *Unbound* (Grand Rapids: Chosen Books, 2003).

[36] Lozano, *Unbound*, 12f.

demon to oppress is removed;[37] the power encounter is marginalised as are demonic manifestations.[38] He does not advocate speaking with demons or extended periods of struggle to evict them.[39] All of this closely resembles the neo-Evangelical approach of Anderson (considered above).[40]

Lozano cites three main influences upon his ministry of deliverance. Firstly, Francis MacNutt though he appears to have some reservations here,[41] secondly, his cousin, Michael Scanlan[42] and thirdly, Pablo Bottari.[43] Bottari oversaw deliverance ministry during Carlos Annacondia's campaigns.[44] Lozano met him at a time when he had 'backed away from it [deliverance ministry] for years.'[45] Lozano had become dissatisfied with enthusiastic power encounter deliverance; Bottari managed to steer him towards a truth encounter approach. Whilst Lozano still expects to evict demons with a word of command and requires that ministers of deliverance have 'received the power of the Holy Spirit',[46] the emphasis is clearly upon repentance and renunciation.

The fact that Lozano is a Roman Catholic makes it tempting to suggest that he represents the emergence of an ultimate rapprochement between sacramental and enthusiastic exorcism incorporating features of Charismatic and neo-Evangelical deliverance. Whilst there is a seed of truth in this, it is important to remember that Lozano, like MacNutt and Scanlan, advocated Charismatic deliverance, rather than the sacramental forms advocated by Malachi Martin or Scott Peck. Consequently, Lozano's true significance lies in his transition from a Charismatic practitioner to his adoption of a routinised neo-Evangelical approach.

Conclusion: The Triumph and Defeat of Enthusiastic Exorcism / Deliverance

The motivation for, and effect of, these rapprochements was actually the creeping routinisation of exorcism/deliverance; after the explosion of enthusiastic versions marked by typically assertive and mutually exclusive approaches, the fire of enthusiasm gradually dissipated and the rite began to bed down, integrating the various perspectives into a more moderate, less

---

[37] Lozano, *Unbound*, 201.

[38] Lozano, *Unbound*, 199, 205f, 38, 162, 219.

[39] Lozano, *Unbound*, 217,199.

[40] Examine Lozano, *Unbound*, 96, 102, 170, 234.

[41] Lozano, *Unbound*, 250.

[42] Lozano, *Unbound*, 250, cf. 143.

[43] Lozano, *Unbound*, 175f, 214-220, 250.

[44] Lozano, *Unbound*, 175. Which places Bottari within the 'Third wave' stream of Charismatic enthusiasm.

[45] Lozano, *Unbound*, 214.

[46] Lozano, *Unbound*, 157, 202. These may be understood as the vestiges of his previous Charismatic approach.

contentious version. Herein lies the simultaneous victory and defeat of exorcism / deliverance. Like countless aspects of Christian spirituality that surf a wave of enthusiasm and achieve brief prominence, exorcism / deliverance was by the 1990s largely washed up on the beach in a somewhat more acceptable form having had many of its hard edges worn away during its brief but turbulent ride. It may have enjoyed an exhilarating voyage, drawn great attention to itself and earned the right to be taken more seriously on the broader Christian scene. Nevertheless, the metaphor holds; by the late 1990s enthusiastic deliverance / exorcism was to a large extent washed up in the church settings under examination here.

CHAPTER 7

Conclusion

Exorcism / Deliverance and Christian Enthusiasm

Following comprehensive analysis of exorcism / deliverance within the three main streams of Western, twentieth century Christian enthusiasm, the conclusion that the latter provides an environment conducive to exorcism / deliverance may now be drawn with some confidence. Repeated examples have indicated that the fundamental enthusiastic appeal to religious experience lies at the heart of the practice of exorcism / deliverance wherever it is encountered. Furthermore, it has been demonstrated that it tends to emerge alongside other ubiquitous characteristics of enthusiasm such as dramatic, ecstatic physical manifestations,[1] imminent eschatology,[2] schism,[3] and perfectionism.[4]

In theological terms, most practitioners of exorcism / deliverance at least implicitly perceive demons as the prime mover in human evil rather than a more traditional model which would make the sinful nature the prime mover and the demonic a contributory, exacerbating stimulus.[5] In this light, the following quote from Knox appears almost prophetic in its perception of the heart of enthusiastic exorcism / deliverance (which was certainly not the focus of his study):

we have observed, in the foregoing chapters, other... symptoms which are... recurrent... native to its [enthusiasm's] genius. The chief of these is

---

[1] Knox, *Enthusiasm*, 4.

[2] Knox, *Enthusiasm*, 357.

[3] 'It is an old dream of the enthusiast (not extinct in our time) that he can start a new religion without starting a new denomination.' Knox, *Enthusiasm*, 403. It is hard to imagine a better description of the activity of many of those involved with exorcism / deliverance.

[4] Knox, *Enthusiasm*, 570.

[5] Some of the more theologically articulate advocates of exorcism / deliverance protest otherwise and include sections on discipleship, nevertheless, this runs against the tide of the implications of practising deliverance. Once the problem of human sin is cut off at it's demonic root, the process of overcoming the flesh is at best a secondary (and at worst an unnecessary) requirement.

– and it largely subsumes the others – is what I have termed ultrasupernaturalism. It is the attempt to root up nature and plant the seed of grace, in fallow soil, instead of grafting the supernatural on to the natural, after the timorous fashion of orthodoxy.'[6]

In the case of exorcism / deliverance, the flesh is almost entirely subsumed and the human person functions merely as an arena for the cosmic battle between the Holy Spirit and the satanic hordes. In this sense, the flesh is 'rooted up', and when demons have been evicted, the Holy Spirit may indeed be planted 'in fallow soil'.

That Charismatic deliverance ministry is a clear symptom of enthusiasm is, in the light of the extensive evidence considered above, beyond question. Moreover, it has been clearly demonstrated that Evangelical Fundamentalism emerged as an enthusiastic rejection of the early Pentecostal Movement. The fact that deliverance ministry emerged within Evangelical Fundamentalism, which so strongly rejected all things Charismatic, gives further indication of the essentially enthusiastic nature of the practice. Furthermore, this conclusion is lent yet more support from the evidence to show that it similarly emerged though somewhat later within a very different brand of enthusiasm, namely sacramental enthusiasm. The time lag of twenty years or so is accounted for by the much greater commitment to the anti-enthusiastic institution of the Church on the part of enthusiastic sacramentalists.

Once exorcism / deliverance is properly understood as a possible consequence of Christian enthusiasm, it may be concluded that further studies of its significance, theological, sociological and psychological are more likely to yield helpful results. Conversely, the scarce academic analyses produced to date have often failed to appreciate the enthusiastic context in which exorcism / deliverance functions. As a consequence they have to a greater or lesser extent failed to accurately understand and identify its true significance.

Secondary Conclusions

Knox observed the essentially tidal nature of enthusiasm, a theme which has been developed by Stackhouse in his study of Charismatic faddism. One may certainly conclude that Charismatic deliverance ministry is a clear example of the fads that have marked the Charismatic Movement. Whilst Stackhouse paints with a broader brush, this study of the emergence, progress and ultimate routinisation of enthusiastic deliverance provides a detailed picture of the progress of one particular fad.

The role of itinerant ministries in the propagation of enthusiastic deliverance

---

[6] Knox, *Enthusiasm*, 584.

ministry has been identified and established. Itinerants may be viewed as those who escape the routinising clutches of the denomination to reignite and fan the flames of enthusiasm from the sidelines, or as a destructive unaccountable influence, diverting Christians into spiritual sidings, depending upon one's perspective.

Late century approaches to exorcism / deliverance demonstrate cross-fertilisation across the various streams of enthusiasm. To some this may appear to be the triumph of enthusiasm as it crosses hardened institutional and denominational boundaries, bringing a degree of unity to those who contend with the secularising forces at work within and without the church. However, a more perceptive onlooker will discern the decline of enthusiastic exorcism / deliverance in this rapprochement. Unity, or at least mutual respect, among previously contending practitioners of enthusiastic exorcism / deliverance is usually motivated by the marginalisation of the rite, even among the enthusiastic groups from whence it sprung. This decline is most clearly demonstrated in the routinised versions of exorcism / deliverance that now enjoy far more widespread appeal than classic enthusiastic approaches.

Possibilities for Further Study

This study throws up a number of issues that demand further consideration:

- The presentation of religious experience. Whilst agreeing (in Chapter 4, above) with Middlemiss in his contention that religious experience is equivocal, this study has indicated the manner in which enthusiasts sometimes relate such experience. Frequently, incidents are presented in such a manner that one if one accepts the validity of the experience then one can only draw the conclusion that is desired by the teller, or better, the interpretation of the experience becomes embedded in the memory of the experience itself. One can only conclude that some sort of unconscious revision has taken place after the event. There is scope for some field-work here, namely, the observation of exorcism / deliverance later compared to the manner in which it is recorded by participants over time thereafter. However, the likelihood is that such revisions only take place when the incident is retold as part of a case for the universal validity of exorcism / deliverance. Further research could lend helpful results in understanding this process further and improving understanding of the enthusiastic psyche.
- Exorcism / deliverance and millenarianism. The relationship between exorcism / deliverance and millenarianism is intriguing. A superficial analysis suggests that the pessimistic environment generated by premillenialism seems very conducive towards traditional forms of deliverance whilst postmillenialism drives an incorporation of exorcism / deliverance into a more optimistic, triumphalistic even, schema for

Spiritual Warfare. It would be of great interest to explore this further to gain greater insight into the way in which these different forms of eschatology motivate and interpret religious experience.

- Exorcism / deliverance in non-Western churches. This is an area of great interest due to growing awareness of the existence of isolated incidents of child abuse due to syncretistic Christian / animist rites of exorcism / deliverance. It is hoped that the current study might provide a platform for much needed investigation of this sensitive issue. By charting the course of Western exorcism / deliverance it should prove possible to contrast and compare the forms of Christian exorcism / deliverance that exist within non-Western churches.

APPENDIX 1

References to the Eviction of Evil Spirits and Related Themes in Early Pentecostal Journals

The Apostolic Faith Magazine

(published out of Asuza St – lots of reports as Pentecost spread around the world)

Edition 1 – September 1906

A brother who had been a spiritualist medium and who was so possessed with demons that he had no rest, and was on the point of committing suicide, was instantly delivered of demon power. He then sought God for the pardon of his sins and sanctification, and is now filled with a different spirit. (page 6)

A drunkard got under conviction in a street meeting, and raised his hand to be prayed for. They prayed for the devil of drink to be cast out, and the appetite was gone. (page 24)

When we leave the Blood out, Satan has power to switch us into fanaticism, but no powers out of hell are able to make their way through the Blood. (page 33)

Edition 2 – October 1906

A mother brought her son to the Mission to be healed of epileptic fits. He is about twenty-one years old and has been suffering for years, like the boy that was brought to Jesus whom the devil had often caused to fall into the fire and into the water. The boy was so wrecked in mind and body that he was in a semi-conscious condition. Bro. Batman, who is called to Africa, prayed for him, asking the Lord to cast the demon power out of him and give complete healing. The boy raised up from the floor and witnessed that the work was done and went home rejoicing. (page 5)

Edition – November 1906

We find some that are superstitious about seeking the Holy Ghost. They are afraid they are going to get the power of the devil instead of God, but men and women that are walking in the light can quickly see that this is of God. It is easy for the Lord to show them that This is that which was spoken by the prophet Joel. We are living in the last days when He is pouring out His Spirit upon all flesh. (page 13)

The signs are following in Los Angeles. The eyes of the blind have been opened, the lame have been made to walk, and those who have accidentally drunk poison have been healed. One came suffering from poison and was healed instantly. Devils are cast out, and many speak in new tongues. (page 30)

Edition 4 – December 1906

the power of the Holy Ghost in God's people today condemns and swallows up the counterfeit. It digs up and exposes all the power of Satan. (page 24)

If we ask our Father for bread, He will not give us a stone; if we ask Him for a fish, He will not give us a serpent; if we ask for an egg, He will not give us a scorpion. We would not treat our children that way, and how much more will our Father in heaven give good things to them that ask Him. Never let the hosts of hell make you believe that while you live under the blood, honoring the blood, and pleading through the blood for blessings from the throne, that God will let Satan get through the blood and put a serpent into you. There is no way for Satan to make his way through the blood. "And they overcome him by the blood of the Lamb and by the word of their testimony." The devil cannot act through you and talk through you, if you are God's child and baptized with the Holy Ghost. (page 37)

People that have a real knowledge of the Holy Ghost in their hearts by the Holy Spirit, and then go and say this work is of the devil, and people are speaking in tongues by the devil, after they have the knowledge of the truth, such people are in danger of sinning against the Holy Ghost. (page 51)

They are having a real old time Pentecostal revival in San Jose, California. The devil is stirred and doing his best to put out the fire, but they just ignore him and shout the victory. The altars are crowded day and night. Twelve have received their Pentecost and are speaking in tongues. Devils are being cast out and the sick healed. (page 7)

I came from Frisco to Los Angeles five days after the earthquake and heard about these Pentecostal people. I visited their meetings and looked on rather critically. At first I opposed and openly fought them and said it was the devil. The result was I backslid altogether and had to go back and ask forgiveness and do my first works over again, even down to having the devils cast out of me. (page 34)

Spiritualists have come to our meetings and had the demons cast out of them and have been saved and sanctified. Christian Scientists have come to the meetings and had the Christian Science demons cast out of them and have accepted the blood.

People have come to this place full of demons and God has cast them out, and they have gone out crying with loud voices. Then when all the demons were cast out, they got saved, sanctified, and baptized with the Holy Ghost, clothed in their right minds and filled with glory and power. (page 24)

A man that had been possessed with a mad demon and had been in the asylum was delivered. The Lord cast out this demon, clothed him in his right mind and completed the work, baptizing him with the Holy Ghost. (page 7)

Edition 5 – January 1907
Many demons have been cast out and the sick are being healed. (page 6)

We have had some marvelous(sic) cases where those possessed by the devil have been wonderfully and completely delivered and clothed in their right minds. We wish to note one case in particular for the glory of God and the power of our Lord Jesus Christ. A man of German birth came in the meetings, a master in Theosophy and Spiritualism, who claimed he was Christ incarnate - that he was immortal, and had all wisdom and knowledge. The blessed Holy Ghost gave the saints the discerning of Spirits, and they rebuked the devils in him. And the man fell to the floor, trembling from head to foot. The devils were commanded to come out of him in Jesus' name. Immediately he began to confess his sins and crimes, too awful to mention. He continued to pray and call upon God for mercy, and in a few days he found peace. He has since gone on to the cleansing Blood and has received his Pentecost, and in humility is owning Jesus as his perfect Savior, clothed in his right mind, joyful and happy. (page 5)

O I am so glad He has chosen me. The Lord has healed some bad cases. One woman had epileptic fits. When the devil went out of her, she was so weak she could not stand. (page 8)

Edition 6 – February/March 1907
This work seems to be increasing in power, despite all the efforts of self-appointed critics and antagonists. The writer has not a single doubt but that Brother Seymour has more power with God, and more power from God, than all his critics in and out of the city. His strength is in his conscious weakness, and lowliness before God; and, so long as he maintains this attitude, the power of God will, no doubt, continue to flow through him.

We tremble for some of our friends, who claim that God has revealed to them, that "this whole work is of the devil." We can not, dogmatically affirm that these persons have not received a revelation; but we are perfectly sure that such a revelation was not from God. The Almighty doth not pull down with one hand, what He buildeth up with the other. Satan is not in the rescue work; nor does he lead his followers to magnify the atoning blood of Christ, nor fill people with a desire and a passion for saving souls. We have never known Christ more magnified than in Azusa Mission. To ascribe this work to Satan, appears to us to be very much like ascribing the work of Christ, done in power of the Spirit, to Beelzebub. We tremble for all those who have made any such rash decision. May God in his great mercy help them to reverse such decision, and get to the place where he can give them the equivalent of what He is giving many in Azusa Street Mission. (page 47)

To the Saints at Los Angeles and all over the world, Greetings in Jesus name! The work at Dunn, N.C., still continues in His name. In the three weeks I was here, about fifty received the baptism with the Holy Ghost and spoke in tongues, which is thewitness of the baptism as on the Day of Pentecost; and about fifteen of the fifty were ministers of the Gospel. Some are from Georgia, some from South Carolina, and some from North Carolina. Some are called to China to preach this blessed truth. God has blest me in casting out devils, healing the sick and in discerning of spirits. (page 24)

[The following account of a Spiritualist being saved and sanctified, is written by Bro. J.E. Sawders, Homestead, Ohio., in *New Acts*]

We have had some of the most wonderful experiences with demons, that I have ever seen in my life. One woman, a Spiritualist, from the age of sixteen, was possessed with a legion of demons. The devil threw her on the floor where she fought and foamed froth out of her mouth, saying: "I hate Jesus Christ," many times, and blasphemed God in the most diabolic manner possible to imagine. She pointed right up in the faces of those praying for her, with a hellish laugh, challenging and defying God Almighty, saying, "Ha! ha! She is mine, ha! ha! she belongs to me, etc." Well, we prayed in Jesus name till she was gloriously delivered, and settled down like a lamb at the feet of Jesus, and for hours prayed and praised Him, until He forgave her, then cleansed her heart, and since then she has been seeking Pentecost. Last night she got up and told her whole experience, and it was simply wonderful indeed. She is very intelligent and she now feels that God is going to use her for revenge upon the devil and his hellish work in Spiritualism. These cities are full of Spiritualists and no doubt God will use this woman now to expose the thing from an experimental standpoint. (page 26)

Demons have been cast out in the name of Jesus. (page 22)

Praise God, the Holy Ghost came today. A minister slain under the power. Demons cast out of many. (page 27)

They brought many sick and those possessed with demons from far and near and God healed them. (page 43)

I want all of you to know how the Lord has cured me of an incurable disease of about eight years standing, and made me perfectly whole. Glory to God! He also gave me a discernment of spirits, till I could see the epileptic demons, demons that had been tormenting me so long. The Lord sent Sister Kennison from Redlands over to pray for me, and she came and we fasted and prayed for about four days. We had a hard fight with the devil, but thank the Lord, we at last got glorious victory. (page 49)

In spite of the great opposition from church people and holiness professors, many dear hungry souls are launching out into the ocean of God's love, and finding a satisfying portion. A great many were healed. Rheumatic demons and all manner of aches and pains were compelled to fly, at the name of Jesus. (page 23)

Edition 7 – April 1907
Backsliders are being reclaimed and some honest souls being converted, quite a lot of sick ones being healed, and also many demon possessed persons are being delivered in Jesus's name from the power of Satan. Glory to God! (page 5)

The Lord is working here in Bellvernon. People are being healed, devils are being cast out in Jesus' name. People are being baptized with the Holy Ghost and speaking with other tongues. (page 4)

WE are just holding up Jesus before this people, and God is doing the rest. We had quite a scene at the altar last night, when a demon possessed man who was kneeling at the altar was picked up; by demon power, thrown over the altar rail on his head, and when we commanded them to come out of him they barked at us and said that they would not come out of him, but they were cast out in the Nameof Jesus and the man was set free. (page 5f)

Many have received the personal Pentecost and speak and sing in new tongues, and have power over demons to cast them out and to pray the prayer of faith for the healing of the sick. (page 7)

The effect of the manifestation of the Spirit's power was, however, immediate and very marked, for the people came forward to the altar and fell all around under the power of the Holy Spirit, demons being cast out in the name of Jesus. (page 11)

Before they received deliverance in some cases the demon of drink had to be cast out. (page 11)

Those who are attributing the power of the Lord's servants, to speak in other tongues, to demons or evil spirits, seem to me to put themselves in the place of the Pharisees of old, who attributed Christ's supernatural power to the same source. See Matt. XII. 24-32; Mark III. 23-30. (page 17)

Edition 8 – May 1907
There is nothing that makes pure but the Blood of Jesus. God honors nothing but the Blood. This world is a mass of corruption, and there is nothing that keeps satanic power out of people but the Blood of the Lamb. (page 17)

One lady had a legion of demons cast out of her, was saved, sanctified and baptized with the Holy Ghost inside an hour, and spoke in tongues at the night meeting. One Swedish young man here had a demon cast out and received the baptism with the Holy Ghost, speaking in tongues, inside of two and a half hours. (page 7)

Bro. and Sister H. McLain, Sister Agnes Jacobson, and Bro. Harmon Clifford have been called to Chicago from San Jose. They wrote May 1st: "We had a wreck on the road but God saved us all. Praise God! We have not got to work yet only four souls have come to the place where we are stopping to be prayed for. One got the baptism last night and talked in tongues. One was sanctified and one anointed, and we cast out demons from two. Praise God." (page 15)

Edition 9 – June to September 1907
Nothing to note

Edition 10 – September 1907
A girl named Z---- had awful conflicts with the devil. A few friends, believing Z---- to be in some degree under satan's power, prayer earnestly for her deliverance. Later that night there was a meeting in the Church, and after the meeting to the glad surprise of those present, Z---- began to pray intelligently in English. One of the sentences uttered was, "Jesus' Blood make clean." Prayer had been answered and the devil's power broken, and a clear witness given to the Pentecostal baptism. Later, God gave this girl the gift of song which has been described as most sweet the notes of which are like the music of the flute. When singing in this new tongue she immediately translates the words into Marathi. A line which has been recalled is: "Jesus is over all; He is on the throne." (page 30)

Edition 11 – October 1907 to January 1908

Can a child of God be possessed by evil spirits?

No; evil spirits cannot come under the Blood, any more than the Egyptians could pass through the Red Sea-the Red Sea represents the Blood of Jesus Christ. The Blood gives you power over all the power of the enemy. But we must have Christ within us. If the soul is left empty and no "strong man" within, then the evil spirit can just take the house. (Luke 11:21, 26.) Some say that when the soul is sanctified, the house is empty and clean, and if he does not get the Holy Ghost, a wicked spirit can come in. Don't you ever believe that. That empty house represents a man that had a demon cast out (as we see plainly in the 24th verse); and he did not get Christ within. But a man that is sanctified has Christ ruling within. People that are living under the Blood live free from demons and satanic powers. They live pure and holy before the Lord. A man might be a Christian and oppressed by a demon, but that is altogether different from being possessed. Wicked spirits are driven out and repentance and faith wrought in the heart, when a man if justified. Then Christ comes in and keeps them out. A demon might be in the flesh as in the case of a cancer. The devil may oppress the body with sickness but that is very different from possessing the soul. (page 15f)

Remember, when the Lord works the devil works too, but when Satan presents anything to you, just tell him you are under the Blood. Just plead the blood, and he will flee. (page 30)

What is the real evidence that a man or woman has received the baptism with the Holy Ghost?

Divine love, which is charity. Charity is the Spirit of Jesus. They will have the fruits of the Spirit. Gal. 5:22. "The fruit of the Spirit is love, joy, peace, longsuffering, gentleness, goodness, meekness, faith, temperance; against such there is no law. And they that are Christ's have crucified the flesh with the affections and lusts." This is the real Bible evidence in their daily walk and conversation; and the outward manifestations; speaking in tongues and the signs following; casting out devils, laying hands on the sick and the sick being healed, and the love of God for souls increasing in their hearts. (page 11)

Edition 12 – January 1908

All prayer should be directed to the Father through Jesus. In casting out devils, it is through the name of our Lord and Savior Jesus Christ. In laying hands on the sick, it is in His name. All prayer must be in the name of Jesus. (page 24)

After that I went to Shanghai with the intention of finding some one in the Centennial Missionary Conference that had the baptism of the Holy Ghost who could help me out. Instead of that I met opposition from every side, and one from Los Angeles that had attended the meetings denounced the whole thing as of the devil. (page 25)

The Lord is casting out devils, healing the sick, and singing the sweetest songs. (page 30)

Demons were cast out of those bound by them. (page 5)

Edition 13 – May 1908

People have told me that it is all of the devil; but the Jesus I serve and trust will not allow Satan to deceive me. It is now over six months since I received this baptism, and I know that Satan does not give the peace, joy, and happiness that I have got. (page 8)

Jesus brought the living, burning words of the Father into this old world, and bless His dear name, He has left them here for those that love Him and keep His commandments, and walk softly before Him. O, to think He has given us this power and these words of the Father that bring instant healing, and rebuke demons and bring salvation to poor perishing souls. (page 12)

Confidence Magazine 1908-1911

(Early British Pentecostal magazine pioneered by A. A. Boddy)

April 1908

Pentecost 'arouses Satanic opposition in the least likely quarters.' (page 3)

We have seen demons cast out, and the very devil of disease rebuked, and the continual power and blessing fully resembling Mark xvi., 17. (page 7)

People say they do not believe in 'Tongues,' and because of their unbelief aittribute them to the devil. Let them come down here and see with the naked eye the wonderful works of God. 'By their fruits ye shall know them." (page 14)

'Pleading the Blood'. (page 12f)

May 1908

But worst of all is the Devil's cunning, using God's children to inject fears and doubts as to our Heavenly Father's love, and as to the almightiness of our Christ. Especially has he succeeded of late in making men afraid of seeking the Baptism of the Holy Ghost "with the Scriptural evidences." (page 3)

Other voices say, ('It is more than likely that, when you ask for the Holy Spirit, you will get a very unholy spirit instead. You are seeking the Holy Ghost, but you are going to get a devil." Shall we believe Jesus, our unfailing Saviour, who said, '(I will send you another Comforter, and He shall abide with you for ever," or shall we yield to man-made doubts and fears, and open the door thus to Satan's emmissaries? (page 3)

Best of all, let us magnify Jesus until he is so great as to completely shut out the Devil from our thoughts. A GREAT CHRIST means a very small devil. (page 4)

June 1908
We then spoke of discernment and of casting out devils, and how one had recently been delivered from the drug fiend and the drink devil. (page 15)

An ex-soldier, who had walked from Birmingham to be present at the Conference Meetings, cried out for help. He said he had back-slidden, and the Enemy had possessed him. We carried him into another room after the demons had been cast out. At the end of the Conference he set off to march back to Birmingham, looking very bright and well. (page 8)

Souls are being saved and sanctified, bodies healed, demons cast out, and the Holy Ghost poured-out. (page 13)

During the Conference there were several cases of Divine Heating, of casting out of demons. (page 18)

She has charge of boys who are mentally affected and have become almost criminal, and she asked for the prayers of God's people for them, that the demons might be bound, especially on Fridays when they always seem worse. (page 19)

August 1908
One woman who is baptized [in the Holy Spirit] had been an ordinary sailor's wife, very rough, and before her conversion was always fighting with her neighbours and swearing and cursing, and often used the knife. Last year, on Whitsuntide, she was converted **in** one of **our** meetings, her husband **also** converted and healed of a rupture of 10 years' standing. Her child **also** was healed of epileptic fits, when my husband consecrated it to God. God wonderfully blessed that family, and now she is baptized [in the Holy Spirit] and gloriously happy. What **a** change has come over her; truly we often find pearls in the mud. She was wonderfully used by God in casting the devil out of one of her children last Monday. (page 18)

The Devil is loose also, but we keep victory through the Blood. (page 19)

We are to yield, to let go, to cease, to step aside, to stop trying, and at all times and in all things rejoice in Christ and believe in the almighty and ever-present Spirit of God within you. Hallelujah! He will assert His sway and make Himself known. Do not fear that the devil will possess you; it is impossible under the blood. (page 24)

During one of our evening meetings not long ago I became conscious in my spirit that there was some hindrance to God's workings in those present. Without in the least expecting suchan answer as came to me, I prayed "0 Lord, show me what hinders Thee!" At once a voice seemed to say in my car, "Come, and I will show you" Then I seemed to be taken in spirit with Jesus into the air where I could look into the room and see the people kneeling there, myself one of the number. I soon noticed that the upper part of the room was filled with a vast number of very large bees which looked to be about 2½ feet across their outstretched wings, having stings in their tails which were 5 or 6 inches long. I said, "Oh, *see* all those bees! The Lord replied, "They are not bees. They are made to, look like bees to you, but they are demons. I saw that they were stinging one and another in the most terrible manner until nearly everyone in the room was attacked, and was in dreadful suffering in consequence. The Lord spoke to me again and said, "If you will Iook closely you will see that they have their names on their backs. "I looked and read these words on different bees: Fear, Envy, Pride, Dread, Doubts, Unbelief, Jealousy, the Opinion of Others, Lack of Love, etc. Jesus said, These are the things that are hindering my work.

Just then at one side I saw what seemed to me to be smoke, and I asked, 'What is burning? He said, "Nothing is burning: I will show you what it is." Then I saw Heaven opened and the Throne of God, with God Himself sitting on the Throne. The smoke I had seen was rising before the Throne, and Jesus said, "This is the prayers of the saints that rise as sweet
incense before the Throne of God." Then He told me to look into the room again, and this time I saw the bees falling dead, here one and there another, then in increasing numbers till they fell by dozens from the effects of the smoke. Jesus said to me, Prayer is the power that will kill these bees, and *so* let Me have My perfect right of way in these hearts" (page 20f).

September 1908

A sister (the first to receive 'Pentecost' with Tongues a year ago, and who has had sore trials since) said, "It's better every day. All the day long it is the precious blood of Jesus. It is all Jesus. The nearer we are to the Lord the more He shines upon us and then we reflect His Light." She felt she must tell of a recent vision she had had in which she had seen all the grinning demons cast down into the abyss. Then she saw *a* wonderful avenue of light and at the end of it was the Lord Himself standing-all victorious and ready to help. (page 5f)

Why do you want the baptism in the Holy Ghost ? Do you want it because your friends have it? Because you will then have more power to cast out demons, heal the sick, preach better, conduct bigger meetings? Your friends may turn you down. You may never do any of these things openly. You may be called to isolated suffering. Whatever minor motive prompts you to seek this glorious enduement, or enclothment, the one supreme motive should be that you may fully, whole-heartedly and constantly please God by letting Him reveal **His** Son in you. (page 18f)

October 1908
God will not forsake an honest soul, neither will He let you get into the hands of the devil if you are earnest and love to do His will, seeking only His glory. (page 11)

November 1908
If a real baptism of fire makes them better equipped to serve God and fight the Devil, then what they have received, if it is as some people say "Of the Devil," it ought to make them more useful in the Devil's service. Such a mighty experience as this, through which they have passed, if of the Devil, must absolutely make them Devilish and Satanic, and that in a very extreme measure. They find instead of that, that their delight is in the Lord and His statutes are their songs in the house of their pilgrimage." (page 7)

There is nothing the Devil and his hosts are attacking so much now as this movement; he knows that his time is short and that this fight is real. He is using Bible, pen, papers (religious and secular), halfhearted Christians, and even honest, though misguided Christians are in his service. (page 8)

December 1908
The last two weeks have been weeks of victory, but also of fight against the wiles of the devil. He is still alive and fights us fiercely, but we are overcomers through the precious Blood of the Lamb. (page 21)

We are daily witnessing to the work being done. Demons are being cast out, the sick are healed, and sinners turn to Jesus. (page 9)

The great difference between hypnotic, mesmeric or demon power and that of the Holy Spirit is, that the former control us, causing people to act against their will. (page 14)

February 1909
A. A. B. [A. A. Boddy] told how he had been led to cast out demons (St. Mark

xvi., 15), and how, in a meeting, the word of command in the name of the Lord had brought liberty to several, and to some who had not expected deliverance. (page 16f)

March 1909

He had been warned against our meetings and told it was of the devil. (page10)

April 1909

He explained that in many parts of the world-in Los Angeles, China, Japan, India, Africa, Germany, in England (Sunderland, London, Southsea, Bournemouth), and many other parts of the world God was pouring out His Spirit, and people were prophesying, seeing visions, speaking in new tongues, casting out devils, healing the sick, the blind, the deaf, the lame--all in the name of the Holy Child Jesus. (page 11)

May 1909

This Pentecostal Tree is God's own planting and the Fruit is the Lord's. Satan, knowing that his time is short, tries his very hardest to (I) slip in now and again something of his own, or *(2)* make the Lord's people afraid of what is not so much of Satan, but rather the flesh stirred up by emotion. (page 12)

June 1909

By Mrs. Lockhart, of Winnipeg, who has been so marvellously used out there in healing the sick, casting out of demons, etc., and who has known this blessed experience of the Pentecostal Baptism for many years; who, when she first received her Baptism, spoke in Tongues... (page 13)

In various places many have been delivered from demons of torment and infirmity, the lame have walked, the blind have seen, the most incurable diseases have been healed, and thousands upon thousands of souls have confessed Christ. (page 25)

throughout the world, some of high profession, who, before God, have the awful and fearless daring to hunt this work like Saul hunted David, and to brand this whole movement as of the Devil and every one in it as either deceived or a deceiver. (page 25)

And neither does the Devil's work in connection with the Pentecostal movement make it from beneath. (page 27)

July 1909

"Get on your knees, and tell the Devil that Jesus is Lord I' (1 John iv., *2)*. This he could only do when the demons had been cast out. So he was delivered and saved and baptized with the Holy Ghost. "Yes, they need to be delivered first from the devil," continued Bro. Murdoch; "They must then go on to get saved, sanctified, and baptized in the Holy Ghost. (page 13)

August 1909
some were of the opinion that the old recognized Christian leaders of England had made a very *sad mistake* in denouncing this whole movement as of the devil, instead of attempting to co-operate with its leaders. (page 21)

September 1909
When he heard that Pastor Paul had received his Baptism and spoke in Tongues, he thought, "Was it possible that a man so fully given up to God could be taken possession of by a demon?" (page 25)

Fear is from the devil. Be more afraid to fear than afraid of the tongues. Some people say, 'When the tongues came I commenced to be afraid.' But this fear is not from God as they imagine, but from the devil. (page 10)

October 1909
We wish to acknowledge that, even as in all revivals, also in **this** movement, we see manifested not only the things of God, but also soulish, viz., human and in some cases demoniacal manifestations. (page 13)

I give you these Scriptures to shew that the Gift of the Holy Spirit, attended with the miraculous speaking of Tongues, is clearly God's will, and not to be either despised, criticised, or objected to, much less to be feared or classed with that of having communion with evil spirits, which latter some are doing, and attributing the Holy Spirit's work to that of Satan, and *so* committing an unpardonable sin (Matt. xii., 31, 32). (page 18)

November 1909
As we landed and were walking into the busy streets, a tall young lady in black in front of us suddenly crashed to the ground in what seemed to be an epileptic fit. A crowd rushed together, and many did what they could, but we stood by and prayed. At one point it seemed as if she had died. All life seemed to go, and her face was as if she were really dead, and her eyes turned back. But I rebuked the demons in the name of Jesus continually, and life returned. (page 7)

Heavy tribulations have befallen us. The leading brethren of the German Gemeinschaftsbewegung, in a public declaration issued from Berlin, have condemned the Pentecostal movement as being from the Devil, and, by this step, have caused a real persecution to break in upon the children of God who are connected with this movement. Also these brethren have denounced our beloved brother Paul *as* a heretic teaching false Doctrines. (page 18)

December 1909

There was a case of Jesus casting out devils also that night. A young woman that had been troubled for a long time, in the Name of Jesus, he, the evil spirit, was commanded to depart. And truly it was *so* in a very similar way that we read in Mark ix. This dear one was Baptized by Jesus with the Holy Ghost and Fire. (page 14f)

January 1910

(It is most necessary at this point, when casting out the demon of disease, or any other demon, to bid it depart far away and not enter into any other being, human or animal, as strange occurrences otherwise may happen). (page 10)

February 1910

We had a solemn and powerful after-meeting, when the sick were prayed with, demons were rebuked, and prayer was made for the outpouring of the Spirit. The power of the Lord was present to heal and bless. (page 6)

It was good to hear Beloved Pastor Paul, he puts me in mind of his namesake, the Apostle Paul. Self-forgetful, full of zeal and fire, yet full of love and tenderness. How the German pastors can say he is of the devil, I do not know. (page 20)

March 1910

Just to touch upon demon-possession, I am convinced that there is much demoniacal power at work both at home and abroad, and even where there is not demon-possession there is in many cases strong obsession or the persistent attack from some demon who has hopes of entering in. Dr. Nevius, in 1897, published a very valuable work "Demon possession and allied theories." He was a missionary in China for forty years, and he came into touch with many cases of demon-possession in that great Empire over which waves significantly the Banner of the Dragon. One of the lands of which it might be written as of Pergamum *"where Satan's seat is."* He gives instances where, when Christianity came into a village, the presence of an ill informed Christian of no great spiritual attainments had a tremendous effect upon Demon-possessed Temple attendants -really spiritualistic mediums--so that their power of divination was injured. In other cases the demons went out of the possessed ones, acknowledging that Jesus was mightier than they. It is a valuable book to study upon this subject, but we would venture to say that the subject should only be studied when we are consciously in union with the Almighty Lord who can protect us even from the Demons we might possibly rouse by light and careless thoughts concerning them. (page 22) .

April 1910

Our asylums and prisons are crowded with thousands of devil-possessed and oppressed degenerates. (page 11)

June 1910
Tongues with interpretations. Messages in the Spirit. The wonderful Heavenly Anthem. Healing of the Sick. Casting out of Demons. All these were in evidence during the Whitsuntide Convention. (page 7)

This Pentecostal work *is* discovering and exposing the devils. (page 15)

God Himself is purifying this work, defeating Satan's attempts to overthrow or to counterfeit. God Himself is shewing His children that His Gift of "Tongues" is more for personal edification than for public use, unless He gives interpretation. (page 17)

"Brother Hutchinson made some remarkable statements. He declared with much force that demons of disease were being driven out of the human body by the name of Christ. (page 18)

'A woman had fits. She was torn with demons. I rebuked Satan. I commanded the demons to come out of her. Three came out at different times, and when the third came she fell down in the dust. (page 18)

July 1910
Several demons have been cast out in the name of the Lord. (page 15)

August 1910
Attacking demons of disease should be rebuked in the Name of the Triumphant Jesus. (page 7)

"From Below." Can it be that the movement is really *from below,* but that our friends have just gone *down* one stage too far in their hasty zeal to defend God's cause? Supposing that the revival is "From Below," namely, from *the* DUST, and that our friends have gone just a bit too deep in *looking down* on the movement and called it FROM THE DEVIL. God brings *all* His new creations from *the dust,* but none from the DEVIL. (page 11)

This Movement is from Below. BY ARTHUR S. BOOTH-CLIBBORN. --
Such was the solemn declaration made in 1909 by a number of German Pastors. That which some 100,000 true Christians believed to be a revival coming from above, they declared (with incredibly little real. evidence before them) to be a revival of Satanic power coming from below. (page 10)

September 1910
Then, standing upon Mark 16 teaching, we have seen devils cast out and many

cases of suffering relieved, and healing of the body, through laying on of hands, and, praise God, honest seekers are being delivered from fear and inquiring the way of God more perfectly. (page 19)

October 1910

Some were very difficult cases-most anxious to be true to the Lord. Demons were cast out, and sick ones were prayed with, and hands laid upon them in the Name which is above every name. (page 6)

The great difference between demon control and God-control is that God will not work without our co-operation. (page 13)

December 1910

Our strongest opponents denounced the whole movement as being FROM BELOW, and those of us who have received spiritual gifts as being possessed by demons. (page 20)

January 1911

I would ask you to pray also for power and wisdom to be given for laying on of hands for the sick, and for the demon-possessed. We have many such among the natives. (page 16)

March 1911

They have a young fellow here, a Chinaman who formerly WAS in the Boxer riots, and was a very terrible character. He was prayed for by the brethren, and the demons were cast out in the name of the Lord Jesus Christ. (page 21)

June 1911

Then there were requests that prayers might be offered for the casting out of demons, of whom certain persons were stated to **be** possessed... Then there was a solemn praying manifestation. Amid fervent murmurs, gesticulations, and genuflections, prayers were offered up for all those afflicted, and especially that demons might be cast out. (page 6)

September 1911

To-day the world is girdled by a religious revival called "The Tongue Movement." Its advocates assert it is the work of the Holy Ghost. Its opponents seem to be quite sure it is of the devil. (page 11)

There are some lamentable features connected with the "Tongue Movement" of to-day. We refer to a few... That Satan is counterfeiting this gift of God, and thus deceiving many precious souls, besides putting the real work of God in a false light before those who hear. Great prejudice and opposition is the result. (page 15)

November 1911

by Dr. C. Williams (The Ambrose Co., *55,* Wigmore St., London, W.). This book contains several papers read at important meetings in London, before medical men and others. He hoped to persuade his fellow-practitioners as to the reality of Demon powers. Those who are baptized in the Holy Ghost generally learn quickly the reality of demon-powers. and how safe we are in union with the Lord, and sheltered **by** His Blood. (page 17)

Redemption Tidings 1924 - 1930

October 1924

We are not defending every manifestation which has been witnessed during the past 18 years. As stated previously every revival attracts cranks and fanatics; while it would be wrong to say that every physical manifestation is of God, it is absolutely wrong and very serious to say that any great proportion is from the devil. There are too many people ready to do this and if asked for proof, they simply say, " O God would never work in that way," as though they were authority on what God will or will not do. (Page 15)

The 44th Chapter of Isaiah, verses 13 to 17, is a true picture of India. In many of the houses you will see images, also under some of the trees near the villages you will find them. The people place offerings of food and flowers before these idols, they fall down and worship them and ask them to deliver them from evil, harm and sickness. Theirs is a religion of fear, not a religion of love. Many of the Sacthu's (holy men) are demon possessed. You can see the devil shining out of their eyes. (page 17)

June 1925

After that. I began to seek my baptism. I had not given up smoking yet. In one of the meetings I had a vision of a handsome black man whom I recognised as the devil, and I said to myself, there must be something wrong with me. About this time, in course of conversation, a relation said to me, how can a man with cigarettes in his pocket expect to receive the baptism in the Holy Spirit. After that remark I dropped two or three packets on the road, and told my cousin that I intended to give up smoking. But later the devil gained an advantage, and I am ashamed to say that I bought a packet and had a smoke on the quiet. That very evening something said, throw those cigarettes away. At first I resisted, but presently got up and threw the cigarettes out of the window. (page 4)

July 1925

I know the fact that God declares it to us by His own Son is this, that the new birth is a perfect place of royalty, reigning, over the powers of darkness, bringing everything to perfect submission to the rightful owner, and that is- the Lord. (page 4)

December 1925

A man and his wife came to me troubled about things taking place in their meeting. I said: You two can be so perfectly joined in unity, as to take victory for every meeting, not a thing could stand against you, a perfect fellowship, which the devil is not able to break, if any two of you agree. Dare on the authority of God's Word to bind every spirit in the meeting. (Page 3)

April 1926

Extended article on demon possession by Donald Gee which downplays the fear of the demonic and the possibility of a believer being possessed. (page 3ff)

March 1926

Donald Gee continues optimistically insisting that the power of the HS transcends that of the demons (page 2-3) S Wigglesworth then continues insisting that the presence of the HS evicts imitiations (page 4). He also asserts that the spirit filled believer is invulnerable to Satanic attack. (page 5)

July 1926

Baptism in HS = 'power to deal with the devil' (page 3) Smith Wigglesworth highlights his experience in evicting demons (page 6) in the name of Jesus – optimistic and serving his ministry.

February 1927

Donald Gee notes that those baptised with the HS will endure more testing from Satanic activity (page 3) 'Two great personalities are interested when you are baptised in the Holy Spirit, Satan is interested, and God is interested, but mark you, Satan has something to fear when a man is filled with the Spirit.' (page 3)

March 1927

A Roman Catholic converted at a Stephen Jeffries revival says '" Ah, sure enough this Place is too Hot for old Nick (Satan) to live, Shure, this man Jeffries, has kicked Nick right out of the place, Nick hath not one inch to stand on.' (page 16)

August 1927

May God keep us in Himself where Satan has no power or victory. (page 8) Harold Horton.

January 1928

Amongst some of God's most spiritual and devoted children there is a strangely perverted and exaggerated dread of demon-power and spiritual deception. As though the Lord left the man sincerely seeking a closer walk with Himself to become the sport of the fiends of hell! Such should ponder Luke xi. 11-13. They appear to prefer no experience of the supernatural at all, lest it should prove wrong. They forget that there are plain tests for the supernatural given in the New Testament within the reach of every believer, and that a spirit of fear is specially deprecated. It has been Satan's master-stroke to so raise fears of deception, that he is thereby able to keep many of God's dear children out of their inheritance on this line. The saddest part is that he has actually found tools for this work among some of the finest Christian teachers of the hour. (page 17)

October 1928
Demons may drive along the unfortunate persons they possess in a frenzy or a stupor; but the Holy Spirit will never operate through a believer except along the line of his willing, active, and intelligent co-operation. (page 17)

December 1928
the "Fundamentalist" teachers who make a hobby of demonology, and scare believers away from any form of the supernatural in their Christian experience, will ascribe the whole thing [Montanism] to deceiving spirits. (page 5)

April 1929
Do not say with regard to me (as some did about —) that I have received a "deceiving spirit." Does a "deceiving spirit" acknowledge Christ as the Son of God, come in the flesh to be our Saviour; exalt His Name; light up God's Word in a manner never before experienced; and put such a reality and joy into the Prayer Life that the hours spent in communion fly past like minutes? Does a "deceiving spirit" give one power, real living power, over hitherto unconquered habits, and put into practical experience the truth that we are "crucified with Christ"? No, this is not the work of a "deceiving spirit"—it is the work of the blessed Third Person of the Trinity, the Holy Ghost Himself. "He shall glorify Me." One who attributes this blessed Baptism of the Spirit to the work of the devil approaches very near indeed to that unpardonable sin of blasphemy against the Holy Ghost. (page 14)

May 1929
There are some who declare a readiness to believe that God will do these things to-day, yet they very inconsistently maintain that the Pentecostal Movement is "all of the devil." Such opponents usually write and talk of nothing else but "counterfeits" and "deceiving spirits," and seem to have a far more exalted view of the power of Satan than they have of the Risen Christ. They are afraid of having anything to do with the supernatural in present-day Christian experience lest it should prove wrong. They seem to have an altogether morbid and exaggerated fear of demon-power, far removed from the healthy

watchfulness enjoined in the New Testament. They see in the Pentecostal Movement nothing but "grave danger," etc., etc. Doubtless they would have felt at home with certain Israelites of old who would have kept the whole nation out of the Promised Land because there were some giants there! These folk should' be buckling on their armour to help, not to oppose (page 6).

July 1929

Faith applied can rise to the level of "whatsoever we are called to meet with— difficulty, trial, infirmity, or sickness, and is the shield to quench all the fiery darts of the devil (page 8).

October 1929

Thus when Christ fills us with His blessed Spirit our hearts should gush forth with a spring of divine water that should never cease flowing lull and plenty till the very end of our days. And so powerful this leaping stream should be that, every time the devil endeavours to throw something in, he gets it thrown hack at him, with a rebuff bath of divine power in the bargain (page 4).

May 1930

At last in February, 1910, we held a four days' convention, and invited some Spirit-filled saints to come and minister. I felt that the time had come and that I must claim my blessing now. How I rejoiced when another Christian worker about my own age fell to the ground, smitten down by the power of God, and was soon praising the Lord in New Tongues. I was staying with a godly couple, and when I reached home that night they were indignant with the whole convention. "Don't tell us that that is of God," they said; "whoever heard tell of people shaking, laughing, crying, singing, and even falling to the ground under the Power of the Holy Spirit? No, it must all be of the devil."

It was useless to argue with them. Souls were being saved, and bodies healed in every meeting. Could that be the devil? I read in the Bible of special visitations from God being accompanied by trembling, falling on one's face to the ground, all strength being taken away, by laughing, dancing and leaping. Yet these dear people had become so accustomed to a stereotyped, unemotional form of religion that any experience too great to be trammelled by their particular notions must be regarded as of the devil (page 2). W. F. P. Burton

December 1930

If satanic or demoniac counterfeits have, in the case of some seekers after the special Scriptural Gifts of the Holy Spirit been substituted by the evil one for the divine blessings (and not a single authentic case has been known), even that circumstance could not render the commands concerning this subject in God's Word, null and void, nor could it stultify the faith and devotion of those who have attached themselves to this Movement (page 3).

Optimistic Reference to the Demonic

1928	March page 7
	April page 2
	May page 1
1929	March page 8
1930	June page 8
	November page 1

Reference to the Demonic Causing Illness

1925	December page 4
1926	January page 2
	February page 20
	March page 3
	May page 4
	June page 16
	July page 10
	August page 16, 18 (demon possession and illness closely identified)
	October page 4
	November page 2
1927	January page 5
	May page 4
	July page 18 (healing equated with deliverance from Satan)
	October page 7
1928	January page 2
	April page 2
	September page 4
1929	January page 18
	May page 6, 18
	November page 4
1930	July page 11
	November page 1
	December page 6
	December page 11, 13

Reference to the Demonic Darkness of or Demon Activity in Heathen Lands

1925	December page 10, 11
1926	February page 12
	June page 16
	November page 11
1927	January page 12
	July page 10

Bibliography

Primary Sources

Allen, A. A., *Demon Possession Today and How to be Free* (Miracle Valley: A. A. Allen, 1953).
- *Invasion from Hell* (Miracle Valley: A. A. Allen, 1953).
- *The Tormenting Demon of Fear* (no publication details available).
- *It Pays to Serve the Devil* (no publication details available).
- *Witchcraft, Wizards and Witches* (Miracle Valley: A. A. Allen, 1968).
- 'Demon Possession Today' in *Voice of Healing*, May 1953.
Amorth, G., *An Exorcist Tells His Story* (San Francisco: Ignatius Press,1999).
- *An Exorcist: More Stories* (San Francisco: Ignatius Press, 2002).
Anderson, N. T., *The Bondage Breaker* (London: Monarch, 2002).
- *Living Free in Christ* (Harpenden: Monarch, 1993).
Anderson, P., *Talk About the Devil* (London: Word, 1973).
Arnold, C., *Spiritual Warfare* (London: Marshall Pickering, 1997).
- *3 Crucial Questions about Spiritual Warfare* (Grand Rapids: Baker, 1997).
Bartleman, F., *Azusa Street* (New Kensington: Whittaker House, 1982).
- *Way of Faith* (October 1906).
Basham, D., *Deliver Us From Evil* (London: Hodder and Stoughton, 1972).
- *Face Up with a Miracle* (Northridge: Voice Christian Publications, 1967).
Branham, W., *Demonology* (Jefferson: Spoken Word, 1976).
Brittle, G. D., *The Demonologist* (Lincoln: BackinPrint, 2002).
Brown, R., *He Came to Set the Captives Free* (Chino: Chick, 1986).
Bubeck, M. I., *The Adversary* (Chicago: Moody Press, 1975).
- *The Rise of Fallen Angels* (Chicago: Moody Press, 1991).
Cain, P., 'I was not disobedient to the Heavenly Vision' in *Voice of Healing* (August 1951).
Cerullo, M., *The Back Side of Satan* (Carol Stream, Illinois: Creation House, 1973).
Cruz, N., *Satan on the Loose* (London: Oliphants 1973).
Dickason, C. F., *Angels: Elect and Evil* (Chicago: Moody, 1975).
- *Demon Possession and the Christian* (Westchester: Crossway, 1987).
Dow, G., *Those Troublesome Intruders* (Nottingham: Grove, 1990).
- *Deliverance* (Tonbridge: Sovereign, 2003).
DuPlessis, D., 'Foreword' in W. R. McAlister *The Dilemma: Deliverance or Discipline* (Plainfield: Logos, 1976).
Foster, T. N., 'Divine Deliverance in the Local Churches' in *Voice of Healing* (September 1953).
Friesen, G., *Uncovering the Mystery of MPD* (Nashville: Nelson, 1991).
Green, M., *I Believe in Satan's Downfall* (London: Hodder and Stoughton, 1981).
Hagin, K., 'A Vision of the End-Time' in *Voice of Healing* (September 1963).

- *Demons and How to Deal with Them* (Tulsa: Kenneth Hagin Ministries, 1979).
- *Ministering to the Oppressed* (Tulsa: Kenneth Hagin Ministries, 1986).
Hammond, F., *Pigs in the Parlour: A Practical Guide to Deliverance* (Kirkwood: Impact Books, 1973).
Hampel, H., 'I Met the Devil Face to Face' in *Voice of Healing* (June 1956).
Harper, M., *Spiritual Warfare* (London: Hodder and Stoughton, 1970).
Harris, L. C., 'Deliverance from Evil Spirits' in *Voice of Healing* (July 1954).
Hayes, N., *How to Cast out Devils* (Tulsa: Harrison, 1982).
Horrobin, P., *Healing Through Deliverance Volume 1: The Foundation of Deliverance Ministry* (Grand Rapids: Chosen, 2003).
- *Healing Through Deliverance Volume 2: The Practice of Deliverance Ministry* (Grand Rapids: Chosen, 2003).
Irvine, D., *From Witchcraft to Christ* (Cambridge: Concordia, 1973).
- *Set Free to Serve Christ* (Cambridge: Concordia, 1979).
- *Spiritual Warfare* (Newton Abbot: Nova, 1992).
Israel, M., *Exorcism: The Removal of Evil Influences* (London: SPCK, 1997).
Jackson, J. P., *Unmasking the Jezebel Spirit* (Eastbourne: Kingsway, 2001).
Jeevaratnam, L., *Concerning Demons (Questions and Answers)* (Allahabad: Mission Press, no date available).
Koch, K., *Between Christ and Satan* (Berghausen: Evangelisation, 1972).
- *The Coming One* (Grand Rapids: Kregel, 1972).
- *Day X* (Grand Rapids: Kregel, 1971).
- *Demonology, Past and Present* (Grand Rapids: Kregel, 1973).
- *The Devil's Alphabet* (Grand Rapids: Kregel, 1971).
- *Occult Bondage and Deliverance* (Berghausen: Evangelization, 1970).
- *World Without Chance?* (Grand Rapids: Kregel, 1974).
Lake, J. G., *John G Lake: His Life, His Sermons, His Boldness of Faith* (Fort Worth: Kenneth Copeland, 1994).
Lindsay, G., (ed.) *The New John G Lake Sermons* (Dallas: CFN, 1979).
- *Satan, Fallen Angels and Demons (and how to have power over them)* (Dallas: The *Voice of Healing*, no date available).
Lindsey, H., *The Late Great Planet Earth* (London: Lakeland, 1971).
- *Satan is Alive and Well on Planet Earth* (London: Lakeland, 1973).
Lozano, N., *Unbound* (Grand Rapids: Chosen Books, 2003).
MacNutt, F., *Healing* (New York: Bantam, 1997).
- *Deliverance from Evil Spirits*, (Grand Rapids: Chosen, 1995).
Martin, M., *Hostage to the Devil* (New York: Reader's Digest, 1976).
Maxwell Whyte, H. A., 'Delivering a Haunted House' in *Voice of Healing* (November 1958).
- *The Kiss of Satan* (Monroeville: Whitaker, 1973).
- *Return to the Pattern* (no publication details).
- *The Body is for the Lord* (first published in 1969, no other publication details).
- *Pulling Down Strongholds* (no publication details).
- *Dominion Over Demons* (Monroeville: Banner,1973).
- 'The Imperative Need of Deliverance Pastors' in *Voice of Healing* (January 1955).

Murphy, E. F., *The Handbook for Spiritual Warfare* (Nashville: Thomas Nelson, 2003).

Nee, W., *Sit Walk Stand* (Eastbourne: Kingsway, 2002).

– *Love Not the World* (Eastbourne: Kingsway, 2000).

Neil, A., *Aid Us in Our Strife* (no location given: Heath, 1989).

– *Aid Us in Our Strife: Volume 2* (Newton Abbot: Nova, 1990).

Neil-Smith, C., *The Exorcist and the Possessed* (Andover: James Pike, 1974).

Nevius, J. L., *Demon Possession and Allied Themes* (London: Revell, circa 1894).

Peck, M. S., *Glimpses of the* Devil (New York: Free Press, 2005).

– *People of the Lie* (New York: Touchstone, 1985).

– *The Road Less Travelled* (London: Arrow, 1990).

Penn-Lewis, J., *War on the Saints* (Leicester: Excelsior, 1912).

Peretti, F., *This Present Darkness* (Eastbourne: Monarch, 1986).

– *Piercing the Darkness*, Eastbourne: Monarch, 1989.

Perry, M., *Deliverance* (London: SPCK, 1987).

Pethrus, L., *The Wind Bloweth Where it Listeth* (Chicago: Philapdelphia, 1945).

Petitpierre, R., *Exorcising Devils* (London: Robert Hale, 1976).

Petitpierre, R., (ed.), *Exorcism: The Findings of a Commission Convened by the Bishop of Exeter* (London: SPCK, 1972).

Prince, D., *They Shall Expel Demons* (Grand Rapids: Chosen Books, 1998).

– Ministry Cassettes 6001-6 (Derek Prince Ministries, no date given)

– *Deliverance and Demonology Study Note Outline DD1* (Derek Prince Ministries, no date given).

– *Blessing or Curse: You Can Choose!* (Harpenden: Word, 1990).

Richards, J., *But Deliver Us From Evil* (London: Darton, Longman and Todd, 1980).

Roberts, O., *My Story* (Tulsa: Summit, 1961).

– *My Twenty Years of a Miracle Ministry* (Tulsa: Oral Roberts, 1967).

– *The Call: An Autobiography* (New York: Doubleday, 1972).

– 'Demon Possession' in *Voice of Healing* (November 1951)

– *How to Resist the Devil and His Demons* (Tulsa: Oral Roberts, 1989).

– *If You Want Healing Do These Things* (Tulsa: Healing Waters, 1954).

Sandford, J., *The Transformation of the Inner Man* (Tulsa: Victory House, 1982).

– *Healing the Wounded Spirit* (New Jersey: Logos, 1985).

Sandford, J and M., *A Comprehensive Guide to Deliverance and Inner Healing* (Grand Rapids: Chosen, 1992).

Scanlan, M., *Inner Healing* (New York: Paulist, 1974).

– *Deliverance From Evil Spirits* (Cincinnati: Servant, 1980).

Shakarian, D., *The Happiest People on Earth* (London: Hodder and Stoughton, 1975).

Subritzky, W., *Demons Defeated* (Tonbridge: Sovereign, 1985).

Suenens, L., *Renewal and the Powers of Darkness* (London: DLT, 1983).

Sumrall, L., *The True Story of Clarita Villaneuva* (Manilla: Lester Sumrall, 1955).

– 'An Evil Spirit was Starving a Girl to Death' in *Voice of Healing* (September 1955).

- *The Gates of Hell* (South Bend: World Harvest Press, no date available).
Trinkle, G., *Delivered to Declare* (London: Hodder, 1986).
Unger, M. F., *Biblical Demonology* (Grand Rapids: Kregel, 1994).
- *Demons in the World Today* (Wheaton: Tyndale, 1971).
- *What Demons can do to Saints* (Chicago: Moody, 1991).
Wagner, C. P., 'Territorial Spirits' in C P Wagner (ed.), *Wrestling With Dark Angels* (Speldhurst: Monarch, 1990, 83-125).
- 'Spiritual Warfare' in C P Wagner (ed.), *Territorial Spirits* (Chichester, Sovereign, 1991, 3-27).
Walker, D., *The Ministry of Deliverance* (London: DLT, 1997).
Warnke, M., *The Satan Seller* (Plainfield: Logos International, 1972).
Wimber, J., *Kingdom of God* (Placentia: Vineyard Ministries, 1985).
- 'Power Evangelism' in C. P. Wagner and F. D. Pennoyer (eds.), *Wrestling With Dark Angels* (Speldhurst: Monarch, 1990) 19-49.
- *Power Evangelism* (London: Hodder and Stoughton, 1985).
- *Power Healing* (London: Hodder and Stoughton, 1986).
Wink, W., *Engaging the Powers* (Minneapolis: Fortress, 1992).
Woolmer, J., *Healing and Deliverance* (Crowborough: Monarch, 1999).
Zuendel, F., *The Awakening* (Robertsbridge: Plough, 1999).
No author, *Demon Experiences in Many Lands* (Chicago: Moody Press, 1960).
No author, *Roman Ritual, Rite of Exorcisms 22nd November 1998* (Vatican City, 1999).

Pentecostal Journals

The Apostolic Faith Magazine (see Appendix 1 for exhaustive list of references)
Confidence (see Appendix 1 for exhaustive list of references)
Voice of Healing (December 1948); (October 1952); (July 1953); (August 1953); (October 1953); (October 1954).

Secondary Works (Books and Articles)

Adams, K., *A Diary of Revival* (Farnham: CWR, 2004).
- *A Pictorial History of Revival* (Farnham: CWR, 2004).
Almond, P., *Heaven and Hell in Enlightenment England* (Cambridge: Cambridge University Press, 1994).
Anderson, R. M., *Vision of the Disinherited: The Making of American Pentecostalism* (New York: Oxford University Press, 1979).
Balmer, R., *Mine Eyes Have Seen the Glory* (New York: OUP, 2000).
Barling, M., 'Satan, the church and a con-man' in *Renewal*, (124, August/September 1986) 4-7.
Bebbington, D., *Evangelicalism in Modern Britain* (London: Routledge, 1989).
Bowman, R. M., *The Word-Faith Controversy: Understanding the Health and Wealth Gospel* (Grand Rapids: Baker, 2001).

Brandreth, G., *The Devil is Gaining Ground* (Daily Telegraph, 29 October, 2000) Review Section 1-2.

Breese, D., *Know the Marks of Cults* (Wheaton: Victor, 1975).

Bruce, S., *Religion in Modern Britain* (OUP: Oxford, 1995).

Buchanan, C., *Encountering Charismatic Worship* (Bramcote: Grove, 1997).

Burnett, D., *Dawning of the Pagan Moon* (Eastbourne: MARC, 1991).

Cavendish, R., *The Powers of Evil in Western Religion, Magic and Folk Belief* (London: Routledge & Keegan Paul Ltd, 1975).

Cohn, N., *Europe's Inner Demons* (London: Pimlico, 1993).

Cook, P. L., *Zion City, Illinois: Twentieth Century Utopia* (NewYork: Syracuse University Press 1996).

Cuneo, M. W., *American Exorcism* (London: Bantam, 2001).

Dawson, L. L., *Comprehending Cults* (Ontario: Oxford University Press, 1998).

Dayton, D. W., *Theological Roots of Pentecostalism* (Metuchen: Hendrickson, 1987).

Evans, E., *The Welsh Revival of 1904* (London: Evangelical Press, 1969).

Finis, T., 'Appendix 1,The Berlin Declaration, 1909' in T. Finis, *A Quest for Holiness* (unpublished MTh thesis, 1998).

Finlay, A., *Demons!* (London: Blandford, 1999).

Harrell, D. E., *All Things are Possible* (Bloomington: Indiana University Press, 1975).

– 'Healers and Televangelists after World War II' in V. Synan (ed.), *The Century of the Holy Spirit* (Nashville: Thomas Nelson, 2001) 325-347.

– *Oral Roberts: An American Life* (Bloomington: Indiana University Press, 1985).

Harris, H. A., 'How Helpful Is The Term Fundamentalist?' in C. H. Partridge (ed.), *Fundamentalisms* (Carlisle: Paternoster, 2001) 3-18.

Hathaway, M. R.,'The Elim Pentecostal Church: Origins, Development and Distinctives' in K. Warrington (ed.), *Pentecostal Perspectives* (Carlisle: Paternoster, 1998) 1-39.

Hertenstein, M., *Selling Satan* (Chicago: Cornerstone, 1993).

Heyd, M., *Be Sober and Reasonable* (Leiden: E J Brill, 1995).

Hocken, P., *Streams of Renewal* (Carlisle: Paternoster, 1986).

Hollenweger, W. J., *The Pentecostals* (Massachusetts:Hendrickson, 1988).

Howard, R., *Charismania* (London: Mowbray, 1997).

Hunt, D., *The Cult Explosion* (Eugene: Harvest House, 1980).

Hunt, S., 'Deliverance: The Evolution of a Doctrine' in *Themelios*, 21(1) (October 1995) 10-13.

– 'The Devil's Advocates: The Function of Demonology in the World View of Fundamentalist Christianity' in M. Percy and I. Jones (eds.), *Fundamentalism: Church and Society,* (London: SPCK, 2002) 66-87.

Jones, B. P., *The Trials and Triumphs of Mrs Jessie Penn-Lewis* (North Brunswick: Bridge-Logos, 1997).

Kay W. K., *Pentecostals in Britain* (Carlisle: Paternoster, 2000).

Kinnear, A. I., *Against the Tide: The Story of Watchman Nee* (Eastbourne: Victory Press, 1973).

Knox, R. A., *Enthusiasm, A Chapter in the History of Religion* (Oxford: Oxford University Press, 1949).

Latourette, K. S., *A History of Christianity Volume 2: Reformation to the Present* (London: Harper and Row, 1975).

Lindermayer, O., 'Europe as Antichrist: North American Pre-Millenarianism' in S. Hunt (ed.), *Christian Millenarianism* (London: Hurst, 2001) 39-49.

Lindsay, G., *John Alexander Dowie* (Texas: CFN, 1986).

- *The Gordon Lindsay Story* (Dallas: CFN, 1992).

Lovelace, R. F., *Dynamics of Spiritual Life* (Exeter: Paternoster, 1979).

Lowe, C., *Territorial Spirits and World Evangelisation?* (Sevenoaks: OMF International, 1998).

Luhrman, T. M., *Persuasion of the Witch's Craft* (Oxford: Blackwell, 1989).

McGee, G. B., 'To the Regions Beyond: The Global Expansion of Pentecostalism' in V. Synan (ed.), *The Century of the Holy Spirit* (Nashville: Thomas Nelson, 2001) 69-95.

McDowell, J., *Understanding the Cults* (San Bernadino: Here's Life, 1986).

Martin, W., *The Kingdom of the Cults* (Minneapolis: Bethany House, 1985).

Melton, J. G., 'Anti-Cultists in the United States' in B. Wilson and J. Cresswell (eds.), *New Religious Movements: Challenges and Response* (London: Routledge, 1999).

- *Encyclopedic Handbook of Cults in America* (New York: Garland, 1986).

Middlemiss, D., *Interpreting Charismatic Experience* (London: S.C.M, 1996).

Moore, S. D., *The Shepherding Movement* (London: T. and T. Clark, 2003).

Orr, J. E., *The Light of the Nation* (Exeter: Paternoster, 1965).

Owens, R., 'The Azusa Street Revival: The Pentecostal Movement begins in America' in V. Synan (ed.), *The Century of the Holy Spirit* (Nashville: Thomas Nelson, 2001) 39-68.

Partridge, C. H., 'Pagan Fundamentalism?' in C. H. Partridge (ed.), *Fundamentalisms* (Carlisle: Paternoster, 2001) 155-180.

Percy, M., *Words, Wonders and Power* (London: S.P.C.K., 1996).

Poloma, M., *The Assemblies of God at the Crossroads* (Knoxville: University of Tennessee, 1989).

- 'The Millenarianism of the Pentecostal Movement' in S. Hunt (ed.), *Christian Millenarianism* (London: Hurst, 2001) 166-186.

Powlison, D., *Power Encounters* (Grand Rapids: Baker Books,1995).

Price, C., *Transforming Keswick* (Carlisle: O.M., 2000).

Rack, H. D., *Reasonable Enthusiast: John Wesley and the Rise of Methodism* (London: Epworth Press, 1989).

Randall, I., 'When the Spirit Comes in Power' in *Out of Control* (Milton Keynes: Authentica, 2004).

Redwood, J., *Reason, Ridicule and Religion* (London: Thames and Hudson, 1976).

Ross, C., *Satanic Ritual Abuse* (Toronto: University of Toronto Press, 1995).

Sanders, R. G. W., *William Joseph Seymour* (Sandusky: Alexandria, 2003).

Scotland, N., *Charismatics and the New Millennium* (Guildford: Hodder and Stoughton, 2000).

Smith, M., *When the Fire Fell* (Nevada: Preparedness Publications, 1996).

Stackhouse, I., *The Gospel Driven Church* (Milton Keynes: Paternoster, 2004).

Stanley, B., *The Bible and The Flag* (Leicester: Apollos, 1990).

Taylor, H., *Pastor Hsi: Confucian Scholar and Christian* (London:

Lutterworth, 1900).

Theron, J., 'A Critical Overview of the Church's Ministry of Deliverance from Evil Spirits' *Pneuma*, 18(1) (Spring 1996) 79-92.

Thomas, J. C., *The Devil, Disease and Deliverance* (London: Sheffield Academic Press, 1998).

Victor, J. S., *Satanic Panic: the Creation of a Contemporary Legend* (Peru, Illinois: Open Court, 1996).

Wacker, G., *Heaven Below: Early Pentecostals and American Culture* (Harvard: Cambridge, 2003).

– 'Marching to Zion: Religion in a Modern Utopian Community' *Church History* 54 (December 1985) 496-511.

Walker, A., 'The Devil You Think You Know: Demonology and the Charismatic Movement' in T. Smail *et al* (eds.), *Charismatic Renewal* (London: S.P.C.K., 1995) 86-105.

– *Restoring the Kingdom* (Guildford: Eagle, 1998).

– *Enemy Territory* (London: Hodder and Stoughton, 1987).

Wallace, A., *A Modern Pentecost* (Salem: Convention, 1970).

Warrington, K., 'Healing and Exorcism: The Path to Wholeness' in K. Warrington (ed.), *Pentecostal Perspectives* (Carlisle: Paternoster, 1998) 147-176.

Watson, D., *Fear no Evil* (London: Hodder and Stoughton, 1984).

Weaver, C. D., *The Healer-Prophet* (Macon: Mercer University Press, 1987).

Weber, M., *The Theory of Social and Economic Organisation* (New York: Free Press, 1947).

White, J., *When the Spirit Comes with Power* (London: Hodder and Stoughton, 1992).

Williams, G. H., *Radical Reformation* (Missouri: Sixteenth Century Journal, 1992).

Wright, N. G., *A Theology of the Dark Side* (Carlisle: Paternoster, 2003).

– 'Does Revival Quicken or Deaden the Church?' in A. Walker and K. Aune (eds.), *On Revival* (Carlisle: Paternoster, 2003) 121-135.

York, M., 'New Age Millenarianism and its Christian Influences' in S. Hunt (ed.), *Christian Millenarianism* (London: Hurst, 2001) 224-238.

No author, *De Oorlog Tegen de Heiligen* (Amsterdam: CHEV, 2005).

General Index

www.ingramcontent.com/pod-product-compliance
Lightning Source LLC
Chambersburg PA
CBHW060332100426
42812CB00003B/967